Second Edition

ORAL COMMUNICATION

Second Edition

ORAL COMMUNICATION

Skills, Choices, and Consequences

Kathryn Sue Young
Professor, Mansfield University

Howard Paul Travis
Emeritus, Mansfield University

WAVELAND

PRESS, INC.

Long Grove, Illinois

For information about this book, contact:
    Waveland Press, Inc.
    4180 IL Route 83, Suite 101
    Long Grove, IL 60047-9580
    (847) 634-0081
    info@waveland.com
    www.waveland.com

The crossword puzzles in the text were created using the criss-cross puzzle template available at http://www.puzzlemaker.com

About the Authors

Kathryn Sue Young has taught at the college level for over 20 years at The Pennsylvania State University, Clarion University, University of Central Arkansas, and is currently a full professor at Mansfield University. She has published *Group Discussion: A Practical Guide to Participation and Leadership*, 4th edition with Wood, Phillips, and Pedersen, which is also available in Korean. She has published numerous articles, including an article in a joint American–Russian publication, and has presented numerous papers at national conferences. She is active in the community, sharing her expertise in parliamentary procedure.

Howard Travis taught at the university level for 37 years. His former students work nationally and globally in electronic media as on-air talent, writers, producers, directors, technicians, sales executives, lawyers, public relations/promotion practitioners, media managers, and media CEOs. He retired early from his teaching career in 2002. Mansfield University of Pennsylvania awarded him professor emeritus status, and he holds the rank of Honorary Professor of Communication, Volgograd State University, Volgograd, Russia.

Acknowledgments

Inspiration challenges the human spirit to achieve the impossible. My willingness to take risks and do new things reflects the enthusiasm of unique people who crossed my path on life's journey.

The idea for this book came from Dr. Kathryn Sue Young, a former colleague of mine. An innocent phone call to discuss a book idea led to a joyful collaboration. Her enthusiasm, intelligence, and patience made the writing process tons of fun. Thank you, Sue!

The book also allowed me to reconnect with friends and Montclair State alumni who shared my enthusiasm for this project. Their professional experience and thoughts are used as sidebars throughout the text. It's comforting to know so many corporate executives are interested in sharing what they have learned with future generations. Their lives continue to inspire me and make me glad to be alive.

Finally, teachers who open the door to information, imagination, professional discipline and global culture are remarkable gifts. Edward Stasheff, Zelma Weisfeld, Ralph Herbert, and Frederic W. Ziv were inspirational gifts to me. Thank you. Each one enriched my life and my academic career.

—Howard Paul Travis

Together, we would like to express a debt of gratitude to Bia Bernum, Assistant Professor of Communication, Mansfield University of Pennsylvania, for creating, developing, and writing a professional and innovative online instructor's manual for our book. In addition, she provided a criteria example in the reflective thinking section, the reasonable goals list in persuasive speaking, and innovative terms and concepts such as a "key" for organization. When we moved on to the second edition, she continued to supply unique examples from her classroom experiences for us to use. She also provided the new information in the second edition about the feedback and self-disclosure continuums in the Johari Window and the addition of the categories bullying, delaying and withdrawing in the conflict-resolution model. She is a valued colleague and extremely creative teacher.

In addition, Holly Pieper, Assistant Professor of Communication, Mansfield University of Pennsylvania, gave us thoughtful insights and suggested new sections such as preparing for the interview that greatly enhanced the second edition. We would like to thank the professors who wrote to Waveland Press with suggestions for changes as well. Finally, we would like to thank Jonathan "Patches" Yard who suggested changes for chapter 5 and Raymond R. Ozley whose thoughtful editing and insightful commentary about the first edition provided excellent guidance for us.

—Kathryn Sue Young and Howard Paul Travis

First and foremost, this book is dedicated to all of my students who continue to inspire me. I thank you for being in the classroom, for engaging with the material, and for continuing to teach me about communication and the world. Without you, I couldn't do the job I love.

Second, this book is dedicated to the people who have guided me to this profession or believed in me and mentored me. To Gerald M. Phillips who educated, encouraged, and challenged me, to Arlie Parks who guided me to graduate school, to Julia Wood, Douglas Pedersen, and Nancy Phillips who gave me my first opportunity to write a book, to Herman Cohen who always treated me as though I had something important to say, to all of my professors at Penn State University who taught me how to think and instilled a love of this field, and to Carol Rowe and the editors at Waveland Press who continue to teach me about writing effectively, I am eternally grateful.

Third, this book is dedicated to the people who give me strength in my life: my husband, daughters, my parents, my friends, you all know who you are.

Finally, I dedicate this book to my coauthor Howard P. Travis. This project is a great journey, and the synergy we experience is tremendous.

—Kathryn Sue Young

PROFESSIONAL CONTRIBUTORS ACKNOWLEDGMENTS

The authors gratefully acknowledge the professional men and women who enthusiastically supported the development of the book. They share their thoughts with you as encouragement to pursue your dream. Your dream lies in the future, and you must walk forward. Your present and past experiences are your history. Learn from them, but never take your eyes off your dream.

Mandy Aikens, NCAA Compliance Coordinator & Head Softball Coach, Nyack College
Julie Allen, Senior Human Resources Specialist, The Summit Federal Credit Union
Vincent Andaloro, President and Founder, Latin-Pak Direct Marketing
T. W. Anderson, Adolescent Therapist
Jeffrey M. Andrulonis, President, Colonial Radio Group, Inc.
Anonymous (a member of the professional staff at a large museum)
Maureen C. Baker, President, Highland Ventures, Inc.
Jim Benson, President, Vision Quest Productions
Helene B., Lead Programmer Analyst
Bia Bernum, Assistant Professor, Mansfield University of Pennsylvania
Robert Buchanan, Producer, NBC News/*Dateline*
Lori L. Burrows, Staff Attorney, Arkansas Public Service Commission. Former Peace Corps Volunteer (1999–2001), Pohnpei State, Federated States of Micronesia
Greg Chesterton, former undergraduate student, The Pennsylvania State University
Robert H. Christie, Senior Public Relations Manager, Dow Jones and Company

viii Acknowledgments

Carrie L. Clarke, stay-at-home parent
Kathleen Corrigan, Legal Clearances, Grey Global Group
Jana Polsky Deneroff, Writer/Producer, Creative Services, CBS/Westwood One
  Radio Networks
Dean De Peri, Director, Human Resources, CIGNA HealthCare
Christina DeVries, Senior Account Manager, Spotlight Payroll Inc.
Angela Dickson, Senior Coordinator of Communications, American Architec-
  tural Manufacturers Association
Tom Donahue, Assignment Manager, Court TV
Edward Gallardo, Playwright
Allynn Gooen, International Performance Artist
Dr. Aparna G. Hebbani, Lecturer, School of Journalism and Communication,
  University of Queensland, Brisbane, Australia.
Hyun Mook Kim, former international student, Mansfield University
Maryellen Lurie, Principal, Maryellen Lurie & Associates, Inc.
Timothy I. Martindale, President, Kiemle-Hankins Co., Captain, U.S. Army (Retired)
Barry McCauliff, Account Executive, The Investment Center
Cami McCormick, Network Correspondent, CBS Network Radio News
Dr. Larry Miller, Professor Emeritus, Mansfield University of Pennsylvania
Roberta J. Miller, Casework Supervisor, Retired
Wes Moon, Interior Designer
John W. Nichols, Executive Director, The Art Museum Partnership
Raymond R. Ozley, Lecturer, University of Montevallo
Colleen Quinn, Video Technician, CBS/BET Television
Gene R. Sower, Vice President, Production, West Glen Communications, Inc.
David P. Strus, Law Enforcement Officer, Nutley, New Jersey
Tracy Synowsky, stay-at-home parent
Evan Tripoli, Motion Picture Talent Agent, International Creative Management,
  Inc., A Talent and Literary Agency
Joe Tucker, Senior Vice President, The Walt Disney Company
Lance Walden, Northwest Regional Radio Promotions, Universal Republic
  Records
Raymond Weaver, Residential Care Supervisor, The Sage House, former sec-
  ondary English teacher, Ilsan, South Korea.
Robert C. Weigand, Technical Manager, Studio and Field Operations, ABC
Corey D. Welch, Operations Supervisor, Arkansas Student Loan Authority
Stacy Wolfe, college student

Contents

Preface

Welcome to the study of communication. Our goals for this undergraduate communication textbook are to: (1) engage you to think about the skills, choices, and consequences of your communication; (2) create a book you will want to read; and (3) convince you that success can be yours if you make solid choices in your communication style. You may not realize how important a good communication style can be. The strength of this book is the inclusion of communication observations from the careers of corporate professionals. These professional sidebars give relevance to the academic concepts and encourage you to improve your communication skills for success. Since you are ultimately preparing for a career, we hope you find the insights valuable and enjoy reading the shared comments of our professional contributors.

This book is designed to help you recognize the importance of your words and actions in communication. We cover topic areas such as intrapersonal communication, language, nonverbal communication, interpersonal communication, presentational speaking, persuasion, interviewing, and team orientation. Each section of the book helps you to appreciate the value of appropriate communication in your personal and professional lives. We use a chatty style to make communication fun for you to learn.

Career opportunities are lost when you fail to recognize your role in the communication process or to use appropriate skills. The ability to talk seems so simple. But, it is not. Once you master the skills of interpersonal and pre-

— Professional Perspective —

My decision to program the radio station WCIE in Fayetteville, North Carolina, with a Latino-tropical format was made after careful market analysis. *La Caliente* quickly developed a loyal following among Hispanic soldiers at Fort Bragg and Hispanic wives of some American soldiers. But, I quickly discovered that my inability to communicate fluently in Spanish was a business obstacle. I sold the station a year later. I was personally enriched by the opportunity to connect with the Hispanic culture in North Carolina. It's amazing what you can learn by simply taking a calculated risk.

—Jeffrey M. Andrulonis
President
Colonial Radio Group, Inc.

sentational communication, speaking becomes as simple as it looks. The discussions in this book will prepare you to make effective communication choices throughout your life.

— Professional Perspective —

Some of the professional people contributing to this book work with the international community. They translated their remarks into the language they use with some clients. We included the translations to encourage you to study foreign language and to remind you of the importance of speaking more than one language.

As companies enter global markets, English-only speakers will find themselves at a competitive disadvantage. Technology makes direct contact with customers and suppliers in other countries much more likely even if you never leave your office. In addition, one in five people in the United States speaks a language other than English. (Coombes, 2004). At Nicholas Senn High School in Chicago, two in five students were born outside the United States. The graduates from the school in 2007 spoke forty-six languages and came from sixty countries (Brotman, 2007). People seeking jobs will find that foreign language fluency is increasingly necessary as companies recognize the importance of understanding the cultures of other markets. "The important thing about speaking another language is it allows you to stand in the shoes of that other culture and see the world from their point of view," states Thomas Zweifel, chief executive of a cross-cultural coaching firm in New York (Coombes, 2004, p. 4).

Zweifel describes two examples where lack of cultural understanding is very costly. In the first example, the problem was lack of familiarity with the language. Clairol marketed a curling iron called "Mist Stick" in Germany. Sales were terrible because "mist" means "manure" in German. Buyers weren't tempted to curl their hair with a manure stick. In the second example, Microsoft hired programmers from Taiwan to translate Windows software for sale to China. While knowledge of the language wasn't a problem in this example, the programmers failed to set aside their political preferences and inserted pop-ups such as "Take back the mainland" and "Communist bandits." The Chinese government chose Linux over Microsoft—jeopardizing potential sales to 1.3 billion people (Coombes, 2004, p. 4).

In an increasingly competitive job market, knowledge of a foreign language will make you more attractive to potential employers. Expanding your language skills also enhances your communication skills, making you more competent interculturally and interpersonally.

—Howard Paul Travis

CHAPTER 1

Communicating for Life

OBJECTIVES

After reading this chapter, you should be able to:
- Explain the importance of studying communication
- Identify and describe the parts of the communication process
- Identify four types of communication
- Identify four principles of communication
- Understand the ethical considerations of being a competent communicator
- Explain the importance of adaptability

Eric enters his residence hall room for the first time. There are two beds: one by the window; the other next to the wall in the middle of the room. There are two permanent closets. One is next to the door, and the other is next to the sink. Two portable desks and dressers are across from the beds. As Eric looks around the room, his mother asks him where he wants his stuff. He's not quite sure what he should do. Eric has never met or talked to his roommate. He has some decisions to make: he can choose to arrange the furniture the way he wants it, or he can wait and discuss the arrangement with his roommate.

Eric likes fresh air while he is sleeping, so his mother puts his boxes on the bed by the window. Not wanting to seem pushy or to make a bad first impression, he leaves the rest of the decision making for later. He and his roommate can decide together how the room will look. Imagine what Eric's roommate would think if he walked in to find his new room completely arranged and the spaces assigned. Does Eric's decision not to rearrange the room communicate a message? Absolutely. Do you think Eric's decision to wait will help him develop a more positive relationship with his new roommate?

Only a moment earlier, Eric learned from the RA that his roommate's name is Juan Martinez. Eric looks up just as his roommate arrives. Juan looks

1

Latino, as his name suggested he might be. Before Eric gets a chance to impress his new roommate by greeting him with "Buenos días," Juan introduces himself. He sounds like a typical midwesterner. Eric is relieved to learn Juan speaks English and is glad he didn't embarrass himself by speaking in Spanish. Did Eric's face show signs of surprise? Could he have said anything that would alienate or offend Juan rather than welcome him into what could be a great friendship? Relationships evolve based on the choices we make when communicating: one bad or ineffective choice could impair the development of the relationship between these two roommates.

Choices and Consequences

Should you spend time with your new roommate, walking around campus and getting to know one another? Or should you spend time with a person you know and with whom you already feel comfortable? What kind of impression are you creating with the decision you make? What are the consequences of these choices?

_____

_____

_____

_____

_____

In the two-way *communication process* people share meaning, verbally and nonverbally. You are familiar with verbal messages, but keep in mind every gesture you make, the clothes you wear, or even the way you sit in class communicates a message about you. Communication can be **intentional or unintentional**. For example, most of you can remember making a remark you never intended for someone else to hear. When the person overheard the remark, you communicated a message about your true feelings.

Choices and Consequences

Describe a situation where you said something and then had to convince someone that you didn't really mean it. What were the consequences of your communication?

_____

_____

_____

_____

_____

Finally, it is important to understand that while the goal of communication is to share accurate meaning, communication **occurs whether it is interpreted correctly or incorrectly**. When the meaning is interpreted incorrectly, it is called miscommunication, but it is communication nevertheless.

To communicate effectively for life, you must first understand the:

- Importance of studying communication
- Communication process
- Types of communication
- Basic communication principles

WHY IS COMMUNICATION IMPORTANT?

We communicate to initiate or improve relationships, get things we want, negotiate the best price, conduct business, meet people, function in teams, and learn new things. The more effective we are, the better the outcome. Good, solid communication skills allow us to move through life with self-confidence and a feeling of accomplishment.

Critical Thinking

Why are you taking this class? _____

What is your career goal? _____

If your university mandates this class as a general education requirement, think about the academic reasoning for this choice. Why would a class in communication be so important that everyone in the university must take it in order to graduate?

_____

_____

_____

COMMUNICATION PROCESS

Communication is an ongoing process. In order to be successful, people must effectively share meaning, but this goal is not always possible. Sharing meaning implies a person must comprehend the intended meaning of the other person's use of language. In order to understand communication, we must look at the parts that make up an interaction. Each interaction consists of communicators, messages, a channel, circumstances, feedback, and, in some instances, noise. A good communicator analyzes each of these parts to make the best possible choices in each communication interaction.

If you have a bad communication experience, you can analyze what the cause might be: "Was it me?" "Was it the other person?" "Was it the channel?" "Was the message worded incorrectly?" "Was there noise?" The answers to these questions will help pinpoint a potential problem and enable possible corrections. You can also begin to think ahead to future interactions.

$\Rightarrow$ **Try It!** $\Leftarrow$

Take a moment to list the many situations in which you need to have effective communication skills:

_____

_____

_____

_____

Communicators

Communicators are the people involved in a verbal/nonverbal exchange. Each communicator simultaneously sends and receives messages. During a lecture, for example, a professor sends both nonverbal (smiles, hand gestures, eye contact) and verbal messages (the lecture material). At the same time, each student sends messages to the professor by maintaining eye contact, writing notes, or yawning. Everyone is communicating, whether they like it or not. Effective communicators are aware that they intentionally and unintentionally send and receive messages; they constantly monitor and reflect on their verbal and nonverbal behavior as well as on the behavior of others around them as they fine-tune their skills.

Messages

Communicators deliver both *verbal* and *nonverbal messages*. The process begins with a thought in a person's head. The person encodes the thought into words or actions. *Encoding* means a communicator reviews all of the available symbols or actions that could represent the thought and selects the most appropriate ones. The person then selects a channel to send words or actions to other communicators. The other communicators receive the words or actions and decode them. *Decoding* means thinking about the received symbols or actions, applying meaning to them, and making them into a usable thought.

The more effective we are at encoding our thoughts, the more likely other communicators will decode messages correctly. This results in a better chance for shared meaning. It is important for communicators to be fully aware that other communicators could decode the message with a meaning that wasn't intended by the sender. A slight pause before delivering an important thought could be decoded as "the following statement is not true." However, a pause could also mean the communicator was searching for the right word to start the message. We should be aware that our decoding of meanings can be inaccurate.

Nonverbal messages are actions without words. Nonverbals include our gestures, the way we use our voice (loud, soft, high, low), the clothes we wear, and the car we drive. Delivery can enhance or hinder the effective decoding of a verbal message. Characteristics of delivery include the tone, the pitch, the rate, and the projection we use when we speak. All of these vocal characteristics of a verbal message help to emphasize or de-emphasize key thoughts. If messages are not delivered appropriately, then our meaning may be distorted and decoded incorrectly.

In our example at the beginning of the chapter, Eric realized that if he arranged the room without Juan's input, he might send a nonverbal message that would make him appear to be pushy. In addition his clothes, gestures, haircut, and personal possessions send nonverbal messages to his new roommate. As with verbal messages, nonverbal messages also have the potential to be decoded incorrectly by others.

Channel

Messages must go through a medium to get from one communicator to another. The different mediums are called *channels*. Each channel targets a different sensory receptor and must be chosen appropriately to accomplish your goal. Channels include the telephone, cell phone, pager, computer, newspaper, radio, television, books, notes, sound systems, and face-to-face interaction.

When thinking about channels, remember every communication situation necessitates an appropriate channel choice. For example, Melinda wants to break up with Anthony. She logs onto her computer, finds him on instant messaging (IM), and types in, "I'm breaking up with you. This hasn't been fun for a long time." She hits send and immediately blocks any return messages. Is using e-mail or IM an appropriate channel for this situation? By choosing to use IM, what does Melinda communicate? What will Anthony think of her actions? What message does she send by blocking any further messages from Anthony?

⇨ Try It! ⇦

What would be the most appropriate channel for the following communication situations?

1. A boss needs to inform an employee that she did not receive a raise   _____

2. A groom wants to call off his wedding two weeks prior to the date   _____

3. A student needs to tell a faculty member there has been an emergency at home   _____

4. Campus police need to tell a student there has been an emergency at home   _____

As you choose a channel for certain communication events, think about the purpose of the communication and the consequences of that choice. There are certain situations that warrant direct and immediate involvement with the intended receiver of the message.

Critical Thinking

Describe a recent event where you chose the wrong channel to communicate an important message to someone else.

_____

_____

_____

Circumstances

Circumstances refer to the context of the situation and to the fundamental nature of the communicator. A communicator's background, attitudes, beliefs, and values contribute to his or her **fundamental nature**. As we analyze a communication event, we must remember that people are different. Because Jose's father was verbally and physically abusive, he may react to conflict differently than his significant other, Sally. When Jose gets into an argument with her, he may avoid her eyes and look downward. Because Sally was raised in an environment where family members always asserted themselves, she may not understand why he is so passive.

The context in which communication occurs also contributes to the meaning of a message. What you say in one situation could be completely inappropriate in another. For example, you and your friends feel comfortable using jokes and calling each other names. In the context of your friendships, you are all satisfied with this banter. However, you may feel uncomfortable or be offended if someone from outside your group makes the same type of comments to you. Analyzing your circumstances, including your own fundamental nature and the context of the situation, allows you to encode messages effectively. Reflection about past communication choices will help you think carefully about future interactions.

Feedback

Feedback is the response one communicator gives to another. Feedback can be verbal or nonverbal. Feedback is essential to the communication process; it acknowledges the presence of the other person, lets the communicator know the message was received, and demonstrates that the communication is valued.

Noise

Noise is anything that interrupts communicators from encoding, sending, receiving, and/or decoding a message properly. There are three types of noise: physical, personal, and semantic. *Physical noise* is anything external, from loud construction sounds outside a window to a bug flying around your head at an outdoor concert. At many schools, it is inevitable that the maintenance employees will mow the lawn on the day that students give their final speech, or that the Spring Fling celebration will be blasting live band music during an exam. Physical noise distracts us and competes with our thought processes. Think about turning down the car radio while trying to find a friend's house for the first time; it's easier to concentrate when physical noise is minimized.

⇨ **Try It!** ⇦

How many types of physical noise can you list? _____

_____

_____

_____

Personal noise refers to the ongoing thoughts in our minds. Three types of personal noise can distract us.

- *Prejudice.* To be prejudiced is to "pre-judge," or to have a preconceived, often negative, view of someone or something. If, for example, you have biases against small towns, you may have a negative impression of anyone from a town with a population of less than 3,000. So when you come to college and find your neighbor is from Small Town, U.S.A., you may immediately belittle this person. How will your ability to communicate with your neighbor be affected by your preconceived ideas? Will you be able to learn from her? It is our choice to be aware of our prejudices and to try to refrain from stereotyping. Just as Eric realized how ridiculous he was to have assumed Juan would speak Spanish, we must also be aware of prejudices and choose to work toward eliminating them. If we don't, we will ultimately pay the consequences provoked by our ignorance.

- *Close-mindedness.* Close-mindedness occurs when we refuse to listen to another person's point of view. Think about your view on a topic like immigration. Chances are you feel very strongly about your opinion. Could you learn something by hearing information from the opposing side? Of course. However, many people who believe they are right refuse to listen to any information that conflicts with their own beliefs. This position harms the communication process.

- *Self-centered noise.* Self-centered noise happens when we are more focused on ourselves than on the other person. Think about how often you zone out in class thinking about your friends, the exam you have in two hours, your weekend plans, the party you attended the night before, or even what you will have for dinner. You may have learned the art of smiling and nodding and looking attentive even though you are not paying the least bit of attention to the message.

The third type of noise is *semantic noise.* Semantic noise occurs when the person you are communicating with speaks a different language, uses technical jargon, and/or resorts to emotionally charged words. In the case of a different language, it is easy to understand the difficulties in the communication process. But technical jargon is almost as confusing. It is the specialized language of a profession. If one communicator knows the terminology and the other does not, sharing meaning is difficult. Emotionally charged words also block the communication process. The listener may lock onto a word rather than pay attention to the complete message. If you call a 35-year-old lawyer *honey,* she may not hear anything after that word because she's thinking, "*Honey?* I'm a professional, not a child or a personal friend, and it's demeaning to be addressed as one." As another example, in some regions of the United States, the terms *ma'am* and *sir* refer to people who are in authority positions, even if they are only 30 years old. However, in other areas of the United States, those terms conjure up images of senior citizens. A 30-year-old woman in northern California, for example, could be offended by the term "ma'am," just as a 30-year-old woman in Arkansas could be offended if a younger person didn't use "ma'am" when addressing her.

As you can see, every part of the communication process is important. Select your message and channel carefully. As a communicator, you must be aware of the process and accept responsibility for the choices you make.

— Professional Perspective —

In ethnic direct marketing it is essential to be able to reach prospective Hispanic households in their respective language. Not only must we acknowledge formal languages, such as Spanish, Chinese, French, or Japanese, but also differences and nuances within each language group. For example, Spanish spoken in Spain is different from the Spanish spoken in Mexico or Puerto Rico or Venezuela. This relates to all languages and their dialects. Good marketers speak the language(s) of their customers.

En la venta directa dirigida a los grupos étnicos es muy importante poder llegar a los hogares de los posibles compradores hispanos en su mismo idioma. No sólo debemos reconocer los principales idiomas, tales como español, chino, francés, o japonés, sino también las diferencias y matices dentro de cada grupo idiomático. Por ejemplo, el español hablado en España es distinto al español hablado en México, Puerto Rico o Venezuela. Esto es también cierto con respecto a todos los idiomas y a sus dialectos. Los buenos vendedores hablan el idioma de sus clientes.

—Vincent Andaloro
President and Founder
Latin-Pak Direct Marketing

Always consider the circumstances of the people around you. You should be aware of noise during the interaction and work to eliminate it whenever possible or to adapt to the circumstances to diminish the effects of the noise. And you should do your best to provide proper feedback. These choices will make interactions as smooth and effective as possible.

The communication process consists of many parts. To be an effective communicator, you must make appropriate choices as you become aware of how each part influences the others.

TYPES OF COMMUNICATION

There are four basic types of communication.

- Intrapersonal communication: Communicating within yourself
- Interpersonal communication: Communicating with another person
- Small group communication: Communicating with 3–20 people (with 5– 8 as the ideal size) who have a common goal
- Public communication: Communicating with a large audience

When we mentally review or rehearse conversations or experiences, we are engaging in ***intrapersonal communication.*** Think how often you do this. Before you meet with your professor, do you think about what you are going to say? When your alarm goes off in the morning, do you think, "If I hit the snooze button, I can give up the shower, sleep for another 18 minutes, and wear a hat"? We communicate intrapersonally when we meditate, reflect, and strategize. Intrapersonal communication helps us to be in tune with ourselves, to practice important communication scenarios, to analyze everything around us (including our own actions), and to think critically of past and future events.

In contrast to the internal dialogue of intrapersonal communication, ***interpersonal communication*** takes place when two people speak with one another. Can you remember the discussion you had with a classmate about the final exam in one of your classes? The complaints you shared with someone about your roommate? The person you smiled at in the cafeteria? You should be able to list at least 50 exchanges in the last 24 hours. We use interpersonal communication constantly to help create and maintain our relationships.

⇨ **Try It!** ⇦

How many interpersonal interactions have you already had today? List as many as you can.

_____

_____

_____

Interpersonal communication becomes *small group communication* when the number of people increases. Generally, groups are defined as having 3–20 members. Group members share a sense of belonging and have common beliefs, goals, or reasons for getting together. Group members work together to accomplish tasks and/or relationship goals.

Groups with task goals meet to solve a problem or to complete an assignment. This type of group can be found in the workplace or in the classroom and generally consists of 5–8 people. When your company asks five of you to develop a marketing plan for a new product, you are in a task group. On the other end of the spectrum, the primary purpose of groups with relationship goals is to fulfill personal needs of conversation and belonging. These groups may consist of close friends who eat dinner together or colleagues who go dancing every Friday night. Sometimes groups have both task and relationship goals. These blended groups can include a social fraternity/sorority, book club, study groups, and/or a religious gathering. In addition to relationship functions, these groups also perform tasks such as fundraising, social service projects, reading assignments, and so forth.

Teams are a type of small group. Teams work on tasks designed to accomplish a specific goal. The members of teams employ a procedure to accomplish their goal. Teams are prevalent in many workplace environments. In this text, we focus exclusively on communication within teams rather than on the broader concept of small group communication.

Public communication occurs when a communicator informs, persuades, and/or entertains a group of people. Speakers have an organized message and an official audience, and they prepare for the event. Typically public communication comes in the form of school assemblies, oral presentations, political speeches, a keynote address at a conference, high school announcements, sermons, corporate announcements via in-house television, and messages delivered through electronic media. You may think you will never have to give a speech except in this class; however, chances are public communication is in your future. You should learn the skills for effective public speaking so that you will be prepared when opportunities arise in both your professional and personal life.

| ⇨   **Try It!**   ⇦ |

List five instances of public communication that have occurred on your campus since school began.

_____

_____

_____

_____

_____

BASIC COMMUNICATION PRINCIPLES

Improving your communication skills takes time and dedication. It involves thinking before acting, making the best choices, and dealing with the consequences of those choices. Below are four principles to keep in mind when thinking about communication.

We cannot not communicate. Everything we do is received and interpreted by someone, somewhere. Even if we isolate ourselves, thinking we won't have to communicate, the very act of not interacting communicates a message. We communicate with family members, friends, coworkers, peers, professors, service personnel, significant others, and many more. Our communication skills are put to the test every minute of every day.

— Professional Perspective —

The world is such a hurried place today. We rush here, we rush there, we rush, rush everywhere! We are, at the same time, inundated with communication. We get it by television at home or, now (WOW!), in the car, by phone, at the movies, on a plane, and even sides of trains; we get it via the Internet or magazines, in our mail and even the halls, and, of course, at the malls. At all times someone or something, somehow, somewhere is speaking in an attempt to convince us.

—Corey D. Welch
Operations Supervisor
Arkansas Student Loan Authority

Communication is irreversible—whether it is intentional or unintentional. If you say something or do something that upsets another person, you can't change it. Once the words are out of your mouth, the damage has been done. You can apologize and hope to lessen the impact, but the communication can't be changed. When you choose certain words or act a certain way, there are consequences, some positive and some negative. Effective communicators understand this principle and think carefully before they speak. They monitor and reflect on all of their communication.

Communication is a process. The bits of information we collect become part of our circumstances and affect our future communication. By being more aware we can improve our communication style and learn other perspectives. We all experience the world a little differently, so in addition to understanding and improving our own style, we need to remember that other people have unique styles. No one is a perfect communicator; instead, we have varying degrees of success in certain situations. Effective communicators are flexible because they adapt their messages to the circumstances they encounter.

— Professional Perspective —

Adaptability is also important in facing the unexpected in terms of the twists and turns your personal career can take.

—Christina DeVries
Senior Account Manager
Spotlight Payroll Inc.

Improving your communication skills is a life-long commitment. You already possess communication skills; by increasing your repertoire you'll be able to handle the diverse situations you will encounter. When doing so, you don't need to imitate others or to compromise your values and ethical standards. Increased skills allow you to communicate effectively and to adjust to unexpected circumstances.

Communication involves ethical considerations. As you think about the fact that communication is an ongoing, irreversible process, you'll also want to think about ethical considerations. According to Pamela Shockley-Zalabak (2006), ethics are "moral principles that guide judgments about good and bad, right and wrong, not just effectiveness or efficiency" (p. 118).

Many communication situations we face on a daily basis include ethical choices. For example, do we repeat gossip we heard about someone? Or do we take the time to investigate the comment prior to passing it along? Or do we refrain from sharing the information altogether? On another day, do we refrain from communicating that we have a crush on another friend? Or do we hide our feelings by remaining silent? Each of these choices has considerable ethical consequences related to your credibility and judgment.

We can also use communication to uphold personal ethics and moral standards. We do so, for instance, in a grocery store when we inform the clerk that the register undercharged us, or when we tell a server that the dessert we ordered is missing from the bill. Our reaction to these situations reveal our ethical standards to others.

The better you understand your intrapersonal communication and the more you practice communicating interpersonally, the better equipped you will be to handle these common situations.

SUMMARY

Think back to Eric and Juan. They have a lot of work ahead of them, but with some thinking, acceptance, and patience they will get to know one another and may develop a life-long friendship. Eric is already aware that nonverbal communication plays an important role in the perception of others. If he continues to monitor and reflect on his communication choices, he will have the opportunity to share meaning and to develop a satisfying friendship. The knowledge you gain from this book will help you review and improve your current skills so you will be a more successful communicator in a variety of situations.

Key Words

channel
circumstances
close-mindedness
communication process
communicators
decoding
encoding
feedback
interpersonal communication
intrapersonal communication
noise

nonverbal messages
personal noise
physical noise
prejudice
public communication
self-centered noise
semantic noise
small group communication
teams
verbal messages

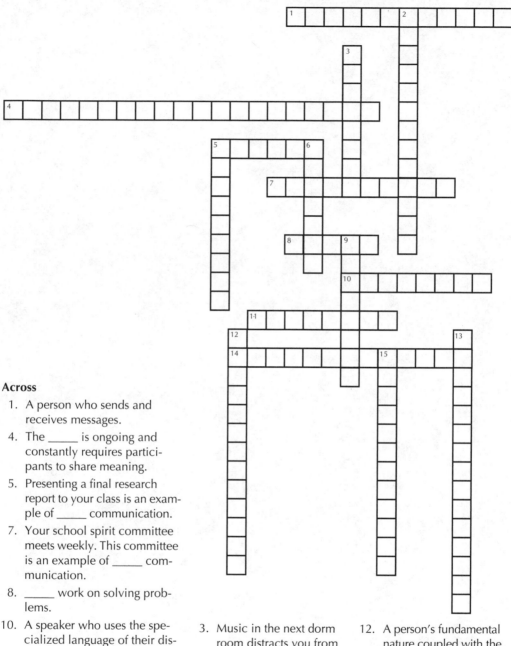

Across

1. A person who sends and receives messages.
4. The _____ is ongoing and constantly requires participants to share meaning.
5. Presenting a final research report to your class is an example of _____ communication.
7. Your school spirit committee meets weekly. This committee is an example of _____ communication.
8. _____ work on solving problems.
10. A speaker who uses the specialized language of their discipline without defining it creates _____ noise.
11. The response one communicator gives to another.
14. Thinking of ways to solve a problem is an example of _____ communication.

Down

2. Instant messaging with your friend is an example of _____ communication.

3. Music in the next dorm room distracts you from studying. This is an example of _____ noise.
5. A bias tainting your judgment about people, objects, or situations.
6. The medium through which a message moves from one communicator to another.
9. Verbal and nonverbal codes.

12. A person's fundamental nature coupled with the situation.
13. The inability to listen to someone because their view is different from yours.
15. Thinking about a party instead of focusing on a lecture is an example of _____ noise.

CHAPTER 2

Perception

OBJECTIVES

After reading this chapter, you should be able to:

- Define the perceptual process
- Explain how people can have varying perceptions of the same phenomena
- Recognize instances of stereotyping and explain its relationship to the perceptual process
- Explain the difference between fact and inference
- Recognize communication problems caused by attributing meaning
- Explain the perception-checking process and practice the skill
- Explain how perception relates to self-concept and self-esteem

Imagine three people witnessing a car accident. When interviewed by the police, they give three different eyewitness reports. How can that be? Although each person saw the same event, they did not *perceive* the event in the same way. Therefore, perception is more than seeing. Because we all have different experiences and expectations, we all perceive events and behaviors differently. Competent communicators understand that perception affects how we encode and decode messages and are savvy enough to assess potential communication errors due to perceptual differences.

THE PERCEPTUAL PROCESS

While walking down the street talking to a friend, you encounter numerous sensory stimuli. You hear the sounds of cars, the honking of horns, your friend's voice. You see other people and perhaps notice some of their characteristics and personal belongings. You also see store window displays, buildings, and vehicles; you smell hot pretzels, perfume, bakery goods, and fumes from a passing bus. Your conversational stroll down the street is filled with distractions and sensory input. However, you notice only a few of these things.

If we acknowledged all of the sensory stimuli around us, we'd be so overwhelmed we would have trouble existing. Perception helps us sort through external stimuli for relevance. We compare newly received messages to past experiences we've had with similar situations. Past experiences help us to interpret what we sense in our daily lives. This *perceptual process* occurs in three stages: (1) selection; (2) organization; and (3) interpretation (McGaan, 2003).

In the first step of the perceptual process, your mind decides which of the numerous distractions are worth recognizing. As you walk with your friend, you pay strict attention to the conversation because you haven't seen each other in a long time. You are aware of people walking toward you in order to avoid bumping into them. You may notice a particularly nice car go by, or an outfit on a specific person in the crowd, or even a parent with a child. These choices capture your attention based on your personality, your background, what is unique in a particular object and sound, and what seems important to you at the time. At one point, you notice a pregnant woman with an armload of groceries moving through the crowd to a parked car. She reminds you of your pregnant sister who is in her eighth month. This woman stands out because you've watched your sister's physical condition change and have become more sensitive to pregnant women. Your personal interest in pregnancy makes this woman noticeable to you, but not to the person with whom you are walking. This process of focusing on specific stimuli and ignoring others is called *selective attention*. While numerous other stimuli are there, you do not choose to pay attention to them.

Reality ✔

Selective attention is natural for most people. However, someone who lost their hearing and then regained it (such as with a cochlear implant) has to relearn the selective-attention skill. Once the hearing is regained, an individual can suffer from an overwhelming amount of aural stimuli. He or she will hear every sound that others easily filter out. Imagine hearing every hum, buzz, plink, or rustle. The process of relearning to filter out extraneous sound can take weeks to accomplish and cause great distress to the person.

In the second step of the perceptual process, your brain *organizes* the stimuli you receive by grouping them in meaningful ways. Recently we received the following anonymous e-mail:

> aoccdrnig to a rscheeahcr at an Elingsh uinervtisy, it deosn't mttaer in waht oredr the ltteers in a wrod are, the olny iprmoetnt tihng is that frist and lsat ltteer is at the rghit pclae. The rset can be a toatl mses and you can sitll raed it wouthit porbelm. Tihs is bcuseae we do not raed ervey lteter by itslef but the wrod as a wlohe.

This is a perfect example of how our minds group information. Most people can read this paragraph with little or no trouble at all. Our minds fill in blanks when we group information. What do you see below?

Most people would say this is a triangle. In fact, it is only three connected lines. However, our minds fill in the piece of missing information during the organizing process. We organize messages by comparing them with the information we have from past experiences. We think about similar situations, incidences, or behaviors from our past and use them to categorize the new information before assigning meaning. We expect future events to be similar to previous experiences. This helps us select and organize stimuli, but it also potentially limits our ability to perceive things properly. If we cannot view new perceptual input with an open mind, it is difficult to be an effective communicator. Our previous judgments can cloud our willingness to be open to new information. Have you ever seen this puzzle?

.   .   .

.   .   .

.   .   .

The instructions are to connect all of the dots using four straight lines without lifting your pencil from the paper. Most people can't do it. Even after having previously seen this puzzle in various classes during their academic life, people often can't remember how to accomplish the task. The concept of staying inside the imaginary square is so ingrained that we conceptualize the problem by comparing it to past experiences, and we can't do the puzzle. (After trying the puzzle, see page 29 for the solution.)

How does this apply to communication? Well, when you see a 300-pound, macho football player, what kind of voice do you expect the person to have? Chances are most large men you meet have deep, baritone voices. What is your reaction when this person starts to talk in a high-pitched, wispy voice? His voice violates your expectation of how he should sound and may make you uncomfortable.

Think about being in a business setting and management announces that a new administrative assistant starts today. Everyone is excited and immediately has a picture and expectations of what this person will look like. When the new assistant appears and is an obese man, would you be surprised? Upset? Bewildered? Would your nonverbal reaction give away your feelings to the new assistant? Would your face convey a message to the new person? Are there possible consequences for these reactions? If we are not flexible and adaptive, we may experience difficulties communicating if we rely solely on past experiences for organizing perceptual stimuli.

Once you have organized information by grouping it and comparing it to past experiences, you move into the third step of the perceptual process. Here you *interpret* what you sense; you assign meaning to it. Let's return to our

---

Critical Thinking

What does an administrative assistant look like? If we used a term from the past, such as *secretary,* would your description change?

_____

_____

How did you come up with this image?

_____

_____

---

street scene: Your friend's cell phone rings, and she decides to answer it. You pay attention to the call for a moment, but you become angry. The meaning you assign to your friend's nonverbal communication is that you are less important than the incoming call. Your attention shifts away from her toward other activities going on around you. Suddenly, you see a car coming toward you. It is weaving in and out of traffic. Without warning it veers to the right and runs up over the curb hitting a pedestrian who is waiting to cross the street. You hear screeching brakes. You smell burning rubber. You hear the scream as the person is hit. Your friend also witnesses the incident; each of you sees the accident but assigns meaning differently. The police question you separately. After providing a description of what you saw, you decide to go for coffee with your friend. You say, "I think the driver must have been drunk because he was losing control of the car before hitting the man." Your friend says, "What are you talking about? He obviously swerved to avoid hitting another car coming into his lane." Both you and your friend saw the car weave, but you assigned meaning to the event differently. Your selective attention also plays a role here. You focused on the accident, but your friend was involved in a phone conversation while the car was weaving back and forth. She only noticed the accident for a limited time.

VARYING PERCEPTIONS

People do not perceive the same sensory input in a similar way for a variety of reasons. For example, you receive the same sensory input from your instructor as the rest of your class. However, you may have different perceptions of the teacher. Some of you may think the instructor is funny—others may think he is a total bore and his jokes are cheesy.

So why do perceptions vary? How can two individuals assign meaning differently? Think back to the communication process and our discussion of circumstances. We talked about the fact that everyone has different backgrounds and experiences. Now, add that personal component to the perceptual process. In the organizing step, we are comparing sensory stimuli to our past experiences. So if people have different experiences, it is reasonable to deduce that they can have different assignments of meaning for the same

— **Professional Perspective** —

As retirement approached, I reviewed my evaluations by students over the years. One thing that stood out was the diversity of opinions that students expressed about my teaching. A comment that I particularly enjoyed was made by a CJA major who wrote, "I'm a senior, and I thought the course was very interesting. Some of the freshmen thought the course was boring. They haven't seen boring yet."

—Dr. Larry Miller
Professor Emeritus
Mansfield University of Pennsylvania

event when involved in interpersonal communication. If you look at the previous sidebar, the senior student had experiences that the first-year students did not when evaluating the same class. Therefore, the students' reactions to the course were different.

Think about your instructor again for a moment. Based on your limited exposure to this person, do you think the instructor owns a pet? If so, what kind of pet? Now, think about your answer. Obviously you have no way of knowing the answer to this question, yet you probably have an opinion. How did you form this opinion? Chances are you looked for physical evidence (cat or dog hair) or based your opinion on something the instructor said. You may think about things the instructor has revealed in class that would indicate a lifestyle that is or isn't pet oriented. Or your instructor could remind you of someone who has a pet and that memory influences your perception. You may just look at the teacher and get an intuitive feeling about pet ownership. You may also look at the percentage of other professors you know who have pets and go with a statistical guess.

In other words, there are a variety of personal experiences that shape your perception. You continue to relate new information to your past experiences as you make sense out of it. As each student in the class does this—and you all have different past experiences—you perceive the same phenomenon differently.

Critical Thinking

Think about three people viewing the Rocky Mountains for the first time. They are all witnessing the same physical object. What meaning do they assign to the object? How do they perceive it? Write a brief statement that would likely be the first comment of the individuals described below as they see the Rockies in person for the first time.

An experienced skier _____

A religious leader _____

A person with emphysema _____

STEREOTYPING

Stereotyping is the act of treating everyone with similar characteristics as though they are the same. We use the perceptual process when we stereotype. As stated earlier, we experience sensory stimuli and make sense of it by categorizing the information and comparing it to what we already believe is true. Stereotyping is an important part of the organizing step of the perceptual process. It develops from information we choose to hear and remember from our family, peers, religious establishments, teachers, community, and the entertainment media. Because stereotyping ignores the possibility of individual differences, it can be problematic. For example, thirty years ago men who wore earrings were stereotyped as homosexual. There was a transition period during which people interpreted earrings as a statement of sexual preference depending on whether the earring was worn in the left or the right ear. Today, many men wear earrings without being stereotyped.

— Professional Perspective —

Think about the stereotypes you hold. I was in a grocery store one day and ahead of me was a man with long hair, tattoos, and a worn leather jacket. Sitting in his cart was a boy who appeared to be about four years old. The boy was facing me, and the man was in front of their cart. As I stood there, the boy lifted his feet and pushed my cart. I was a little shocked at the child's behavior. As I looked at the child with disapproval, the man leaned down and whispered in the boy's ear. The child looked at me and said, "I'm very sorry I kicked your cart." Often we hold stereotypes about the competence of a parent/adult based on the manner in which they are dressed. Stereotyping this man based on his attire would have been a serious mistake; he was not a neglectful, uninvolved parent as some would think. By correcting the boy's behavior, he reinforced the expression, "don't judge a book by its cover."

—Belinda A. Bernum
Assistant Professor
Mansfield University

— Professional Perspective —

Although the situation is improving, I believe stereotyping still does exist to some degree for women in the workplace. As a woman and a technician in the male-dominated video industry, I've been very fortunate. Two men mentored me and treated me with the utmost respect. Yet, there were many incidents in my career when I was not taken seriously. I seem to have the most trouble with male engineers. If I was having a machine problem, I often dreaded calling engineering. They usually assumed it was "operator error" and would take their sweet time getting back to me. Many times, they would patronize me and call me "sweetie" or "honey" or simply ignore me. It made me furious, especially when the same engineer would pull a male technician over and ask if he had had any problems with the same machine! I would fume internally, but I soon realized anger didn't accomplish anything. I learned to use humor as my best defense; self-deprecation became my tool of choice! If I made jokes at my own expense, it usually put my supervisor at ease and my video deck would be repaired quickly. If you can maintain your sense of humor, the barriers of gender stereotyping can slowly erode.

—Colleen Quinn
Video Technician
CBS/BET Television

Stereotyping is something many of us do without thinking. Because we must organize stimuli in the perceptual process, stereotyping is a quick and easy way to group and analyze information. However, we have choices when it comes to assigning meaning based on those stereotypes. As Eric learned in chapter 1, his stereotype of people with Latino surnames was totally incorrect. While stereotypes allow us to organize information, they also limit our ability to look at people and situations objectively. This lack of objectivity could lead to communication misunderstandings. Once you become more aware of your stereotypical beliefs and maintain perceptual flexibility, you will be better equipped to communicate effectively with a diverse population.

Ethical Considerations

Is it ethical to live in a community that keeps certain people out? What about joining clubs that are prestigious, but restricted? Do you realize that both of these situations still exist?

_____

_____

Critical Thinking

Do you claim you don't stereotype people? What do the following people look like?

Prostitute _____

Cop _____

Governor _____

Lawyer _____

Medical Examiner _____

Straight-A Student _____

How many people in these categories do you know? Where did you come up with your perceptions of what these people look like?

_____

_____

_____

FACT VERSUS INFERENCE

As you move into the third step of the perceptual process and try to assign meaning to perceived events, it is imperative to realize the difference between facts and inferences. **Facts** are observable phenomena. It is a fact there are clouds in the sky, the grass is green, and oceans contain water. We can observe the truth of these statements. **Inferences** are conclusions we draw about the facts we observe. For instance, if the green grass looks particularly inviting while we are on a trip, we may infer it would be a nice place to stop, spread out a blanket, and have a picnic. We have drawn a conclusion. When we start the picnic and are attacked by fire ants, we realize our inference was wrong. If we act as though a perception is fact when it is actually inference, we can run into numerous communication problems.

Reality ✔

You are driving down a busy highway and see a van on the side of the road with its door open. As you speed by, you see a man grabbing a 2-year-old child.

What are the facts? _____

What are the inferences? _____

What is the truth? _____

Here is another example to think about from an interpersonal setting. It is a fact that Shakespeare wrote plays. It is a fact that Shakespeare's plays appear on your new significant other's bookshelf. Is it a fact that your significant other likes Shakespeare? No. You infer she likes Shakespeare based on the plays on the bookshelf. So, what happens when you give your significant other a ticket to a Shakespearean play for her birthday? The answer depends on whether you made a correct inference about the material you observed on the bookshelf.

Critical Thinking

What have you inferred that led to a communication difficulty? Describe the situation and how you handled it.

_____

_____

_____

_____

_____

Confusing fact with inference directly relates to the interpretation step of the perceptual process. Another concept to be aware of is how our emotional reactions to past and present experiences affect our inferences. We may infer meaning based on how we felt about something rather than on what we actually saw. This conclusion may often be incorrect. Let's say you are supposed to meet your significant other at 3:00 PM. You decide to show up a little early as a surprise only to find when you get close to his house, he is on the front porch hugging an attractive person goodbye. You immediately assign meaning to the sensory input based on your past experiences and state of mind. You feel your significant other must be cheating on you. Once the other person is gone, you confront your partner by yelling accusations. When your significant other finally gets a chance to explain what you thought you saw, you find out the other person is a sibling you haven't met. In this case, emotional reactions clouded the ability to infer accurately.

Choices and Consequences

Describe a situation where you have assigned meaning incorrectly. What happened?

_____

_____

_____

What were the consequences?

_____

_____

_____

What do you wish you had done differently?

_____

_____

_____

ATTRIBUTING MEANING

When we witness behaviors in others, we try to make sense of those behaviors and assign meaning to them. Creating meaning for behaviors is called ***attribution.*** It is very likely that from observation alone we can never know for sure what behaviors mean, but we often feel confident in our own interpretation. The process of attributing meaning can easily result in miscommunication.

For example, Tony sees Tina in the student center and waves hello. Tina looks at him and quickly looks away without responding. He feels hurt and angry. This is an emotional reaction that clouds his judgment. "Fine," he thinks. "Drop dead!" Tony has just created a meaning for Tina's action. He assumes she meant to ignore him. But is his assumption correct?

Tony has choices in this exchange. He can act as though his assumption is fact. Or, he can question his assumption immediately. He may also brainstorm for other reasons that would explain Tina's action. Or, he can be more direct and active by checking his perceptions (perception checking is discussed in the next section).

Critical Thinking

What are some other reasons for Tina's behavior? Can you list three? Six?

_____

_____

_____

_____

_____

_____

What do you think the consequences will be for Tony if he acts on his assumption that Tina has deliberately hurt him? What will he do next? Will he ignore her the next time he sees her? Yell at her? How will this affect their future interactions? You can see that nothing good will occur if he acts on an incorrect assumption. Tony would benefit, therefore, from either recognizing other possibilities for Tina's actions or doing a perception check immediately.

Critical Thinking

Identify an instance of attribution theory in the description of the two friends walking down the street and witnessing the car accident.

_____

_____

Describe an instance where someone incorrectly attributed meaning to your behavior.

_____

_____

PERCEPTION CHECKING

Many of us choose to act on attributions, inferences, or perceptions without checking to see if they are correct. **_Perception checking_** is a skill that is used to double-check your understanding of what is going on with another person. Let's take a look at an example where perception checking would be valuable.

Judy is a 35-year-old who lives in a rural community where power outages are common. Judy decides to go on a brief trip five hours from her home. Judy has the type of relationship with her mother where she always e-mails her mom after she returns from a trip. The e-mail message lets her mother know she is home safely.

When Judy arrives home at 11:00 PM, she is exhausted from the trip. She pulls in the driveway and notices the power is out again. She could call her mom instead, but she knows her mom is often sound asleep by 9:00 PM. She assumes the power will probably be on within the hour, but she is so tired she falls asleep on the couch. Judy's mother, who is expecting an e-mail from Judy, doesn't find one when she wakes up. She calls Judy at 5:00 AM when she doesn't see the e-mail. Judy is groggy as she answers the phone and tries to process why her mother is yelling at her. Her mother says, "How can you be so irresponsible? All I ask for is a little e-mail message so I know you are okay. I haven't slept all night because I was worried about you. You are so inconsiderate of my feelings. It only takes a minute to send a message." In this case, Judy's mom would be a much more effective communicator if she used the skill of perception checking instead of making assumptions and acting on them as though they were fact. Imagine how awful she will feel when Judy says, "Mom, I tried to e-mail, but our power was out. I was waiting for the electricity to come back on, but I fell asleep on the couch. I'm so sorry."

Perception checking consists of three parts. First, you give an **objective description** of what you sensed; second, you give an **interpretation** of what the situation meant to you; and, finally, you ask a **question**. In the previous example, Judy's mom could have said, "I noticed you didn't send an e-mail last night when you got home, so that I would know you were safe. I feel as though you are inconsiderate of my feelings. What is going on?" This would incorporate all three elements, but could alienate Judy. A simplified inquiry would be, "I was really worried when your e-mail didn't come in last night— did you send one?"

Here is another example. Your significant other comes home from school-work and seems to be in a bad mood. He hasn't even looked in your direction. Yelling, "Hey, aren't you going to pay any attention to me?" or "What's YOUR problem?" normally leads to ineffective exchanges. If you question the observed behavior by asking, "Are you mad?" the likely response is a defensive "no," or "Why would I be mad at you?" The "no" response stops communication and doesn't address your feelings of being ignored. You might say, "I'm getting the sense that you are mad at me" or "I feel you're mad at me when you don't talk to me. Are you?" Perception checking, in the majority of cases, is useful in creating a nonaccusatory, and therefore a nondefensive, communication environment.

Keep in mind, you should only use perception checking if there is a chance your attribution of meaning is incorrect. For example, it would be inappropriate to use perception checking in the following example:

Instructor: Michael, would you please close the door?
Michael: I'm getting the sense you would like to have the door closed. Would you?

It is also inappropriate to over-use perception checking. Think of how annoying it would be to have someone constantly perception checking to see if you are mad at them. Sometimes people over-use perception checking when they really need to simply stop and think for a minute about the situation. In our example above, if your significant other comes home and isn't talking, why is your first perception that the person is mad at you? Why wouldn't you assume she/he is tired or had a bad experience at work? Some people tend to think that everything is their fault when really they need to think through the other reasons that might trigger the other person's behavior. You should also use perception checking when you truly want to understand what is going on with the other person. If they are in a bad mood, and you are in a close relationship, sometimes you can choose to just let it go and stay out of their way. But if the situation continues to worry you, and you need to clarify whether you are the cause, then go ahead and check it out.

Critical Thinking

Describe a recent misunderstanding in your life that would have resolved itself more effectively if you had simply used perception checking.

_____

_____

_____

_____

Finally, there are many people who feel awkward using the perception-checking skill. If you are reluctant to talk about feelings, then this skill will take a lot of practice before you can use it comfortably. Many people choose to simply ignore their own feelings and just accept their interpretation of the other communicator's actions. This is unfair to you as well as to the other person whose actions may be misinterpreted. Another reason people are reluctant to use the perception-checking skill is because it is easier to assume what another person means than to ask questions. Although asking someone to explain his or her behavior may be awkward initially, the value of accuracy in communication is immeasurable.

PERCEPTION RELATED TO SELF-CONCEPT

Self-concept refers to what we think about ourselves, including our physical attributes (short or tall, big or small), our aptitudes (good at math or at getting along with others), our physical coordination (good at sports or video games), and our skills (tying flies or gourmet cooking). Most of these attributes are factual assessments. We recognize whether we are tall or short, good at games, etc. We reach these conclusions as we assess and evaluate ourselves intrapersonally.

We also assess ourselves through comments others make about us. We take into consideration evaluations made by teachers, family members, significant others, friends, siblings, other relatives, coaches, and religious leaders. If, as a child, you hear that you are "pretty" or "smart" or "stupid" or "lazy," these labels shape your perception of yourself. Nicknames such as "chubby," "slim," "bubba," or "princess" also affect our self-concept. If we see ourselves through the labels given to us by others, we may develop a self-concept based on illusion rather than on reality.

Critical Thinking

List five adjectives that you would use to describe yourself. (This is a frequently used interview question.)

_____

_____

How did you come up with the adjectives that you used? (From personal observation? Communication with others?)

_____

_____

Self-concept influences your communication skills with the external world. Our presentational style, use of nonverbal communication, ability to interact on an interpersonal level, or our ability to function in a team environment grows out of our self-concept. If our self-concept is that we are shy, we are likely to have non-animated nonverbals, a quiet disposition and presentational style, and we may be afraid to participate in teams. On the other hand, if our self-concept is that we are confident, we will stand tall, speak loudly, and actively participate in teams.

⇨ Try It! ⇦

If your instructor perceives he is shy, what kind of behaviors will he exhibit in the classroom?

_____

If you hear you are stupid and unlikable all of your life, how will you interact with others at college?

_____

— Professional Perspective —

As a professional therapist it has been my experience that our self-concept is a result of the feedback we receive from others, especially those we love and trust. Their words are the chisel that forms the person we become. If the feedback is constantly negative, we can change "chisel" to "weapon." _The Dead Poet's Society_ gives the example of an adolescent who chooses suicide because he can't meet his father's expectations. I wish I could tell you this is fiction, but it is not. I write crisis intervention plans for my clients every day. And I shudder when I think of the millions of other therapists who must do the same. Feedback kills self-concept every day. Choose your words carefully and choose how other people's words will affect you. It is never all one person's fault. Choose only your level of responsibility. What your loved ones say is only their opinion, it is not fact. And focus on your positives. After all, your yesterday, today, and tomorrow is a matter of your choice. Choose wisely.

—T. W. Anderson
Adolescent Therapist

PERCEPTION RELATED TO SELF-ESTEEM

Self-esteem refers to the value we place on self-concept observations. For example, Rachel, who is 5′3″ tall, thinks she's short. Her self-esteem related to this concept depends on the value she places on height. In U.S. culture, research shows that tall people have an advantage in interviews, presidential elections, and promotions (Knapp & Hall, 2002, pp. 198–199). If Rachel thinks only tall people are attractive and desirable, her self-esteem will probably be low because there is nothing she can do to change her height. However, if she believes attractiveness does not depend on height, then being short will not affect her self-esteem.

Sometimes, we can be our own worst enemy. We can be either extremely critical or extremely supportive of ourselves. How you communicate intrapersonally affects your self-esteem. What do you say to yourself when you get an "F" on an exam? Do you say, "I can't believe how stupid I am! I can never do anything right." This negative internal communication can damage your self-esteem and affect future behavior. Or, do you say something positive to yourself, "Wow. I sure wasn't expecting an 'F.' I need to figure out what to do differently so I can improve my grades." It is important to remain positive in your self-criticism so you can solve your problem and improve performance.

Self-esteem and how we feel about ourselves influences our willingness and ability to communicate effectively. If you feel good about yourself, you may be more likely to approach and meet new people, to assert your ideas in a team situation, to stand confidently before an audience, and to try new communication strategies. If you don't trust yourself to discover new talents and instead rely only on past skills that make you feel comfortable, you constrict personal growth. If you feel your self-concept or self-esteem need to be stronger, there are numerous books and articles outlining the skills you can practice to strengthen your views of yourself. You may also want to seek professional assistance.

SUMMARY

Understanding the perceptual process is critical to becoming an effective communicator. You must understand why you assign meaning the way you do to words, actions, situations, and people so you can improve your communication style and avoid miscommunication. Once you understand your own perceptions and how the perceptual process works, you'll be better able to analyze why other communicators perceive phenomena and assign meaning the way they do. You should be able to think more critically about concepts such as stereotyping and attribution.

There are fascinating challenges waiting for you as you acclimate to new situations, perhaps even new regions of the country with their unique cultures and people. As you work through the perceptual process of organizing and assigning meaning to unfamiliar behaviors and events, you must be aware of the potential for saying or doing the wrong thing. As you gain a more acute awareness about yourself and your ability to communicate effectively with other people, don't jump to conclusions.

Do your best to manage the perceptual process within yourself so others see you as a solid communicator and someone they would like to get to know. Take nothing for granted. The things that look easy are normally the hardest to conquer.

[Nine-dot puzzle solution: Start (1) a diagonal line from *outside* the lower right-hand dot (at a distance similar to the spacing between the nine dots) up to the upper left-hand dot; (2) draw a horizontal line to the right through the upper dots extending, again, outside the area; (3) draw a diagonal line through the middle right-hand dot and the middle lower dot, extending the line to below the left-hand row of dots; (4) draw a vertical line up through the left-hand row of dots.]

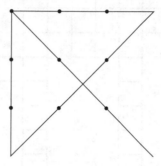

Key Words

attribution
fact
inference
perception checking
perceptual process

selective attention
self-concept
self-esteem
stereotyping

Crossword 2: Perception

Across

2. Paying attention to only the stimuli that are unique or unusual.
7. A conclusion drawn from an observed fact is a(n) _____.
8. Observable phenomena.
9. The process of verifying whether our attributions of meaning are correct.

Down

1. When Eric believed that his Latino roommate, Juan, would speak Spanish, he was _____.

3. If Juan thought that Eric was self-centered because Eric chose the bed by the window, Juan would be using _____ for that assumption.
4. The general perception we have of our physical attributes and abilities.
5. A process of encountering sensory stimuli such as sounds or sights or touches, deciding which you will recognize, and assigning meaning to them.
6. How we feel about ourselves.

CHAPTER 3

Language

OBJECTIVES

After reading this chapter, you should be able to:

• Explain the concept of symbols

• Define denotative and connotative meaning

• Understand content and relationship levels of meaning

• Describe how language influences our thoughts

• Explain the concept of rhetorical sensitivity

• Analyze your own use of rhetorical sensitivity

Lupita is attending your school for the first time. She speaks Spanish as her native language, and she is becoming quite fluent in conversational English. She has occasional difficulty, however, with some colloquial expressions used in the United States. Lupita attends a party in a room full of U.S. students. She notices her friend Maria preparing food at the refreshment table. She turns to Mark and says, "Oh, isn't that nice, Maria just cut the cheese for everyone." Mark spits his drink out on the floor and erupts in laughter. Four other friends who overheard her remark are also laughing hysterically. Lupita has no idea what is going on, but she is embarrassed by their reaction to her remark.

On another occasion, Lupita is shopping at the mall with Anita. They stop for a bite to eat in the food court. Anita notices an overweight man consuming three burgers, a large order of fries, a shake, onion rings, and dessert. Anita says, "Wow! Will you look at that couch potato?" Lupita is very confused because she can't see a sofa or a potato and wonders what Anita is trying to say to her. Anita proceeds to explain that this is a U.S. expression for people who don't move around much and are usually overweight from the consumption of too much junk food.

Language is the common tool everyone uses to communicate. In a basic communication course it is important for you to understand the fundamentals of the language process so you can make the appropriate choices in your remarks and avoid misunderstandings when speaking to others. Since communication is a daily process, solid language skills are essential for everyone.

SYMBOLS

We cannot simply pour the information from our minds into other people's heads. We use **symbols** to communicate with others. All words are symbols. Symbols are arbitrary representations; we choose a word to represent an object or concept and then send the word across a channel to someone else. Because effective meaning relies on mutual understanding of symbols, we must be as clear as possible when we encode words. When someone says, "I saw an animal on my way to work this morning," what image do you see? Animal is a vague symbol—it could represent: deer, bear, squirrel, bird, cat, dog, and so on. Let's say the statement is narrowed to, "I saw a cat on my way to work." Do you have an accurate picture of the animal? How about, "I saw a black cat." Maybe we need to say, "I saw a big, black cat with a white spot on its chest." Now, we all have the same basic picture, but does your image of the cat have three legs? In other words, the clearer you are in selecting the proper symbols for a thought sequence, the greater chance you have of other people understanding your meaning.

Even when we carefully select symbols, we can run into problems conveying meaning because symbols are **arbitrary** and **ambiguous**. Symbols are arbitrary because there is no innate connection between an object or thought and the word we use to represent it. We say a patch of soil where plants, vegetables, or flowers are planted is a "garden." However, there is nothing about the site that necessitates it being called a garden. This is why other languages have different symbolic representations for the same word: in German, it is *der garten*; in Italian, it is *giardino*; in Spanish and French, it is *jardin*; in Japanese, it is *niva*; and in Russian, it is *сад*. Every language uses a different symbol, yet each word represents the same tangible concept—a piece of land where something grows.

— Professional Perspective —

I once performed *The Three Little Pigs* in Japan, and the translator didn't show up. Not being able to translate "Little Pig, Little Pig, let me come in . . ." I just had the Wolf say, "Roar!" That worked until I told the pig to say "Oink, Oink!" That baffled a little Japanese boy . . . since only U.S. kids associate the sound "oink" with a pig.

—Allynn Gooen
International Performance Artist

Technically, we can use any symbol we want to represent an object or concept. If Lisa raises her young daughters to call a "desk" a "pickle," she could say, "Please sit down at the pickle and do your homework." They would understand their mother's meaning and use the word the same way. The only way the daughters would learn that their meaning for "pickle" is not a universally accepted definition would be when they interact with other children who have been taught to say "desk." While this is a highly unlikely scenario, it illustrates the arbitrariness of symbols, which we often mistakenly assume have universal meaning. We need to be aware that differences in symbols exist from region to region in the United States and from country to country. Can you think of a time when someone used a symbol that was unfamiliar to you?

Critical Thinking

A hot sandwich can be called a hoagie, a grinder, a cosmo, or a sub. You might recognize only one of these symbols. List some symbols you have heard people use that were not familiar to you.

_____

_____

Can you identify the following from a region in Pennsylvania?

Gob _____

"Go red up your room." _____

What are some of the local symbols you have heard?

_____

_____

Another problem in trying to create meaning for another person is that symbols are ambiguous. Because meanings are in people and not in words, this language vagueness blends with the concept of perception to make effective communication an exciting challenge. Each communicator decides what certain phrases mean.

⇨ Try It! ⇦

Take a minute to jot down a numerical answer to the following questions.

1. Roberto has a lot of money. How much money does he have?

_____

2. Alisha spends a lot of time on instant messenger. How much time does she spend?

_____

3. The temperature outside during Mark's vacation was unbearable. What was the temperature?

_____

4. When I graduate and get a job, my five-year goal is to own an expensive car. How much will the car cost?

_____

Think about phrases such as "a lot" or words such as "expensive." Such words and phrases are all vague and ambiguous without a context. Compare your answers to the questions in the Try It! box with those of other students in your classroom. Who has the highest number and who has the lowest number? Is the difference substantial? How can that happen? Think about everyone's perceptions and backgrounds. If I say, "That sure is a tall building," you might think of a fifteen-story building. If you are from New York City, you might think of an 80-story building. That is a huge discrepancy. Speakers should be careful to choose the most concrete terms that are available when creating their message. For instance, "That 75-story building sure is tall" is a concrete way of explaining the picture that is in your mind to another person. The other person may not agree with your definition, but at least you have been clear. Clarity should be the driving force for any speaker when selecting symbols to express meaning.

— Professional Perspective —

Clear expression is important in business and is critical in the advertising/public relations industries. Most people don't realize it takes weeks—even months—to find the right words to successfully market a product. The problem facing advertising executives is how to "focus" on the one selling point that is going to generate new sales for the client while staying within the confines of the law and, at the same time, be "brilliant" for the consumer. Clients love to win awards and relish praise from their peers for an innovative campaign. Conversely, clients do not like to spend time in court defending their claims. The simple expression of an idea could lead to either outcome. Writers must be original yet critical of the ways they express their ideas in order to satisfy agency management, the client, and industry watchdogs. Remember the next time you fast forward through a commercial on a program you recorded that what you perceive as simply 30 seconds of denture cleaner is the end result of a long, thought-out, creative process. For the writers, the dentures aren't the only things that need to "shine."

Chiarezza dell' espressione e' importante in affari, ed e' critica nell' industria delle pubbliche relazioni e nella pubblicita'. La maggior parte del pubblico non realizza che si impiegano settimane, se non mesi, per trovare le parole giuste per commercializzare con successo un prodotto sul mercato. Il problema che si presenta agli operatori del settore e' su quale qualita' del prodotto focalizzare la campagna pubblicitaria per convincere il consumatore restando nei parametri di legge e allo stesso tempo soddisfare i propri clienti con successivo incremento delle vendite. Lo scopo e' di ricevere premiazioni e riconoscimenti sia da colleghi che da concorrenti per una campagna innovativa, e non di dover passare ore in tribunale per difendere i propri interessi. La semplice espressione di un'idea puo' portare ad uno o all' altro risultato. Per i produttori e' importante essere originali, ma anche attenti nella maniera in cui esprimono la loro idea, per cosi' soddisfare il cliente, l'amministrazione dell agenzia e i critici del settore. La prossima volta che, usando il telecomando, magari vi soffermate su uno spot pubblicitario per un prodotto di igiene delle dentiere, ricordate che se per voi e' solo un filmato di 30 secondi, per gli addetti ai lavori e' il risultato finale di un lungo e creativo processo di produzione, dove non e' solo l'oggetto pubblicizzato a dover brillare.

—Kathleen Corrigan
Legal Clearances
Grey Global Group

There is an exception, however. There are times when speakers specifically choose ***creative ambiguity*** to mask a message that might be hurtful. If someone says, "How do you like my new shirt?" and you are not impressed, rather than hurt their feelings you might opt for a creatively ambiguous message: "Oh, it's really interesting." Once someone uses a creatively ambiguous message, the receiver generally can tell that the person isn't as excited about the shirt as they are. If the receiver is perceptive, this allows both parties to get out of the exchange gracefully and without any hurt feelings.

Critical Thinking

What are some other creatively ambiguous lines that you have heard or used?

_____

_____

The discussion about word ambiguity becomes more challenging when a speaker uses abstract terms such as "love." What does the following exchange mean: "I love you." "I love you, too." Do these two people mean the same thing? Maybe yes, but probably not. If you have 100 people state their meaning for this exchange, you will probably find many variations. Some possibilities include:

- "I want to be with you until I find someone better."
- "I get goose bumps when I see you across a room."
- "I can't imagine living without you."
- "You are a part of my soul."
- "I will hold your head when you are miserably sick and throwing up into a toilet."

It can be very important to ask for clarification when talking about an important issue with another person. Asking questions can make conversational meaning clearer. Once both people fully understand each other, it is easier to continue the discussion and the relationship. As a speaker, you can use concrete terms to make your message more clear. By understanding the nature of symbols and the inherent problems of ambiguity and arbitrariness, you will be able to recognize potential miscommunications more easily.

DENOTATIVE AND CONNOTATIVE MEANINGS

Another important distinction when analyzing language usage is the difference between the denotative and connotative meanings of symbols. A **denotative meaning** is the dictionary definition of a word. The **connotative meaning** includes the feelings and emotions people attach to a word. If communicators don't share connotative meanings for the symbols in the interaction, communication misunderstandings will occur. Because there are so many connotative meanings for almost every symbol, the possibility of misunderstanding is immense.

For example, think about the term "family." A denotative definition for family is "a set of parents and children, or of relations, living together or not" (*The Oxford American Dictionary and Thesaurus*, 2003).

Family experiences are different for every individual in our culture, including siblings raised by the same parents. For Samantha, the connotative meaning for "family" is very cheerful and happy. It is a place of support, encouragement, and love. In her experience, families eat dinner together, talk about their day, play games, and go to sporting events together. For Tim, the connotative meaning for the word family may be horrifying. His concept of family may be a place of physical and/or verbal abuse, sarcastic put-downs, or absolute emotional neglect. His parents never gave him any attention; often, they would come right out and tell him that he was stupid and would never amount to anything. If Samantha and Tim are in a long-term relationship, imagine the difference in perception when Samantha says, "I can't wait to get married and start a family." Tim will probably have an immediate negative reaction to her statement. Samantha may interpret his reaction as an indication that he doesn't like her well enough to have a family with her. Instead, Tim is reacting to his connotative meaning of family, not to what she is saying.

This kind of misunderstanding happens all the time. For instance, Johnny and Ruth have been married for a year. Johnny says, "I can't wait until my birthday. It's the most special day of the year to me. I love birthday celebrations." Johnny grew up in a family where birthday parties were attended by lots of friends and included elaborate entertainment, decorations, favors, party hats, and fancy table settings. Ruth, on the other hand, grew up in a family where if she got a card on her birthday, she considered herself lucky. So on Johnny's birthday, Ruth hands him a very extravagant card, which she found after reading every card in the shop. She also went to a nearby specialty store and bought him a box of fancy chocolates. He appears confused and upset by her gifts. She has no idea why he seems so disappointed despite her generosity and effort. Ruth and Johnny have different meanings for the words birthday and celebration. You can see how different connotative meanings, coupled with the fact that language is ambiguous, can lead to communication difficulties in a relationship.

Critical Thinking

Describe a time in your life when language ambiguity led to a communication misunderstanding in one of your interpersonal relationships.

_____

_____

_____

_____

Because of denotative and connotative word meanings, we need to remember that word meaning is ingrained in people, not in the word itself. The best-intentioned communicator cannot guarantee how another communicator will receive and interpret spoken language. For example, Juliette visited her brother and his wife for a holiday. They had just purchased a French press coffeemaker, a new concept at that time. She was very impressed and said, "Wow, you guys are so trendy." Her brother was so angry he refused to speak to her for the rest of the day. While she had intended her comment to be a compliment, he interpreted the word "trendy" as a decidedly negative label. When they could finally talk about their misunderstanding, Juliette learned her brother felt the word trendy meant "following along with the crowd and not having a mind of his own." He was a person who strongly valued his individualism; therefore, "trendy" was a total insult. This misunderstanding would not have occurred, however, if her brother had simply used perception checking to discover her meaning for trendy. He might have said, "Are you saying that I follow the crowd?" This would have allowed them to discuss the issue immediately. This example reminds us that the meaning of words resides in people, not in the symbol itself, and illustrates the value of perception-checking skills.

CONTENT AND RELATIONSHIP LEVELS OF MEANING

Are you aware that there are at least two levels of meaning for every statement? The **content level** of meaning refers to the factual interpretation of the words. If you say to your significant other, "So I see you didn't do the dishes," the content level of meaning is that there are dirty dishes in the sink. However, you could also be trying to communicate something about your relationship. On the **relationship level**, the statement could mean, "You lazy person, what have you been doing all day?" Your tone of voice would distinguish that possible meaning from another, such as, "Oh my, is everything ok?" In the second case, your inflection would be different and you would probably speak in a hesitant, questioning tone with lots of pauses.

The relationship level of meaning is particularly ambiguous and can lead to serious misunderstanding. Even when messages seem clear and direct, people may look for "hidden" meaning rather than accepting the content level of meaning. On the other hand, some people "hint" at their meaning by using the relationship level rather than just being honest and direct. Let's examine two scenarios.

Laura asks Scott if he is mad at her. Scott says, "No." Instead of accepting the content level of meaning, Laura begins an analysis in her head. "Well, he said that in a funny way, I wonder if he really is mad?" So she asks, "Are you sure you are not mad at me?" Scott, who just answered that question, is irritated to be asked again, and so he raises his voice a little, "No, I'm not mad." When Laura hears the raised inflection, she interprets the irritated tone as evidence her doubts were correct. She may even ask him a third time, which if you examine the situation from Scott's point of view is totally irritating. Laura would have done better to accept the content level of meaning in the message.

Another scenario involves people who insinuate meaning through the inflection and tone of the words. In this case, Kristen asks her partner Todd if he is upset about something. Todd says, "No" in a cynical tone. He is trying to get across that he really is mad without coming out and saying the words. This is a no-win situation for everyone involved. If Kristen reacts to the content level of meaning and says, "Oh good" and walks away, Todd will be angry. If Kristen recognizes the game he is playing with the language and continues the conversation to find out what is bothering him, she is likely to be irritated because he didn't just come out and state the problem.

— Professional Perspective —

Why should we learn foreign languages? "They should just speak English," I said! Then I became president of an international company working with Russian culture and sports. I found the language barrier had more to do with our use of slang than their inability to speak English.

U.S. English is riddled with idioms. When speaking to people who do not speak U.S. English, leave out sports metaphors ("slam dunk"), Valley speak ("whatever"), and today's favorite buzzword (which, by the time you read this, will be yesterday's buzzword so you fill in the blank!).

English-as-a-second-language speakers are not deaf so speaking loudly will not help them understand English better. Speak slowly, choose words wisely, and never be disrespectful.

When correcting foreigners, do so diplomatically! When the Russian culture minister said the Met was "so mickey mouse," he meant Mickey Mouse was a great American export, and he genuinely thought it was a good metaphor for one of the world's greatest museums.

Зачем нам изучать иностранные языки? – «Они сами должны говорить по - английски », – думал я. Но вот я стал президентом международной компании, деятельность которой связана с Россией в сфере культуры и спорта. И я понял, что языковой барьер обусловлен не столько неспособностью людей говорить по - английски, а скорее тем, что мы сами используем сленг.

Американский вариант английского языка наполнен идиомами. При разговоре с людьми других национальностей американцам следует избегать спортивных метафор («slam dunk» – *термин, описывающий действия баскетбольного игрока**), слов, заполняющих паузу («whatever» – *слово, имеющее различные оттенки значений, от «ладно » до «что бы то ни было »* *) и современных модных словечек (которые выйдут из моды к тому времени, когда Вы будете читать этот текст, так что решайте сами, какие слова можно было бы привести в качестве примера).

Если для кого -то английский язык не является родным, это еще не означает, что такой человек плохо слышит - соответственно, повышение громкости разговора не будет способствовать лучшему пониманию английской речи. Говорите медленно, правильно подбирайте слова и никогда не проявляйте неуважения.

Если Вы поправляете иностранцев, делайте это дипломатично! Когда Министр культуры России сказал, что Нью -йоркский «Metropolitan Museum of Art» похож на Микки -Мауса, министр имел в виду, что Микки -Маус был прекрасным примером распространения американской культуры и искренне полагал, что нашел хорошую метафору для описания одного из самых известных музеев мира.

[* курсивом выделены примечания переводчика]

—Maureen C. Baker, President
Highland Ventures, Inc.

Think carefully about content and relationship levels of meaning. You should look for them and respond to each when appropriate. You should also try to say what you mean. Most people get annoyed quickly with people who play language games.

Ethical Considerations

How ethical is it to be indirect and hint at your meaning rather than coming out and saying what you mean?

_____

_____

How difficult is it to really say what you mean instead of hinting around?

_____

_____

THE INFLUENCE OF LANGUAGE

The language we choose influences the way we think about things (Boroditsky, 2001). As we make symbol choices, it is imperative to think about how we view the world based on the words we use to describe it. For instance, think of a person on a diet who eats six chocolate chip cookies one day. There is a big difference in how the person will view the situation if he chooses the words "I cheated" versus "I made an unhealthy eating choice." Notice that "I cheated" has moral connotations. It makes the person seem unethical, weak, or appalling. On the other hand, the words "I made an unhealthy eating choice" focuses on the event itself rather than making a judgment. An individual can perceive the event as an unfortunate incident under his control or as evidence of a personality flaw. This choice of language will influence how the person thinks about himself.

⇨ Try It! ⇦

Think about the influence of language and relate it to the previous chapter on perception and self-esteem. As we communicate intrapersonally, our word choices can make a difference on how we see ourselves. Keep track of how you talk to yourself for a day. Record the types of things you say and the word choices you use. Are the words positive or negative? Reflect on how those choices influence your self-esteem. Is it high or low?

_____

_____

_____

_____

_____

Another problem occurs when we don't have a word to describe an event or a feeling. It is difficult for us to talk about something if we don't have any symbols to communicate our impressions. We avoid discussion and pretend the event or feeling isn't there. Julia Wood (2001, p. 114) points out that before there was a term for the horrendous behavior of date rape, victims didn't know what to call it or how to talk about it. Once the term developed, many people could begin to describe what had happened to them.

A more current language example is the word "non-divorce." This term appeared in the media in 2007 to describe couples who are married but no longer in love. They are amicable, almost like roommates or brother/sisters. They have platonic relationships and no intent to divorce because of financial reasons, religious commitment, and/or issues with child-rearing/custody. While many of you may have experienced the ups and downs of a relationship, these couples have been on the down side for a number of years with little hope of an upswing. However, they are content with their circumstances. Until now, there has never been a term to describe this situation among married people. Do you know a couple who fits this description?

In addition to the difficulties presented by the ambiguity of our language, we should also be aware of how *polarized* language is. We have words for opposing emotional positions, but no words for the "in-betweens." How do you describe someone who is 450 pounds? We might use the words "fat" or "obese." How do you describe someone who is 95 pounds? We might use the words "skinny" or "thin." How do you describe someone who is 165 pounds and 5´10´´ tall? We don't have appropriately descriptive words for this condition. The person is "of average weight." But, the phrase "average weight" doesn't have the dramatic impact of obese or skinny to a listener. Sometimes phrases polarize our language to set up an either/or way of thinking. A group on our campus recently suggested using the following phrase to get people to vote: "It's a man's world unless women vote." While we agree that women should vote, we are not certain that we need to polarize men versus women in order to do it. The fact that our language is polarized on numerous issues sometimes makes it difficult to find the appropriate symbols for proper communication.

When we create new symbols, we change how people think. Let's focus on a medical example. Some human characteristics have been reclassified as medical conditions so they can be treated. Freedman states:

> The medical community is giving names to "conditions" that used to be simply characteristics. So, what was previously a flat chest, for example, is called micromastia. . . . If doctors give something a name that implies illness, then they have something to treat. (cited in Fellingham, 2003, p. 160)

The creation of a medical symbol for a natural characteristic of certain people spurs thinking about the characteristic as a disease. Will this change the way people think about themselves? Of course!

Language influences the way we think; this is why words are so important. However, meaning always resides in people. Some words are instantly offensive to some people while others have little or no reaction to the very same symbol. Rhetorical sensitivity is a concept that helps us navigate through fluctuating communication situations.

RHETORICAL SENSITIVITY

Communicators must make thoughtful choices when using symbols, mindful of the difficulties created by language ambiguity and connotative meanings. Often you'll hear people talk about using "politically correct" (PC) language. Many people roll their eyes when PC is mentioned. What is the connotative meaning of being politically correct? Many people become outraged and state, "The First Amendment guarantees my right to say anything I want!" They are correct, of course. Others feel PC is "too much hassle." Roderick Hart and Don Burks (1972) introduced the term *rhetorical sensitivity* in an effort to help people cooperate. The term has come to mean reviewing all of the available symbols and using the one that is least likely to be offensive to the listener. That's not unreasonable, is it?

Think of the variety of messages you send on any given day. We may choose a *loaded word* without really thinking about it as we communicate with others. A loaded word is one that has a positive or negative connotative meaning in addition to its denotative meaning. For instance, the following words all have the same denotative definition. But which would you say are loaded terms?

cheap	thrifty
tightwad	miserly
frugal	meager
penny-pinching	prudent
stingy	economical

Even though every one of these terms means that a person is careful with money, which terms have a virtuous meaning? Which have an adverse meaning? Being rhetorically sensitive means that we choose the term that would convey the appropriate emotional meaning and be least likely to offend someone.

There are four main categories of potentially offensive language:

• Racist/Religious/Cultural Language

• Sexist/Heterosexist Language

• The Generic He

• Profanity

If you are aware of these potential problem areas, you can avoid them in your own communication and can decode the communication of others with greater understanding.

Racist/Religious/Cultural Language

Racist language includes words that denigrate someone of a particular ethnic background. We are certain you know the obvious examples; however, there are many expressions buried in our language that you may not recognize as racist. A subtle remark such as, "Those people don't belong here" communicates volumes about a communicator's prejudices. During a recent school board meeting in a small town, a community member said in a low voice, "Why don't you go back where you came from?" after an Asian-looking student offered her opinion on the topic under discussion. This student happened to have been born in that small town. The statement provided real insight into the prejudices of that community member. *Religious* expressions such as "I jewed him down" are also prevalent and extremely inappropriate. *Cultural* expressions about "Oriental" people are also offensive. The term Oriental refers to objects such as rugs. People are Asian. Any term that is offensive to a group with different characteristics from the socially accepted norm falls into this category as well. People who say, "Oh that is so retarded," may be perceived as denigrating people with intellectual disabilities.

— Professional Perspective —

Trying to be rhetorically sensitive has many challenges . . .

I have to tell you what happened at work today—a coworker and I put together a flyer announcing the company picnic, and I had to have it approved by our new Director of People Services (formerly human resources). She said it was ok but (and I quote), "On a personal note I prefer the words outing or teambuilding day or event over summer picnic. The historical origins of the word picnic are derogatory. They are from the term pickaninny, 'a black female child,' and evolved to the shortened version when southern whites would gather with their families and friends to hang a black person, and in a few cases Jews, in a lynching. Everyone gathered for the picnic."

Huh? says linguist Helene—isn't picnic derived from the French *pique-nique?* And who would ever connect picnic with pickaninny any more, even if it were true? And did she just throw in the reference to Jews because she knows I'm Jewish? I never heard a Jew object to the word picnic! But Ms. People Services is of course diversity-sensitive, so we were ready to change it to "outing." Then I Googled "picnic word derivation" because I just didn't believe it, and the very first hit was snopes.com, the "urban legends" site, which states unequivocally that the story is FALSE. They also shared an instance where shifting to the term "outing" offended homosexual students at a particular university. (You can read the whole story at http://www.snopes.com/language/offense/picnic.htm)

In the end, we decided to call it a "summer event." It's silly, but better than calling the HR Director an idiot.

Helene B.
Lead Programmer Analyst

Ethical Considerations

Do you believe that you are unbiased? Do you use the phrases "Oh that is so retarded" or "That is so gay"? What kind of ethical compromise do you make when using those phrases? If you don't use these phrases, do you say anything when others use them? If not, what does your silence communicate about your ethical standards?

_____

_____

Sexist/Heterosexist Language

Sexist language denigrates someone based on their sex. For instance, the use of the term "girl" to refer to a grown woman is derogatory because it implies immaturity. Recently a term has been created to refer to the sandals that men wear: *mandals*. This is derogatory because we are denigrating men for wearing a particular type of footwear that should be available to everyone. **Heterosexist** language assumes everyone in society is heterosexual. It is much more rhetorically sensitive and inclusive to say "partner" or "significant other" when talking about people in a marriage or romantic relationship. Also watch out for terms or phrases that denigrate homosexuals or females, such as, "Oh that is so gay" or "You throw like a girl." Others may not appreciate your remarks about their behavior, even if you intended the remark to be humorous. Someone else overhearing the conversation may perceive you to be insensitive, crude, or uneducated.

Reality ✔

You may think that we are overly sensitive by saying that you should think about refraining from the use of these phrases. However, recently at a high school in California, "when a few classmates razzed Rebekah Rice about her Mormon upbringing with questions such as, 'Do you have 10 moms?' she shot back: 'That's so gay.'

"Those three words landed the high school freshman in the principal's office and resulted in a lawsuit that raises this question: When do playground insults used every day all over America cross the line into hate speech that must be stamped out?" ("That's so gay," 2007).

There are some interesting discussion points here. First, let us clarify that according to the article, the school put a reprimand in Rice's file that led to her parents filing a lawsuit against the school to have it removed, saying that she was singled out. Also, the previous year two students were paid to beat up a gay student, prompting action by the school. You can see that there is a combination of religious and heterosexist language issues here. As a group, discuss the following:

1. How often do you hear these types of remarks at your school? _____

2. Do you think she should have been reprimanded for her comment? _____

3. Do you think the religious comments should have been treated in the same way? _____

4. Knowing that a gay student was beaten up in the previous year at this school; do you think these comments should be classified as hate speech? _____

5. If you were the principal how would you have handled the situation? _____

_____

6. What consequences should the students receive? _____

_____

The Generic He

The *generic he* is another use of language that is changing. It used to be appropriate to use the word "he" or "man" to mean both men and women. However, this is no longer considered to be appropriate. Some people do not understand why this gender issue is so important.

Reality ✔

Before you read any further, fill in the rest of these sentences.

1. When an administrative assistant first arrives at the office, _____

2. After a nurse has completed training, _____

3. When a lawyer meets a client, _____

4. When a chef enters the kitchen, _____

5. If a flight attendant is late to work, _____

6. Before a judge can give a final ruling, _____

Wendy Martyna (1978) conducted a study using the phrases in the Reality Check box. Now—look at your answers. Did you:

- conform to traditional stereotypes (using "he" for lawyer and judge, "she" for parent and administrative assistant)?
- flip the pronouns so that "she" was used for the stereotypically male professions and "he" for the stereotypically female positions?
- avoid using "he/she" and substitute "they" or "one"?
- use "he/she" for each of the entries?
- use a random mixture of pronouns or the other choices above?
- use "he" in each case?

Martyna argued that if everyone truly understood the word "he" to be a generic pronoun meaning everyone, then everyone would use "he" in each of the above sentences. In 20 years of using this activity in class, we only encountered one student who used the generic he. The conclusion is, therefore, that people do not use the generic he to mean everyone. If you use specific pronouns, then you don't believe in the generic he. Analyze your responses above carefully and decide whether you really believe the generic he to mean everyone.

When we modify our communication to use language that eliminates the generic he, we are using inclusive language. The importance of inclusive language is reflected in research that suggests parents, teachers, and religious leaders who use male-oriented language in referring to professions limit young females' perceptions of potential career choices (Wood, 2001, p. 111). If you were aware of the effect of using male-oriented language, would you change your language so that you would not limit the choices for your daughter?

⇒ **Try It!** ⇐

How can you change the following to be inclusive?

Fireman _____

Policeman _____

Mailman _____

Waitress _____

Stewardess _____

Religion often uses the generic he. References in religious teaching are frequently to men. Today, there is increased discussion about whether these historic references give the perception of excluding women. Some religious groups are trying to place women in positions of authority within the church hierarchy, while others are against this action. As another example of the changing generic he in religion, notice during the holiday season that some boxes of cards now say, "Peace on Earth, Good Will toward All."

Profanity

Profanity is the utterance of irreverent, vulgar, or obscene language. Opinions about what is profane will vary depending on culture and socioeconomic factors. People normally use profanity for emphasis, shock value, or because it is a learned habit. A communicator takes a level of social risk when using profanity. There was a time when profanity was mainly an urban phenomenon, but this is no longer the case. Many people use profanity openly in communication. And yet, in some regions, such as the South, profanity is rarely used in public.

Think about your group of friends. Do you ever use profanity around them? If so, do you alter your language when you go home and talk to your parents or grandparents? If your language use does change when you go home, then you understand the importance of adapting your communication to your audience. Your use or nonuse of profanity should be an informed choice. Think carefully about the people who can hear you when you use profanity and the potential consequences of your language choices. There are people who will remember only that you use profane language. What if a potential employer calls them to ask about hiring you?

Frustrations

Many people find the discussion of rhetorical sensitivity extremely frustrating. They think it is too difficult to adapt to the ever-changing terminology in language. The cultural progression of language can be quite frustrating. But that does not mean you shouldn't think about it and decide if you should change your communication patterns. In the past, we referred to people with a physical disability as crippled. Then, the term became handicapped. It morphed quickly into physically disabled. To sound more positive, it eventually became physically challenged. Finally, the word "persons" was added to the beginning of the phrase, "persons with physical challenges." The reasoning was that this places the emphasis on the person first.

Reality ✔

Since we wrote the first edition of this book, the terms have changed once again. If you look at the Web site for the Special Olympics, it is interesting to see the changes. In a previous section, we talked about the ethical consequences of using the term "that's so retarded." A perusal of the Web site shows that the organization has realized that people are slow to change the use of this phrase that means "stupid." Therefore, the organization has changed their language. They now refer to their participants as "people with intellectual disabilities."

A lot of our terms and phrases are linked to a specific period of time and to a specific generation. Try not to date yourself in language choices, and avoid offending people as you speak. You should do your best to keep up with the current terminology. Your choice of a correct term should always be appropriate for any occasion, and it should consistently reflect your personal style. Consistency in style helps the perception of credibility.

There is derogatory language for every race, religion, sexual orientation, and economic class in our culture. The obvious response in any discussion of derogatory language is to say, "Do not use words that offend other people." This is easy to say and difficult to execute. How much should we monitor our own language? When should we speak up about the language others are using around us? You'll notice your reactions to the following scenarios differ depending on the people with whom you spend your time. Your answers will also depend on your personal level of sensitivity to others and your geographical location.

Choices and Consequences

These are all real scenarios the authors have encountered. Which of the following situations offend you? Which do not?

1. Three 16-year-old boys appear at a playground and continuously use profanity very loudly in their conversation. You notice there are small children at the playground.

2. You and your friends are using profanity, and you notice there are small children around you.

3. You and your friends are on campus, and someone in your group makes a racist joke.

4. You are in the break room at work, and a colleague makes a joke about homosexuals.

5. Your 90-year-old grandmother makes a racist comment in a restaurant.

6. A stranger on the train makes conversation with you by telling you a racist joke.

7. You walk into an insurance business and you notice a sign hanging on the wall that says, "Unattended children will be sold as slaves."

8. You are at work when an anti-Semitic comment is made in the conference room. You aren't Jewish.

Each of the choices you identified has consequences for your reputation. Discuss with your peers what those consequences might be. What would you do in those offensive situations?

_____

_____

_____

_____

_____

_____

_____

_____

Some people say Americans are too sensitive. Others say they should be able to use profanity, and too bad if there are little kids, professors, or others around who might hear them. What is appropriate varies from region to region and situation to situation. Also, with the diversity of the population, it is quite probable you'll run into a police officer, an employer, or a potential romantic partner who was raised elsewhere and is accustomed to the norms of another place. Our choice of the appropriate language to use with a stranger may be incorrect, but the effort to make an informed choice is essential. It is important to make choices about how you want to monitor your own language in the presence of others. It is your choice. But, don't be surprised if you encounter consequences for using offensive language.

Something else to consider is what to do if you are the offended person. What happens when people speak inappropriately in your presence? Should you blow up? Should you keep quiet? Probably the best answer is somewhere between those extremes.

Choices and Consequences

You are standing with peers around the water cooler when one of them makes a joke about homosexuals. You are not homosexual, but you realize a joke like that can be offensive to homosexuals, to straight people who have relatives or friends who are gay, or to straight people who believe denigrating another group is morally wrong. List four ways you could handle this situation.

_____

_____

_____

_____

List the potential consequences for each of the four recommendations you made above.

_____

_____

_____

_____

Think carefully about the consequences of derogatory remarks spoken within the corporate culture. These remarks could cost you your reputation, a raise, a promotion, and, in some cases, your job.

SUMMARY

Understanding the concept of symbolic representation of thought can help you avoid miscommunication. Recognizing the differences in denotative and connotative meanings allows you to use perception-checking skills to reach a shared understanding rather than escalating into conflict.

Use of appropriate language signals is a personal commitment to interpersonal and professional credibility. The decisions and adjustments you make right now can enable you to be successful in a diverse society or, conversely, limit your career potential. Because technology is bringing the cultures of the world closer together, you will need dynamic, globally-sensitive language choices—both oral and written. The language battles of the twentieth century are now history. Whether you feel committed to rhetorical sensitivity or not, the concepts in this chapter illuminate the new challenges in communicating to the world. Look forward.

Key Words

ambiguous

arbitrary

connotative meaning

content level

creative ambiguity

denotative meaning

generic he

language

loaded word

polarized language

profanity

racist/religious/cultural language

relationship level

rhetorical sensitivity

sexist/heterosexist language

symbol

Across

2. Literature historically uses the _____ to mean everyone.

4. Being aware of and respectful to your audience by choosing symbols least likely to offend them.

5. If Faith says, "I saw a big building," and Don thinks she means something around 10 stories, but she actually saw an 80-story building, this misunderstanding is due to the fact that symbols are _____.

10. Saying, "Oh that is so gay" is an example of language that is _____.

11. The reason why there are different words in different languages to represent the same object is because symbols are _____.

Down

1. If I use the word "deer" to represent the animal I saw on my way to work, I am using a _____.

3. The feelings attached to a particular word. These feelings vary from communicator to communicator.

6. Language composed of directly opposing terms to describe certain phenomena.

7. Language that denigrates individuals of ethnic backgrounds other than your own is called _____.

8. The dictionary definition of a word.

9. Language that denigrates females is _____.

CHAPTER 4

Nonverbal Communication

OBJECTIVES

After reading this chapter, you should be able to:

- Explain the concept of body movement
- Identify uses of emblems, illustrators, affect displays, regulators, and adaptors
- Explain the concept of time communication
- Explain the concept of smell communication
- Explain the concept of touch communication
- Define the term paralanguage
- Explain the concept of space communication and territoriality
- Describe the importance of artifacts

Nonverbal communication radiates from all of the senses but does not include the use of verbal symbols. We can communicate through sight, touch, smell, and sound. We send messages through our use of space, color, and time; our physical characteristics; movement; artifacts (furniture, clothing, and jewelry); and vocal sounds that are not words. Mark Knapp and Judith Hall (2002) remind us of the "inseparable nature of verbal and nonverbal signals" (p. 11). It is important to make adjustments in personal style to make sure our nonverbal messages complement our verbal messages. A solid blend of nonverbal and verbal communication skills enhances your effectiveness with other people.

When we talk about nonverbal communication, it is important to remember one of the basic principles of communication from chapter 1: we cannot not communicate. Communicators assign meaning to all nonverbals. We can control some of these nonverbals, but not others. Although you have no control over some physical characteristics such as height, other communicators will interpret nonverbal messages from physical characteristics. For instance, according to a University of Florida study, taller people earn more money, and "when supervisors were quizzed about how they viewed their staff, they tended to rate taller people as more effective" (BBC News, 2003, para. 8). It is imperative for you to be aware that nonverbals account for a large portion of our total communication package. You need to make careful choices about the nonverbals that you can control so that the overall impression is consistent with your message.

As we begin our exploration of the types of nonverbal communication, keep in mind that we send many nonverbal messages unintentionally. We may fold our arms in a cold room for warmth. However, a communicator observing our nonverbal position may perceive us as guarded and noninvitational. We have no intention of sending a message with our natural reaction to the temperature, but the receiver may perceive a meaning. It is important to be aware of the possible nonverbals we send unintentionally during any interpersonal encounter.

We may also perceive others' nonverbals incorrectly as well. Think back to chapter 2 on perception and all of the inaccuracies that can occur as we assign meaning to behavior. If we assign meaning to nonverbal behavior incorrectly without perception checking, our attributions may lead us to inaccurate conclusions. Learning about the various areas of nonverbal communication can help you to change your behavior and to evaluate the messages you receive from others more effectively.

BODY MOVEMENT—KINESICS

Body movement (also known as ***kinesics***) communicates volumes about who we are. We often don't think about what we are doing with our bodies, but even the smallest gesture or movement communicates information about us. Eye contact, gestures, facial expressions, and even head movements all contribute to the total package of communication and personal credibility.

Direct eye contact with other people is expected in U.S. culture as a sign of respect, but it is considered aggressive and disrespectful in other cultures. For most of us in the United States, a direct gaze makes a positive connection from one person to another. If we turn our eyes away, we communicate that the words we are saying are difficult or we are thinking about other things. How often has someone yelled at you for watching television while the person was talking to you? Although you were listening, your behavior did not communicate attention. Some people feel they cannot judge your communication unless they can see your eyes. For this reason, sunglasses present a problem. When you wear sunglasses in a speaking situation people feel disconnected from you because they can't see your eyes and read your reaction.

During group meetings, some people look away from a lecturer or write notes or use modern technology to send notes to others. This nonverbal behavior can communicate that they are not focused on the speaker's remarks. This is a risky move during a business meeting when the boss is speaking. Eye contact communicates caring and courtesy in U.S. culture.

Extraneous body movements can detract from your message. This is important to remember in public speaking situations, group meetings, and interpersonal encounters. Constant body motion should be controlled. Some people shake a foot or tap a pen during conversations. The person on the

Reality ✔

The following example shows both the expectation of eye contact in U.S. culture as well as how quickly we can misperceive another person's nonverbal choices. In June of 2006, President Bush was holding a press conference when the following interaction occurred:

The President: Yes, Peter. Are you going to ask that question with shades on?

Q: I can take them off.

The President: I'm interested in the shade look, seriously.

Q: All right, I'll keep it, then.

The President: For the viewers, there's no sun. (Laughter.)

Q: I guess it depends on your perspective. (Laughter.) (Bush, 2006)

It was only after the press conference that the president was made aware that the man he was teasing was actually blind.

receiving end of the message may interpret this random behavior as nervousness or an indication of impatience. Shifting body weight is another problem. A weight shift or two to relax is not problematic, but constant shifting is distracting. How do you watch a physically active speaker and still pay attention to her message? Place yourself carefully into a relaxed position and stay there.

— Professional Perspective —

There are several physical characteristics that can make an individual more appealing in corporate culture. Movement is one. In an office environment, a worker who moves quickly may appear to be more productive and efficient than her colleague who moves at a more leisurely pace. However, as with most things in life, balance is key. The executive who whips around the office may appear panicked, jittery, and rushed. Related to movement, body language often speaks louder than words. In a negotiation, the look on one's face will often reveal more than he/she wishes to tell. Posture speaks volumes. An executive who sits up straight with shoulders back in a meeting appears attentive, interested, and confident. The executive who slouches may appear disinterested, aloof, and distant. One's overall appearance is also an important factor. A worker who is well dressed and properly groomed is going to appear infinitely more appealing than one who is not. In corporate culture, as in everyday life, other physical characteristics such as height, weight, size, and shape will have an effect on one's appeal depending on the situation.

—Evan Tripoli
Motion Picture Talent Agent
International Creative Management, Inc., A Talent and Literary Agency

Emblems

Emblems are nonverbal gestures that have a direct verbal translation. Their meaning is agreed upon within specific cultures or groups; emblems do not have a universal meaning across cultures. For example, there is no doubt what your friend means when he gives you a "thumbs-up" gesture after an exam. However, in other cultures, the thumbs-up gesture means the same thing as the "middle finger" gesture in U.S. culture. At the time the United

States invaded Iraq, soldiers had a hard time deciphering the thumbs-up sign they were getting from the Iraqi soldiers. In Iraq, that gesture is the equivalent of our middle finger gesture. Soldiers didn't know if Iraqis were learning our gesture and showing support for the troops or if they were displaying dissatisfaction with them being there (Koerner, 2003).

In the United States the "V" sign stands for peace as well as victory, but in other cultures it is an extremely rude gesture. A former U.S. president visited Australia while a farmers' strike was in progress. As his motorcade drove past farmers gathered by the road to see him, he made the "V" gesture. Unfortunately, he was pressed against the inside door of the car and did not have room to turn his wrist to enable the gesture to be displayed palm forward. He displayed the gesture with the back of his hand visible to the farmers. The reversal of the emblem meant the same as the "middle finger" gesture means to Americans.

U.S. citizens traveling abroad need to understand how the emblems they use at home are interpreted in the culture they are visiting. Many emblems quite common in U.S. culture are considered to be extremely offensive in other cultures. You must understand emblem use prior to your journey and make the necessary nonverbal adjustments to avoid the consequences of an unintentional emblem display.

— Professional Perspective —

When I was in England during my junior year, I quickly learned not to hitchhike American style. The American thumb for hitchhiking was interpreted in England as giving someone the finger.

—Allynn Gooen
International Performance Artist

Illustrators

Illustrators are nonverbals used to enhance the understanding of a message. We can show how big something is with the use of our fingers or hands. We can point to direct the attention of our listeners. We often gesture automatically without thinking. Illustrators save us a lot of verbal banter. Think about being on a camping trip with your family. You are hiking over a mountain and your father sees an amazing rainbow. Instead of saying "turn around and raise your head 45 degrees and look a little to your left and you'll see a beautiful rainbow," he will simply say, "Look at that!" and extend his arm in the direction of the rainbow. You react immediately to his illustrator and discover an incredible rainbow.

You can also misuse illustrators by illustrating the obvious. For instance, when there are only two people on a stage and one person is introducing the other, an introducer may gesture to the other person as they say, "Today, I'd like to introduce Sally. . . ." There is no need for an illustrator in this scenario, because everyone in the audience immediately understands who is being introduced. Another cultural point to keep in mind is that in Asian cultures, pointing is considered to be rude. In many Asian cultures, people point with their thumb while their hand forms a fist, rather than pointing with an extended index finger. To Asians, pointing with their thumb prevents the rude gesture of pointing a finger directly at someone or something.

Be careful not to use too many hand gestures. In many cultures, gesturing for every comment is distracting. Gestures should always reinforce a specific content point in the presentation or assist with a thematic transition.

Affect Displays

Affect displays are facial muscle movements used to convey meaning. We communicate numerous emotions with our faces. Facial expressions reveal whether we are annoyed, happy, sad, angry, and so on. This is another reason why maintaining direct eye contact during a conversation is important. You won't miss facial cues that help you understand what the other person is saying, and he or she will receive feedback about the message. For instance, when talking to friends who tell us something surprising or startling, most of us raise our eyebrows slightly and widen our eyes. This conveys a message of surprise and allows our friends to know their messages were received properly. In a job interview, facial expressions can work for or against you. Imagine sending a message of surprise when you hear the salary range offered for the position. What might the interviewer think? Affect displays are sometimes hard to control because they are very spontaneous. However, many people are adept at masking a reaction to external stimuli of any kind—hence the term "poker face." Some people control their facial expressions so much that their communication partner may have no idea what they are thinking. When we can't read a person's nonverbals, communicating interpersonally is difficult.

Sometimes we emit facial expressions that are perceived incorrectly. For instance, in one of my (KSY) nonverbal classes, I noticed a young woman who had her arms crossed; she was leaning back and had a look of total disgust. I made a joke asking her whether she was tired or angry with the class we were having. This gave her the opportunity to laugh and to say that she was exhausted because her son had been up all night. Perception checking allowed me to get the true message and her to realize the unintentional message she was sending.

Regulators

Regulators are movements that direct the conversation. For instance, when the teacher asks a question and you don't want to be called on, you immediately look down at your desk. In contrast, the student who makes eye contact with the instructor signals a desire to answer. Eye contact is also used to let the conversation partner know whether to keep talking or when it is the listener's turn to speak. You can communicate boredom by avoiding eye contact with the speaker.

Our choices with regulators can communicate attitudes about people as well. We often turn our eyes away from people who look different than we do. People who have had a stroke may have partial paralysis on one side of their face. Some people may have an unusual facial growth. We often avoid eye contact with these people, because we are embarrassed or uncomfortable. We don't realize, however, that we are being disrespectful to them. Imagine feeling shut out of a conversation simply because you've had a stroke. This situation can also occur with people who have physical challenges. Think about how you would feel if you were in a wheelchair and people were always looking down at you. When communicating with a wheelchair user, you may want to sit in a chair next to the person, so your eye contact is at an equal level. This courtesy makes the person with physical challenges more comfortable, and the entire conversation is warmer. Try to put yourself in the other person's position and adjust your behavior to how you would like to be treated if you were in that position.

Head nodding is another potential problem. Women are often socialized to nod their heads in agreement without even thinking about their message. Generally, men do not use this nonverbal technique. During a conversation, females tend to nod their heads so the other person knows to keep talking. However, some men may think a woman using this behavior isn't listening to what they are saying, especially if her head is moving through a portion of the discussion where nonverbal response is deemed inappropriate. This nonverbal movement could become an issue when a man and woman work together in corporate culture. He may interpret her head bobbing as trying to "suck-up" by always appearing to be in agreement. She may interpret his non-expressiveness as disinterest or disagreement. Neither of these assessments may be accurate. So, it is important to be aware of our nonverbal actions as well as those of the people around us and make appropriate choices when analyzing a communication environment.

Adaptors

Adaptors are self-touching behaviors. Adaptors are often interpreted in a negative way by other communicators. A person who is always fussing with hair, glasses, or clothing is perceived to be nervous and/or not paying attention to what is being communicated. In interpersonal communication, it is important to understand that personal habits such as these should be controlled or eliminated. If your nose itches, you can usually scratch it, but in business situations, you may need to resist the temptation. What if your doctor covered her nose with her hand while she sneezed and then extended it to greet you before your examination? Would you shake hands? While the sneeze was involuntary, her choice of subsequent behavior could have been different.

Choices and Consequences

You are speaking to a group of people, and your notecards suddenly fall from your hands to the floor. What are your choices and the consequences of those choices in this situation?

_____

_____

You are part way through your presentation and the power goes off, disabling your electronically-generated visual aids. What are your choices and their consequences?

_____

_____

You are on a job interview and right before you are introduced to a potential colleague, you sneeze. What are your choices and consequences?

_____

_____

Physical control is critical in corporate environments. In a small group meeting when everyone is listening to the discussion, imagine the reaction of other people if you begin to fuss with your hair, jewelry, a pen, or glasses. Their selective attention is drawn to your random movement. People may say nothing, but they notice your behavior and remember it. Sometimes if the wind is blowing you need to check the impulse to fix your hair and simply focus on the conversation; otherwise, you will be perceived to be more interested in your appearance than in the conversation. Pay attention to television reporters during a "live" broadcast as the wind grabs their hair. Do they try to straighten their hair? What impression do they make? If you interpret the nonverbals to symbolize vanity, make sure you don't repeat the same behavior when you are in a similar professional situation.

TIME COMMUNICATION—CHRONEMICS

Kyle goes to a meeting with his graduate professor. The professor is in her office with the door open, but she keeps him waiting in the hall because she is examining a sheet of paper. He waits patiently. She finally invites Kyle in and asks him to sit down while continuing to examine the paper. He can see the paper is actually a menu from a local restaurant. The professor's message is quite clear. She is using time to communicate her priorities.

Time communication (chronemics) is the study of the way that individuals and cultures use time. Our use of time sends messages about our character. Whether we intend these messages or not, people will perceive things about us and make assumptions about us based on our use of time. In the previous example, it is reasonable for Kyle to decide that the teacher is abusing her power as a faculty member and reminding him of his own insignificance in her schedule. Kyle had an established appointment, and she left her door open while reading a menu. As a graduate student, Kyle feels obligated to keep quiet and deal with her inappropriate behavior. He knows a different choice could compromise his ability to succeed in his graduate program. Two thoughts race through his mind: (1) write a letter to report this incident to the dean after he graduates (this may help his self-esteem by knowing he tried to do something); or (2) write a personal letter to the teacher, after graduation, to let her know how inappropriate her actions were.

Kyle also has a couple of intrapersonal choices. He can assume he is unworthy and allow his self-esteem to decline, or he can realize this is strictly a power play and the professor is the one who has issues. With the latter reasoning, his self-esteem remains strong.

Normally, we would encourage perception checking in this situation. However, because of the status differential between a professor and a student, Kyle needs to decide whether it is worth the risk to speak up. Depending on the professor, he may be able to ask, "Do you need to reschedule this meeting so you can finish your task?" That would call attention to the fact that the professor is making him wait. But, Kyle knows, from her past behavior during the term, that she is using a power play, so he decides he is better off smiling internally and keeping his thoughts to himself.

If there is a valid reason why the professor must review the menu (the president of the university called and asked for an immediate decision on a luncheon choice), then the professor should offer that explanation to Kyle,

"I'm so sorry to keep you waiting, but I've had an emergency phone call and must make an immediate decision. Do you have a few minutes or shall we reschedule?" This is appropriate communication. However, she is communicating for control and selects silence.

Critical Thinking

Describe a situation where your time has been manipulated by another person.

_____

_____

Describe how you responded to it.

_____

_____

Would you handle the situation the same way now? Would another choice have been more appropriate?

_____

_____

Think about your own time choices. How often do you walk into class late? We have noticed over the years there are certain students who constantly walk into class five or ten minutes late. If a student can be consistently late every class period, why can't he or she change the pattern to be consistently on time? Think about the assumptions the professor could make about the student. The professor might assume that walking in late demeans what the teacher is saying, distracts the attention of the other students in the class, and demonstrates a lack of respect for the students who arrived on time. The late student is psychologically manipulating the environment to demonstrate importance. Is this true? Probably not. But many professors could interpret the student's use of time to communicate precisely those messages. The reverse scenario is also true. Professors who are constantly late for class are communicating something about themselves as well.

Edward Hall (1966) described two contrasting ways to treat time. **Monochronic cultures** structure time into discrete units (minutes and hours) and treat it like an object. In these cultures, people "save time," "make time," and "have time." Activities are scheduled one at a time and in a linear sequence. Monochronic cultures compartmentalize time, and people are disoriented if they have to focus on too many activities simultaneously. In a business setting, formal appointments are the normal routine, and one "gets down to business" quickly.

Polychronic cultures plan many things at once, but time is unstructured and informal. The rhythms of nature (the weather, the tides, etc.) mark the flow of time. Relationships take precedence over activities. In fact in some cultures, if no relationship has been established, there will be no business activity.

The United States is a monochronic society. Time is extremely valuable, and we operate on a tight time schedule. Events occur at a specific time. What do we do at noon? Eat lunch. Does it matter if you are hungry? No. It's time to eat. Appointments start on time. Classes start on time. What do you do if a teacher begins a new concept three minutes before the scheduled end of class? Most students begin making nonverbal noises: packing up their books, rustling papers, talking to others, and putting on their coats even though the teacher is still talking. If you are a student in the classroom who wants to learn the new concept, do you say something to silence disruptive students? Do you expect the teacher to silence the students?

People in polychronic cultures don't feel pressured by time. If a person is two hours late, no one cares. Tasks are completed no matter how long they take. For instance, if a teacher continues to lecture beyond the posted class time, students sit and listen even though they will be late for another class or meeting. If a business lunch extends into the late afternoon, people would simply be late for any other activity they might have thought they could attend. Anyone waiting for them to appear would do so patiently. That's a difficult time concept for people in monochronic cultures to comprehend.

Think about how irritated we get when things don't go fast enough. Have you ever found yourself angry because your fast food was not in your hands in a minute or two? Think about how angry some of us get when we are standing at a sales counter or sitting at the drive-thru window for more than two minutes. Our hearts beat faster, and we feel angry just because the high-calorie, artery-clogging food is not getting into our hands fast enough. Many Americans become annoyed at the slightest abuse of their time. And yet, these

---

— Professional Perspective —

"Half our life is spent trying to find something to do with the time we have rushed through life trying to save." Will Rogers [1879–1935], *New York Times*, Apr. 29, 1930)

This quotation illuminates the very American concept of time, its ability to control us, and its importance in our cultural marketplace. However, not all parts of the world are moderated by a clock or the need to make time equal money. In the Federated States of Micronesia, a country of tiny northern Pacific islands, time is simply not a driving force in the everyday course of things.

During a typical day in Micronesia, workers arrive two hours late and leave at least an hour early, funerals can last up to forty days, and women awake before dawn to begin the day's cooking and go to sleep well after every other family member has. While I constantly grappled with the efficiency of such a system, locals understood this "island time" so well they could set their clocks by it—if they had a clock.

Time is as much a part of Micronesian culture as it is American, but it plays a different role. In a place where the seasons do not change and the days are long, timelessness is a way of life and that way of life is simple. Now that I am back in the United States I remember to make time work with me rather than rule me. I believe that cultural sensitivity to different conceptions of time makes us all more efficient and more time-effective in the long run.

—Lori L. Burrows, Staff Attorney
Arkansas Public Service Commission
Former Peace Corps Volunteer (1999–2001)
Pohnpei State, Federated States of Micronesia

same individuals don't mind abusing the time of others. The use of time carries over into the business world as well. In corporate America, everything runs on a tight schedule. You will be judged by your respect for time.

SMELL COMMUNICATION—OLFACTICS

Smells give us a lot of sensory input. Smells send strong nonverbal messages. Aromatherapy is a field of study where people research how smells affect our moods and stress levels. While you may think this is humorous, scientific study about *smell communication* (also known as *olfactics*) is actually compelling.

We use smell to communicate messages about ourselves, our homes, our office environments, and our vehicles. Think about the large amount of money we spend on scents to alter our odor. We choose perfumes, colognes, deodorants, laundry detergents, aftershaves, shampoos, conditioners, and other products based on their smells. The problem is people perceive smells differently. The scent you are wearing may not be appealing to a coworker, interviewer, or new acquaintance. If the fragrance is strong, people may immediately try to avoid you.

Now think about situations where there is no escape (sitting next to someone on an airplane or consulting with a coworker). Even worse, what if the receiver has allergies to the smoke lingering on your clothes, a perfume you've chosen, or the incense or eucalyptus in your office? At this point, the communication experience becomes intolerable for the receiver. The receiver may assume you are insensitive to people around you. This is not a good thing if the receiver is the interviewer, your boss, or potential romantic partner.

The smells in our homes (baking bread, cinnamon potpourri, or pet urine) all send messages to the people who enter. Does your home smell clean? Welcoming? The person visiting makes this decision, not you.

Our vehicles also carry smells. Why is this important? Well, you never know when you may be asked to give a ride to a professor, a client, a boss, or an interviewee. If your car carries the scent of smoke, and the passenger has an allergy, she may have to refuse the ride or suffer the consequences of being exposed to the allergens in the car. Neither of these impressions are ones you want someone to remember.

⇨ Try It! ⇦

What do you think of people when you visit their home for the first time and it smells like . . .

Baking bread _____

Pet urine _____

The smells in our offices (incense, eucalyptus, floral sprays) also send messages. What is your impression of a business executive when you walk into her office and it smells like . . .

Incense _____

Floral spray _____

We become desensitized to the smells we enjoy, so we often increase the application. While we barely notice the fragrance of perfume or cologne we've worn for five years, the person we are meeting for the first time is getting an overdose. With the increase in allergy sensitivities, we need to be aware of the communication consequences as we choose appropriate scents for our bodies and our environment.

TOUCH COMMUNICATION—HAPTICS

Touch communication (haptics) is one of the most powerful ways to send nonverbal messages. However, U.S. culture is particularly touch avoidant, and people rarely use touch in public. In fact, many businesses and schools have policies in place to describe inappropriate touching. In some elementary schools, teachers cannot even hug children who have done a good job or fallen on the playground. Teachers risk sexual harassment or abuse charges in these situations. The legal approach dictates no touching.

Women normally can get away with much more touching than men. Think of the times you've seen women dance together. No one thinks anything of it, but two men dancing together would raise eyebrows. Women also tend to hug each other when they meet much more frequently than do men in our culture. Men display touching behaviors in sports, and few observers react in a negative manner to what they do. However, if a male student were to slap another male student on the derriere to congratulate him on an "A," the reaction of observers would be quite negative. Context plays a major role in our determination of whether a touching behavior is appropriate or not.

How do we know when a touch is inappropriate? If it makes you uncomfortable, it is inappropriate. You need to find the words to tell the other person to stop the offending touch. The Human Rights and Equal Opportunity Commission defines sexual harassment as an unwelcome sexual advance, unwelcome request for sexual favors, or other unwelcome conduct of a sexual nature that makes a person feel offended, humiliated, or intimidated where a reasonable person would anticipate that reaction in the circumstances. Sexual harassment involves a patterned behavior. You must tell the person to stop the behavior. If you don't, your silence could be interpreted as consenting to the behavior. If the person continues with the behavior after you've asked or told him or her to stop, you may have grounds for a sexual harassment claim.

Some people attribute any form of unwelcome touching as sexual harassment. Someone who accidentally bumps into you in a public place is not guilty of sexual harassment. We get bumped many times during a day—on the subway, in a computer-training session, in the lunch line, on an elevator, or walking down a crowded street. These types of encounters, while they may be irritating, do not involve any attempt to create a hostile, offensive, intimidating, or abusive environment. Our reaction to touching behaviors, such as having a hand placed on our shoulder or back, often depends on our family experience. If we grew up in families and cultures that were physical—where lots of hugging took place, where mom or dad put an arm around us as we walked down the street—we accept such touching behaviors as signs of affection or camaraderie. If we grew up in families where none of this touching took place, we could be extremely uncomfortable with touching and could even find the behaviors to be threatening. Be observant when involved in making communication choices about touching so that you can recognize and adapt to the comfort level of others.

Touching behavior varies with cultures as well. In general, blacks and Latinos tend to use much more touching in their communication style with family and friends. Europeans are much more reserved. This difference in the use of touch can create barriers among ethnic groups. Please remember there is no one correct touching style. Try to be open-minded as you blend with other cultures.

A handshake is a touching behavior that varies from culture to culture. In U.S. culture, you must practice making your handshake firm (not bone crushing), and extend your arm out straight without bending your elbow. Ideally, your hand should not be sweaty (but avoid wiping it on your clothes first—this gesture sends a negative nonverbal message). If perspiration is a big problem, you can try a spray antiperspirant on your palms before a meeting.

— Professional Perspective —

Ancient cultural traditions are still followed in the Far East. When meeting a Japanese executive for the first time, you should extend your hand, but remember not to squeeze too hard. In Western culture, a firm handshake is considered important. However, in the Asian culture, a firm handshake is considered an aggressive and threatening act—not a good first introduction for your new Japanese boss.

—Robert H. Christie
Senior Public Relations Manager
Dow Jones and Company

You shake men's hands and women's hands in U.S. culture. In Europe, Asia, and Russia you should not shake a woman's hand. When you are traveling abroad, you might place a female business executive in an awkward position if you extend your arm to shake her hand. It is respectful to follow local customs.

In some cultures, you greet men and women by kissing them on the cheek. U.S. men, especially, need to be prepared for a different experience if they visit a foreign country. I (HPT) was at a university reception in Russia. My

---

Choices and Consequences

Think about yourself. Are you comfortable with touch or are you touch-avoidant? In which situations? Can you handle meeting someone in the business world whose touch rules were different from yours? What are the consequences if you can't?

_____

_____

_____

_____

_____

students had completed a study-abroad program, and I had completed a teaching assignment. A male faculty member kissed me on the lips during the reception. In Russia, this touching experience is reserved for men who have been lifelong friends. The moment was a gesture of acceptance and friendship, and I was honored. It made me feel like I had done a good job in an environment where I had been a total stranger. The kiss was unexpected, but I knew its meaning. Had I not understood the cultural meaning, I could have recoiled or been offended. This reaction would have embarrassed my Russian colleague. You need to study the customs of foreign cultures before you travel. It makes your communication much more effective.

PARALANGUAGE

Paralanguage refers to the vocal techniques you use to emphasize and give meaning to words. We can say the same sentence and make it sound angry, happy, romantic, or indifferent just by altering our paralanguage (try it with "Glad to see you could make it"). The words remain the same, but the meaning changes. In addition, unintentional vocal noises can send messages. Have you ever heard anyone add a vocal element to a yawn? During a lecture, this action draws immediate attention and sends a different message from someone who yawns discreetly. Projection, pitch, rate, and pauses contribute to the meaning of the words you use to communicate.

Pitch, projection, and quality of voice play a large part in creating meaning for our message. Think about a petite, giggly young woman who says coyly, "Don't you talk to me like that," versus a large, deep-voiced man yelling it in a loud voice. Would both individuals be conveying the same meaning with the same words? Absolutely not.

Paralanguage definitely influences the way your message is interpreted during interpersonal communication. When a parent said to you, "Don't you use that tone with me!" they were pointing to your inappropriate use of paralanguage for the situation. Try to make sure you are mentally alert as you approach a communication situation so you can be flexible and accurate with your use of paralanguage. In this way, you can remember the conversational techniques you practiced prior to speaking and be comfortable in conveying your intended message to others. Words contain emotional meaning when paralanguage is used effectively. As you listen to different speakers in person and on television, analyze their vocal techniques (projection, pitch, emphasis, rate, and pauses) during their speech. Can you use some of their paralanguage skills to improve your own style?

⇨   **Try It!**   ⇦

Pausing changes the meaning of a phrase. Note the difference in:

Let's talk (pause) until the end of time.

Let's talk until the end (pause) of time.

Let's talk until (pause) the end of time.

⇨   **Try It!**   ⇦

Write in the meaning of the sentence for each example.

Andre didn't say you were obnoxious.

Meaning _____

Andre **didn't** say you were obnoxious.

Meaning _____

Andre didn't **say** you were obnoxious.

Meaning _____

Andre didn't say **you** were obnoxious.

Meaning _____

Andre didn't say you were **obnoxious.**

Meaning _____

Think about the psychological meaning if you whispered the same message?

_____

_____

What if you screamed it?

_____

_____

_____

SPACE COMMUNICATION—PROXEMICS

The use of space communicates numerous messages nonverbally. People in positions of power can use their offices to communicate importance and to command attention. The president of the United States delivers speeches from the Oval Office to increase the impact of the message. In this section we will focus on the use of distance and space between people *(proxemics)* as they communicate.

Think about a couple sitting across from one another at a restaurant. The message they convey is different than if they chose to sit next to one another. Often people don't think much about the messages they send with their use of space, but the use of space influences perceptions—observers draw meaning from actions. Space and distance preferences depend on the particular environment and vary dramatically from culture to culture.

Most communication textbooks talk about research done in the 1960s by Edward T. Hall (1968) about personal distances.

- Intimate distance (0–18 inches)
- Personal distance (18 inches to 4 feet)
- Social distance (4–12 feet)
- Public distance (over 12 feet)

Hall's research used only white males, and his study is now 40 years old. We will combine his historic findings with more current observations and guidelines.

Hall alerted us to the fact that we place an imaginary bubble around ourselves and only certain people may enter that space. The space is usually reserved for people who are close to us interpersonally—possibly our family members, a significant other, children, and close friends. However, there are also people who are not close to us that we must accept into this intimate space, such as doctors, dentists, masseuses, and other professionals. There are additional situations where we allow total strangers into our intimate space as well. Think about being in a crowded elevator. We occasionally touch people we don't know. But what do we do to make the situation feel comfortable? We face forward, so there is no eye contact with strangers. We create the illusion of more space; we look at the floor or the ceiling. We also pull our arms closer to our bodies and try to shrink the amount of space we occupy. We stand shoulder-to-shoulder while remaining in our own world.

Notice the difference in two classmates standing shoulder to shoulder in front of the room versus the same individuals facing one another when the teacher asks them to turn toward each other. Immediately, the students shift eye contact to give themselves more psychological space.

Business conversations take place in vehicles, in offices, at dinners, or on escalators. Physical spaces vary, but you need to pick up on the cues that others are sending. You may need to adjust your comfort zone occasionally to work with business colleagues from other cultures as well as within your own culture. In many cultures, people stand much closer to each other when communicating than we do in U.S. culture. In some cultures, you are not close enough to another person unless they can smell your breath during a conversation. This intimate distance is much too close for most Americans, but be prepared for this experience as you travel.

Space may vary by gender. Women may be more comfortable being close to other women and more uncomfortable being close to men. Men in the United States often do not like to be close to one another publicly—yet in Spain, men feel perfectly comfortable hugging and walking arm in arm.

Too many people are afraid of hurting someone's feelings or making them upset by saying anything about space, so they sit in silence and deal with communication that is uncomfortable. What happens when someone invades your personal space? There is no need to be uncomfortable. A simple statement such as, "Would you mind giving me a little more space please?" stated in a friendly tone can be effective. Or, "I'm sorry, but I feel uncomfortable when we're standing so close to each other. Why don't you have a seat?"

Critical Thinking

Think about a time you felt your personal space was invaded. How did you handle the situation?

_____

_____

_____

_____

Never hesitate to speak up if you are uncomfortable. As you engage in this dialogue, don't forget the importance of paralanguage. Sounding sincere rather than sounding confrontational will help you to solve the problem with less chance for hurt feelings or misunderstanding.

Territoriality

Territoriality refers to the imaginary ownership of a particular space. Most students walk into a classroom on the first day and then feel ownership of the chair they select for the entire term. If you walk in and someone else is in "your" chair, you are annoyed because someone else confiscated your seat. In apartment buildings or workplaces where there is a large parking lot, people often park in the same space. These people are annoyed if you park in "their space" even though the space does not belong to them. Territoriality is an imaginary social concept, but many individuals take the ownership of space seriously.

We also mark our territory by leaving a sweater or book bag on a seat. I (KSY) recently went to a water park where every single seat was marked by a towel. There was not a vacant seat anywhere. I needed to find a seat for my father-in-law, since he was watching our sleeping baby who was in a stroller. Only 10 percent of the chairs were occupied, and yet the other 90 percent were not available either. It was amazing how strong the message of ownership was. We were not willing to move someone else's belongings. Think how angry you might be if you left your towel on a chair, and it wasn't there when you returned. Later in the day, management made an announcement over the loudspeaker that marking chairs did not reserve them for anyone. So in this scenario, the customers and management had to deal with an uncomfortable situation because of a territorial norm.

How territorial are you? Be honest about it. There are people who aren't annoyed when someone takes their space or moves their things occasionally. However, other people will go through the roof if their belongings are moved. Think about the communication difficulties that can occur when two roommates begin a semester together. Marcia sees her roommate's t-shirt on the floor and picks it up and puts it in the hamper. The roommate comes home to see someone has touched her dirty laundry. She is extremely uncomfortable with this and a confrontation ensues. If Marcia isn't a territorial person herself, she will be shocked that this action upset her roommate.

The extent of our territoriality sends a nonverbal message about each of us. Others may think we are bizarre if our behavior varies from theirs. Some people may think we are unreasonable and odd; they may even think we are obsessed. It is important to remember that territoriality may be grounded in family experiences. In families where kids don't have any space of their own, they could become more or less territorial than the social norm when they are adults.

In addition to understanding your own use of space, it is important to respect the territoriality of others. Just as you want people to respect the way you use space, you need to return that respect to others and not question their position if they ask you to refrain from touching them or to give them some more space. This will help you avoid conflict and hard feelings with the other communicators in your life.

Critical Thinking

Do you feel your use of territoriality is reasonable or unreasonable? Describe three ways you use territoriality. Could you change?

_____

_____

_____

_____

_____

ARTIFACTS

Artifacts are the objects we select to represent our identity. There are two categories. *Personal artifacts* include clothing, shoes, hairstyle, jewelry, eyeglasses, and other adornments. *Physical artifacts* include furniture, artwork, rugs, and other objects.

Artifacts are another area where miscommunication can occur. No matter how carefully we select items for ourselves or for our space, we cannot control how another communicator will interpret them. There are also many artifacts that we don't actually choose (Grandma sends you a piece of clothing). In our discussion, we focus on artifacts that are within your control.

Think about your personal artifact choices. What messages do you send with your clothing? How do you choose your clothing? Some people shop frequently so they always have the latest style; others take the first clean item off the laundry pile. Some of you may dress up, even when you could wear casual clothes; others wear only comfortable clothes even in formal situations. Many people select a specific color for most of their clothing. What do bright colors versus dark colors say about a person? Clothing that is tailored to fit sends a much different message than baggy clothing. People who wear colors that complement each other send a different message than people who wear colors that clash.

The social message clothing sends is strong, yet the meaning is not static—it changes with fashion trends. While jeans are a staple of today's wardrobe, they were not always viewed in a positive manner. In the aftermath of the Depression, jeans were considered a sign of poverty. Many people did not allow their children to wear them because they wanted to send a social message to others that they could provide for their children. In the late 1970s, jeans became a status symbol—and prices skyrocketed to match. Many people had to have "the right" designer's name embroidered on the back pockets to communicate that they knew the latest trends and were members of the fashion elite. Brands proliferated, and jeans became so common they went unnoticed. Recently another upsurge in designer jeans has taken place.

Hairstyles send a message as well. Up-to-date hairstyles send a different message than hairstyles from the past. What do you think when you see someone who is still wearing a hairstyle from the 1980s, such as a rattail (a single, thin braid of hair longer than the rest of the cut) or a mullet (short in the front, long in the back)? What is the message sent by people who have multi-color or unnaturally colored hair? What do you think of shaved heads versus a full head of hair? One of our former students talked about the differences in the treatment she received from strangers during the two years she had her head shaved versus the subsequent years when she had a full head of hair. She was the same person, and yet when her head was shaved, the reactions of others were noticeably different. People will react to appearances that they perceive as unusual—even if the reaction is unfair or inaccurate.

Jewelry and eyeglasses and other personal artifacts should be chosen to complement your build, your skin coloring, and your situation. We will talk about this in more detail in chapter 12 on interviewing. Some people like to reveal information about themselves through their use of jewelry, such as wearing a religious symbol. However, there are consequences to every choice. In a job interview, there could be a positive or a negative reaction to such jewelry, depending on the receiver.

Ethical Considerations

What are the ethical considerations when we judge someone based on their personal artifacts? How often does this happen?

_____

_____

_____

Physical objects such as furniture, artwork, pictures, rugs, lighting, curtains, and other special adornments also communicate messages about you. Feng shui is the Chinese practice of configuring space to harmonize with the spiritual forces that inhabit it—the placement and arrangement of space to achieve harmony with the environment. Feng shui is now widely recognized as a guide for placing artifacts in your space to influence how they relate to your energy and production levels. Think about how you feel and what you think about a person who owns a space that is completely cluttered. How about a simply designed space without clutter, some beautifully placed artwork, and a wide-open feeling to it? Where do you feel more comfortable? Where could you accomplish more work? Where could you relax or concentrate? Removing clutter and minimizing the amount of furniture in a space are two of the first steps in generating a flow of positive energy (Ziegler & Lawler, 2003).

Quite often adults design work spaces to reflect their personal taste. We have assigned students to visit different offices on campus and report on how they felt. Student reports have varied from feeling welcome and calm to feeling distracted and claustrophobic. Think about artifacts as you move into the business world and create your own space. Your clients and colleagues will enter your space—send the appropriate message. Artifacts send such strong messages that many corporations have policies stating what employees can or cannot display in their office space. Some corporations will not even allow you to have a family photo in your office space. Other companies encourage people to decorate offices however they like.

— **Professional Perspective** —

Upon entering an interior environment you are instantly affected by it on an emotional level. Color, and its application, is perhaps the strongest element sending signals in a space. The psychological effects of color are complex, as well as greatly underestimated. Further investigation into color psychology can teach you how colors signal aspects such as socioeconomic status and success, life experiences, and trustworthiness. On a subconscious level, color affects our perception of comfort, time, and quality. These perceptions flow beyond interior design and have a substantial effect on the people who inhabit the space.

The overall decoration of a space, in relation to design style, materials, and furnishings, creates an ambience that is a telltale narrative portraying the image of the inhabitants of that space, be it an office or home environment. As an example, when you walk into the lobby of an office, a few observations can quickly tell you if the inhabitants are modern or traditional, liberal or conservative, accomplished or flailing. This can be a useful tool to decide whether or not you wish to work for that organization or do business with them. Conversely, it has the same effect when people are judging you.

Good design is the key to conveying the image you wish to portray.

—Wes Moon
Interior Designer

These policies influence our perceptions of the companies who create them. When you go to a job interview, look closely at the offices. Do they resemble a place where you would feel comfortable working? Use of artifacts can tell you a great deal about the organizational culture. You may decide not to work for a company because you are uncomfortable with the absence of personal artifacts. Other people may decide they like a company that looks clean and neat with no hint of personal belongings in the environment.

Critical Thinking

Think about your current living space. If money were no object, what artifact changes would you make? What is the new message you would be sending to people who enter your room?

_____

_____

_____

_____

SUMMARY

Your nonverbal choices have a huge impact on your ability to communicate effectively. Body language, time, smell, touch, paralanguage, artifacts, and space and territory, all send messages. Understanding how these nonverbal communi-

cation symbols affect other people will help you make choices that will influence your career potential and the success of your interpersonal relationships.
As the Professional Perspective below illustrates, unawareness of cultural norms
for artifacts at a business dinner can create unintended consequences.

— Professional Perspective —

When I was in Japan, I became friends with a woman whose use of artifacts at a dinner party
for a business associate of her husband unwittingly caused embarrassment. The woman
stopped at a florist to bring a pretty assortment of flowers to the hosts. The host politely put
them in a vase of water and placed them next to the table. After the dinner was over, she was
told this was a funeral arrangement of flowers.

—Allynn Gooen
International Performance Artist

Key Words

adaptors
affect displays
artifacts
chronemics
emblems
haptics
illustrators
kinesics
monochronic cultures

nonverbal communication
olfactics
paralanguage
personal artifacts
physical artifacts
polychronic cultures
proxemics
regulators
territoriality

Across

2. Using vocal techniques to emphasize specific words in communicating meaning.

6. _____ is an imaginary comfort zone individuals place around themselves when communicating.

10. A person who plays with her jacket while waiting for an interview is sending a message through _____.

11. Constantly fussing with your hair might be interpreted as egocentric. You should be aware of this type of _____.

12. Jill is irate because someone in the library moved her book bag that she used to reserve a seat. She is reacting to the imaginary ownership of the seat. This is called _____.

Down

1. Hand gestures that convey meaning are called _____.

3. An _____ is a spontaneous facial reaction to communication stimuli.

4. A fisher who uses his or her hands to show the size of the fish he or she caught is using _____.

5. A student who lowers his eyes when a teacher asks a question is using a _____ to avoid being called upon.

7. Walking into your staff meetings 10 minutes late each week is an example of using _____ communication in a disrespectful manner.

8. You leave an elevator early because the person next to you has an overpowering cologne. That person has communicated by _____.

9. The choice to bleach your hair blonde or to hang an expensive piece of artwork on a wall communicates messages. These are examples of communicating with _____.

12. This type of nonverbal communication is extremely powerful, but it also has great potential for being misinterpreted.

CHAPTER 5

Communicating Interpersonally

OBJECTIVES

After reading this chapter, you should be able to:

- Recognize and use self-disclosure
- Discuss effective conversational style
- Explain the Johari Window
- Identify the six listening/feedback styles and practice using them when appropriate
- Discuss the implications of technology on interpersonal communication

Interpersonal communication occurs between two or more people in a personal or professional relationship. From birth, everyone is involved in interpersonal communication, whether with family members, neighbors, educators, religious leaders, doctors, or peers. As we mature, we add friendships, romantic relationships, student-teacher relationships, employer-employee relationships, and professional colleagues to our social sphere. Each interpersonal relationship is unique.

The study of interpersonal communication is complex. Our discussion introduces you to the basic concepts of understanding others. The study of interpersonal communication will help you unravel why past relationships failed or were successful. Not every relationship fails because of another person. Many times, the failure is really yours. Good communication looks easy. You may think you are effective because you've communicated all of your life. Your skills, however, may not be as sophisticated as they need to be for all the encounters ahead of you. Skills improve once you understand the consequences of poor communication. Once you recognize the importance of interpersonal communication, you can understand others better, get along with others, and be more effective in future interpersonal situations. Try to learn from past mistakes and acquire the skills to prevent similar misunderstandings in the future.

SELF-DISCLOSURE

You enter your chemistry class and are assigned to a lab partner. How do you get to know one another? Most people begin with a brief conversation. *Self-disclosure* is the act of giving personal information to another person. You need to disclose information about yourself in order for others to get to know you. Self-disclosure is a key building block in interpersonal relationships. However, effective disclosure of personal information is done slowly and over a long period of time.

What are some of the common things we disclose when we first meet a peer? Our name, size of our family, hometown, high school activities, basic interests, and academic major are typical topics for self-disclosure. Some initial self-disclosures are appropriate or inappropriate depending on the region of the country where people live. For example, when I (KSY) moved to Arkansas, I was in the car with a colleague and her 7-year-old daughter. The daughter looked at me and asked, "What church do you go to?" I waited for the mother to correct her daughter for asking an inappropriate question. From my perspective the question was too intimate for initial self-disclosure. Silence reigned. The mother was actually waiting for me to answer the question since in that region, "What church do you go to?" is usually the second question asked of strangers, immediately after asking, "What is your name?" The silence was extremely awkward because both of us were waiting for the other person to speak.

We have choices about how much we disclose and the amount of intimate self-disclosure we provide for others. There is no specific formula for what is appropriate and what is inappropriate. Every person can disclose certain information about their past, but the choices vary from person to person. For example, very few students in a college classroom would volunteer information about a family member's personal problems, how much money their parents make, or their ultimate sexual fantasy. How do we know what information is appropriate to share with strangers?

Critical Thinking

What has someone disclosed to you that made you feel uncomfortable? How did you react? Do you still communicate with this person?

_____

_____

_____

_____

The more personal the information you choose to share, the greater the trust you must have in the other person. While intimate self-disclosure can make personal relationships closer, it also makes you vulnerable should the other person choose to violate your confidence. You should take only acceptable risks when you share information with another person. The lesson of what is an acceptable risk is learned through life experience. You will get burned occasionally, but it's a risk you must take when you feel someone is worth knowing. All trust involves risk. If your trust is violated, you will at least know that you were willing to participate in open, honest communication. Although withholding information may be prudent in some circumstances, silence will not lead to close relationships.

Historically self-disclosure was only discussed in the context of face-to-face interpersonal communication. However, today we have millions of people who are willing to self-disclose via the Internet to a multitude of unknown receivers. Through MySpace, Facebook, discussion boards, and instant messaging (IM), people are posting all kinds of facts about themselves that were once reserved for sharing with friends.

If there is someone we want to know about, we can quickly look them up and know their hopes, dreams, favorite movies, foods, songs, etc. Quite often, the person will list an IM address; their away messages often list when they are in class, in the cafeteria, and even in the shower.

Ethical Considerations

Is it ethical to keep track of someone through the use of technology? Why or why not?

_____

_____

Is it ethical for professors to look up student profiles? Why or why not?

_____

_____

Keep in mind that many people have access to these self-disclosure sites. A recent graduate reported that she was told to pull up her MySpace site during a job interview. She was fortunate there was nothing compromising on her site. We find that most of our students aren't so prudent. Many of our students post pictures of ethically questionable behavior, poses, and attire; use profanity; and list other information that potential employers could find objectionable.

Certainly, self-disclosing via technology can be used for good purposes. I (KSY) keep track of our alumni accomplishments and career moves easily through the use of Facebook. However, I also choose to post very limited information about myself.

One way to gauge the appropriateness of self-disclosure is by interpreting the nonverbal behavior of our conversation partner. People may demonstrate discomfort with your self-disclosure through their vocalizations, their silence, or an instant change of subject. When this happens, you need to be perceptive enough to stop the disclosure immediately. If you are in a position where someone is disclosing information and expecting you to disclose similar details, you may find it necessary to respond in a very calm manner with something like, "I'm not prepared to talk about that right now. Can we please change the subject?" This is a reasonable way to let the other person know

— **Professional Perspective** —

It is amazing how a very common language term can be misinterpreted. . . .

Most college students are fully aware of the dangers of a Facebook or MySpace account, whether it be the "unbalanced" people that are out there or the companies and organizations that are using it to find out about potential employees. Regardless of the facts, many of us still choose to have an account.

My professor came into class one day with a surprise for us all. She had done some research on everyone in the class. She informed us that she had her own account on Facebook and MySpace! As she walked around the room, she informed us of something that was not appropriate about each one of our accounts. I was on the opposite side of the room thinking that I was in the clear because I had been very careful to keep my profile clean.

Come to find out, I was completely wrong! That day opened my eyes. Of course, as do most students these days, I have an Instant Messenger screen name that was advertised in my account. Are you familiar with a *crotch rocket*? Most people in my generation know this to be a sporty motorcycle. The professor, on the other hand, did not know it was a motorcycle. Until that day, I had not even thought about my screen name as indicating anything but a die-hard motorcycle fan! It totally took me by surprise. I was shocked and embarrassed by what the professor interpreted. So, before you post something, I encourage you to think carefully!

Stacy Wolfe
College Student

Critical Thinking

Do you have a Facebook/MySpace account? _____

What do you like about posting a profile?

_____

How much information do you reveal?

_____

Would you be embarrassed if a professor, parent, police officer, or future employer accessed it?

_____

What would the consequences be if that happened?

_____

she has overstepped the bounds of appropriate discussion without closing off further communication. Many people have different tolerances for what are appropriate topics for discussion. If you have not yet reached the same comfort level for disclosure, communicate how you feel, leaving the door open for the relationship to continue.

Please remember that disclosures must happen for relationships to grow. There are some people who are unwilling to disclose anything personal. It is extremely difficult to build a relationship with people who never self-disclose.

Keep in mind also that gender research supports the general conclusion that men tend to self-disclose much less than women do (Ivy & Backlund, 2004, p. 212). This means two people in an intimate heterosexual relationship will probably disclose at different levels. The female in the relationship may feel the male isn't willing to get close to her emotionally, while the male may feel the female talks too much and too soon. There are certain things about yourself you should share openly with others and certain things you should not share immediately, if ever. This is a decision only you can make. Always be prepared for the consequences of your choices in every relationship.

CONVERSATION

Conversation is an extemporaneous interpersonal exchange. Some communicators are better at participating in conversations than others. Think about the people you enjoy being with while discussing any topic. Then, think about the people you may try to avoid when discussing certain subjects. What makes the difference?

As a relationship develops, a conversation needs to be a somewhat even exchange in self-disclosure. Each individual should share information about themselves so that both people learn more about each other. The information they are exchanging should be similar in both quality and quantity. A one-sided information exchange does not build a working relationship or an intimate relationship.

Effective communicators know there are various stages in the ***conversational process***: the opening, the body, and the closing. The ***opening*** lets the other person know you would like to talk. You might use a smile coupled with eye contact, or you might use a direct verbal phrase, "Hi, my name is Rita."

Sometimes the opening includes ***conversational setup***—the introductory remarks to the conversation that give the other person a sense of what is coming next. Setup is not always necessary, but if the information to be revealed in the conversation is important or surprising, then conversational setup should be present. People may say, "Have you heard what happened?" or, "I have some really bad news to share with you." In this way, the listener is not shocked by the information you share. Keep in mind that if you use a lengthy conversational setup, you lose conversational effectiveness. Many people get annoyed with a person who starts a conversation with, "Oh hi, hey listen, I was meaning to ask you . . . now if you don't want to, please say no, there is no obligation, and I won't mind, so I really want to know what you think about. . . ." The listener may be annoyed by the rambling, disjointed opening and will be less likely to want to respond.

The second stage, the *body*, is the longest section of a conversation. This is where you exchange information, share stories, tell jokes, or try to persuade. You may talk about superficial topics or topics of great intimacy. It depends on the relationship. Your self-disclosure rules apply here. Conversations end quickly if you launch into uncomfortable or insensitive information. If you want the conversation to keep going, you may need to ask questions. (Be sure to incorporate the information about listening and feedback styles discussed later in the chapter.) However, certain questions and styles of feedback are notorious for closing conversations. So, pay attention to nonverbal or verbal cues that indicate you have plunged too quickly into sensitive topics.

Also be aware of your nonverbals during a conversation. While people can certainly listen without making eye contact, the communicator may legitimately feel there is a lack of interest or comprehension without it. Eye contact, in U.S. culture, makes most people feel connected to another person. It makes us feel as though we have the other person's attention. Eye contact and general attentiveness is essential in meaningful conversation. For example, Rowan and Seanan are business associates having dinner together in a restaurant. Rowan always looks Seanan in the eye while they are conversing. Any shift in Seanan's facial tension or eye motion gives Rowan the clues he needs to change or expand a topic. Rowan's eyes never move even though he is aware of everything around him. Seanan has a harder time with this behavior. He finds himself distracted at times by peripheral phenomena. He looks at the servers walking by, people being seated, and couples in other booths. How do you think these business associates perceive each other's nonverbals? What attributions does Rowan create for Seanan's lack of eye contact? Disinterest? Short attention span? What does Seanan think about Rowan's constant gaze? Which of these associates is really listening to the conversation? Every aspect of nonverbal communication sends a message during conversation. Remember, a nonverbal message can support or detract from the message itself.

In addition to nonverbal habits, you also need to be careful regarding your selection of topics and the information you choose to share. Many people just say what is on their mind rather than reflecting on how it will sound. Have you ever been standing in a checkout line at a grocery store and had someone self-disclose inappropriate information to you? Or have you done a double take when a friend has interrupted what you consider a serious revelation with a totally irrelevant point about his day? Or have you been talking to a friend about something important and personal when some friends interrupt your conversation and instantly begin talking enthusiastically about an upcoming event? After monopolizing your time without ever asking if they had interrupted something important, they leave as quickly as they came, leaving you wondering, "What was that all about?" These moments of inappropriate self-disclosure or an irrelevant topic are constant reminders of why you need to monitor what you share with others. Don't repeat behavior you find to be annoying in others. Learn from the communication mistakes around you and apply that knowledge to your own choices.

The third stage is the *closing*. In U.S. culture, we expect conversations to have an informal or formal ending. This brief statement allows the communicators to agree the conversation is coming to a close. A simple "goodbye," "see you later," or "nice chatting with you" is all it takes to alert each other that the conversation has ended. While the phrases may seem to be meaningless (obviously if I walk away from you, our conversation is over), it is a social norm to close a conversation effectively. Many communicators are aggravated by anyone who hangs up a phone without saying "goodbye" to close the conversation. We learn manners at a young age and apply our standards to other people. Years ago, I (KSY) was hanging up laundry when a 7-year-old neighbor was talking to me. I was somewhat distracted, but I did engage in the conversation. However, because of my distraction, when I was done hanging the laundry I picked up my basket and headed back to the house. The little boy called after me in a quiet, sad, and questioning voice, "Well, I'll see you later?" I was mortified at my insensitivity. Everyone expects—and deserves—some kind of closing to a conversation.

Remember, the most effective communicators can adapt to a situation and read nonverbal clues. If someone is giving you the nonverbal signs that she wants to end the conversation (such as glancing at the computer, reaching toward the doorknob, looking at her watch), then it is time to stop talking. We are constantly amazed at the number of people who have not learned this basic skill of observation.

⇨ **Try It!** ⇦

Your mom calls while you are studying for a very important exam. She is still talking after 30 minutes. How do you end the conversation?

_____

_____

_____

You see a great-looking person at a party. How do you open the conversation?

_____

_____

_____

A friend of yours monopolizes the body of the conversation, never pausing long enough to allow you to participate. What do you do?

_____

_____

_____

There are some rules that apply to every conversation. Remember to be polite. Be concise. Do not waste another person's time. Keep the conversation focused. But also keep in mind that conversations vary from person to person and depend on the context. Specific conversational topics depend on whether you are talking to your friends, your teachers, employers, or parents. Preparation for the conversation is important if you must speak with someone for a specific purpose. If you are simply chatting with friends for enjoyment, no preparation is necessary. However, when you speak with a boss or an instructor, you must prepare for the body of the conversation. There have been times when students have come to our offices under the guise of a specific conversation topic, but they end up venting about something that is of no interest to us and is none of our business. You should converse appropriately with the appropriate people.

— Professional Perspective —

There is nothing more frustrating for a manager than an employee coming to a meeting unprepared. Whether the meeting is regularly scheduled or ad hoc, an employee must anticipate a manager's questions and, where appropriate, be prepared to offer solutions or alternatives to company challenges. The employee is expected to thoroughly research the issues.

In any meeting with a manager, the employee must be able to clearly and concisely state their position, without engaging in company politics or emotional outbursts. They may be passionate about an issue, but the passion must be supported with facts. A manager does not want to be asked questions for which an employee has the resources to independently get the answers either from other employees, company documents, or industry literature.

Wasting a manager's time can leave a negative mark on your career for what will seem like an eternity.

—Joe Tucker
Senior Vice President
The Walt Disney Company

Learning effective conversational skills is immensely valuable for every interpersonal relationship. These skills can help you tremendously in friendships, romantic relationships, family relationships, the workplace, and the job interview.

The Johari Window

The Johari Window model was developed by psychologists Joseph Luft and Harry Ingham in the 1950s during research on group dynamics; the title of the model comes from the first names of Luft and Ingham. Once you understand the importance of self-disclosure and feedback in building relationships, the Johari Window is a tool you can use to analyze yourself and others. The *Johari Window* is a diagram of what we know about ourselves and what others know about us. The symbolic representation of that knowledge consists of four areas: information known to others, unknown to others, known to self, and unknown to self. Think of the areas as panes in a window that will vary in size depending on the individual. The Johari Window helps us understand how open or closed we are with others and how aware or unaware we are of information about ourselves.

Self-disclosure and feedback are the two continuums that determine the size of the areas. Your willingness to share personal information with others increases or decreases the size of the "known by others" area. The more you reveal, the more others know about you. People who self-disclose easily are more open; people who rarely self-disclose keep aspects of themselves hidden. Information learned or elicited from others determines the size of the blind area. If we process feedback from others by listening carefully to what they are saying about us, we can learn information about ourselves that we never knew, and our blind area will be smaller.

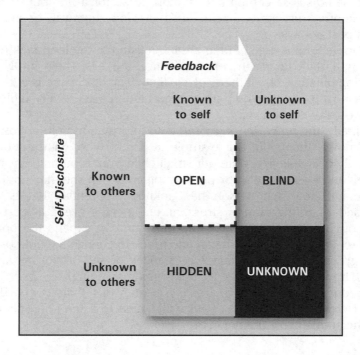

The *open area* refers to what we know about ourselves and what other people know about us: information you have disclosed and information you have learned about yourself from others. As you self-disclose and as you accept feedback, your open area will grow larger. It takes trust to open oneself up to feedback and self-disclosure, but it is necessary for healthy interpersonal relationships.

The *blind area* refers to qualities or characteristics about yourself that others are aware of but that you are not. These elements may include mannerisms, an unusual posture, a unique way of walking, or what your language choices say about you. The best way to discover the image you project (thereby decreasing the blind area) is to listen to and consciously evaluate the feedback others give to you. If you play with your hair when you give a speech and are unaware of it, you will learn about this inappropriate behavior through feedback from classmates and/or your teacher.

People who have a large blind area typically overuse self-disclosure. They desire social relationships but are often unaware that they are talking too much to accept the feedback of others. They are unaware of listener feedback and keep talking because they are socially nervous, self-centered, or refuse to admit that others may have better ideas and thoughts.

A good way to reduce the size of your blind area is to elicit feedback from others through conversation. If you listen to others as they respond to your questions, process their information, your open area will become larger and your blind area smaller.

The *hidden area* refers to information you know about yourself but choose not to share with others. This is private information you never discuss with anyone. For most people, certain thoughts or actions remain hidden, such as an embarrassing incident or a mistake you made in the past. If you have a large hidden area, you are low in self-disclosure. People who choose not to self-disclose certain information do so for a number of reasons: low self-esteem, trust issues based on a previous betrayal, or embarrassment about past behavior.

People with a large hidden area can listen to the feedback of others and actively participate in the communication process. They simply never share anything personal about themselves. Since self-disclosure is a key to building a relationship, the person with a large hidden area is very difficult to get to know on a personal level.

Finally, the ***unknown area*** refers to information neither you nor anyone else knows about you. For example, a parent who, with a sudden burst of adrenaline, is able to rescue her small child from a burning car may surprise herself and everyone else by performing an action she may not have thought she could do. Each person has unknown potential that is occasionally released when triggered by stress, an unexpected event, a burst of creativity, or through self-exploration. Communication can expand the open area and contract the blind area but it can't do much to change the unknown area. The synergy created in meaningful exchanges of self-disclosure and feedback could, however set the stage for better understanding.

Reducing your unknown area is a journey of self-discovery. The more you self-disclose and the greater your willingness to listen to feedback from others, the smaller your unknown area will be.

Choices and Consequences

Have you ever been around someone who was too open? What information did they disclose? How did you feel as a result of the self-disclosure? What were the consequences?

_____

_____

_____

_____

Now that you understand the four symbolic panes of the Johari Window a little better, think of them as a useful analytical tool for improving your interpersonal communication. The panes will not be the same size from one person to the next because people vary greatly in their ability to self-disclose information and listen to feedback from others.

If you analyze yourself and your relationships, you may be able to see whether you need to self-disclose more or less information and process more or less feedback to maintain a positive relationship. You may realize that you haven't been telling your significant other or close friend enough about yourself so she can get to know you. Relationships end when people don't share information about themselves. Maybe you are the socially inept person who can't seem to fit in with others, but you're not sure why. It's possible you might be revealing too much or inappropriate information about yourself. This information or behavior might make other people uncomfortable. We also need to learn about ourselves from others. Are you listening to what others tell you about yourself? Are you listening at all? Or are you always talking? Do you brush off comments that others make about you? As you analyze feedback from others, there is a difference between harmful labels and constructive criticism. For example, if someone suggests that you cut others off when they are talking, you should reflect on that analysis and work on ways to improve your communication skills such as turn-taking. However, if someone has told you all your life that you are stupid, we would recommend that you don't internalize that message.

Personal awareness is the first step in the process of changing communication patterns. You can increase or decrease your self-disclosure as well as your ability to respond to feedback with a little practice. The Johari Window can become a tool for personal growth.

LISTENING

Most of us have the ability to hear from birth, but *listening* is an acquired skill. *Hearing* is a passive action. It is simply the process of sound hitting your eardrums and then being decoded for a possible response.

— Professional Perspective —

To become an articulate verbal communicator, I feel it is necessary to first become an attentive listener. I have always felt that I have been a good listener. But when I became the parent of a hearing-impaired child, my listening skills were immediately challenged. Hearing is an amazing gift, and I was just learning how amazing it really is. I had to listen carefully to my daughter's speech and then teach her how to listen and speak using Auditory Verbal Therapy.

Step one for everyone to become articulate verbal communicators: first listen, then verbalize. It seems very simple but, if you think about it, do you use this rule in your daily life? In every situation and phase of life, be it at school, your place of employment, or at home with family and friends, everyone wants and deserves to be heard. If you find yourself speaking and no one seems to be listening, chances are your auditory skills are lacking. If you interrupt, correct, and speak over people often, your listening skills will need some fine-tuning. And actually just being aware of having these habits is really the only step a person needs to correct them.

Remember, your auditory comprehension of others will not only determine what and how you verbalize your thoughts back to others, it will also determine how others perceive and respond to you. Listen—Think—Speak.

—Tracy Synowsky
Stay-at-Home Parent

Think back to chapter 2 on perception. We talked about the concept of selective attention. Remember how we are constantly bombarded by sounds and choices? We hear everything, but we only pay attention to specific sounds based on personal need and preference. Listening is an active process where you selectively attend to and assign meaning to sounds. If we analyzed every sound within earshot, we'd be exhausted. Once we focus on which sounds interest us, we can process the information and respond appropriately.

⇨ Try It! ⇦

Take a minute and list eight sounds that you can hear right now:

_____   _____   _____   _____

_____   _____   _____   _____

Being an effective listener is a skill that takes practice. Some of us develop this skill to a much finer degree than others. Because every interpersonal relationship is unique, and because each communication situation has different listening requirements, we need to learn multiple listening styles in order to be a strong communicator. Many communicators learn only one listening/ feedback style and use it consistently, but this doesn't allow for the uniqueness of situations. As you progress from situation to situation, flexibility and the ability to adapt to new information immediately helps you to become an effective listener.

Reality ✔

There are some quick and easy ways to improve your listening skills. When you are in a classroom or business meeting, sit up straight, make eye contact with the speaker, and take lots of notes. Note-taking keeps you focused on the message. Make sure that you are briefed on the material of the day (either by reading the textbook or reviewing material for the meeting). Knowing the information makes listening easier. Also make sure to take proper care of your body. If you have adequate rest and proper nutrition, focusing on the message is much easier than if you are concerned with staying awake or a rumbling stomach.

As a speaker, you can help listeners follow your main points by using signposts and transitions (see chapter 8). This will help the audience retain the information more easily as well.

⇨ Try It! ⇦

List all the reasons you can think of why it is hard to listen to others. Think of situations with friends, parents, and teachers.

_____

_____

_____

_____

_____

Listening and Feedback Styles

As you process and respond to information others give you, it is important to remember there are actually six different *listening/feedback* styles. Some of them are more useful than others, but each one serves a purpose. The six styles are judgmental, directive, empathetic, questioning, interpreting, and active. In each of the situations below Frank approaches his friends and says: "I can't believe I got a 62 on my chemistry exam. I needed an 80 to pass the course. I don't understand. I thought I did really well."

A *Judgmental* style of listening/feedback means a listener makes a judgment about both the content and the speaker. Judith, who is a judgmental listener, tells Frank: "Well, I told you that you needed to study more." This response makes Judith sound superior because she "knew it all along." It also implies that Frank failed to do what he needed to do to pass the course.

Directive style means a listener tells the speaker what to do. Giovanni tells Frank: "Well, the first thing you need to do is go talk to the professor. Then you need to. . . ." As a directive listener, Giovanni tries to solve the problem by giving advice.

Empathetic style of listening/feedback means a listener gives the speaker an emotional form of support. Sarah says, "Oh, Frank, I'm so sorry. You must feel awful. Is there anything I can do?" Sarah, an empathetic listener, tries to comfort Frank.

Did you think Giovanni's and Sarah's responses were stereotypical? We intentionally chose to use a male for directive listening and a female for empathetic listening because, in general, women are more likely to be empathetic listeners while men are more likely to be directive listeners (Wood, 2001, pp. 125–130).

Questioning is another listening/feedback style. The listener asks probing questions of the speaker that are not necessarily supportive questions. They sometimes have a hint of accusation in their tone. Frank's brother, Jeff, who is a questioning listener, asks, "Why didn't you study harder?" While he is inviting more conversation, he is also placing a confrontational edge on the communication. He is implying that Frank did something wrong. This leads Frank to reply defensively.

The *Interpreting* style of listening/feedback means a listener tries to offer another explanation of what happened. This style can be very useful in helping the speaker to think of other possible explanations for an event or a better analysis of the problem. Svetlana tells Frank, "Maybe the instructor made a mistake. Did you think about going in to go over the test and make sure the grade is accurate?" As an interpretive listener, Svetlana helps Frank explore other possibilities for his dilemma.

Active listening/feedback means a listener offers supportive questions and makes it clear that he is willing to listen. The listener tries to encourage more communication, using paraphrasing to ensure understanding. There are two types of paraphrasing that can be useful. You may use a content-level paraphrase or a relationship-level paraphrase. A content paraphrase summarizes the message the other person states. The relationship paraphrase checks on the emotional state of the speaker.

Content paraphrase: "Oh wow, I'm sorry, so are you saying you won't be able to graduate?"

Relationship (emotional) paraphrase: "Oh my, you sound really upset, is there anything I can do?"

— Professional Perspective —

As a mom to five kids, I am my children's first teacher and model of communication. Knowing that I am helping to shape their communication skills and habits makes me very aware of what I say and how I say it. However, I often find myself spending more time listening than speaking. Active listening is vital to effective parenting. My kids know that I'm not truly listening to them when I'm reading the newspaper and mumbling "uh huh." Taking the time to use eye contact and interested body language, to ask relevant questions, and to reflect or repeat the thoughts or emotions I'm hearing demonstrates to my kids that I am listening and that they and their ideas are important to me.

—Carrie L. Clarke
Stay-at-Home Parent

The active listener may use either or both of these styles if they are appropriate. In many situations, you may not need either. But if you do use them, you might continue with some other questions, such as, "Would you like to talk?" "Is there anything I can do?" Active listening helps the speaker emotionally process her reaction to a situation. It doesn't superimpose a plan. The active listener acts as a sounding board and allows the speaker to discover the best solution for the dilemma.

Implications of Styles

Communication misunderstandings occur when people don't get the feedback style they are expecting. Think about how defensive you might get if you weren't expecting the questioning or judgmental response. If you are looking for help, sympathy, or an active listener to help you out, a questioning or judgmental listener will make you feel worse or angry. At this point, communication stops or an argument begins.

If you're looking for a shoulder to cry on, and the person begins directing you instead, you may feel the person is not really listening. In this situation, you already feel emotionally down, and if the listener begins to give you directives, you may resent being told what to do. All you really wanted from a listener was some sympathy. But, some people find empathetic listeners to be extremely annoying. These communicators prefer a more directive listening approach to help them solve their problem. They want to be told what to do.

It is critical for you to begin an intrapersonal analysis of the listening style that works best for you. Begin to discover your reasons for communicating with other people and think about the responses you receive. Are you unhappy when you hear the comments and questions peers and colleagues offer you? Could you be looking for one of the listening styles just discussed rather than the one people are giving you? You should tell the people closest to you why a specific listening style works for you. If they can tailor their responses to the listening/feedback style that best suits your needs, you will feel better about the decisions you make and you will be closer to each other in true friendship. Your family, significant other, and close friends can't support you properly if you are not clear about the responses you need during a conversation. We encourage you to think about which listening style will work for you in a given situation. Then, communicate your needs to those around you.

Critical Thinking

Think about the people in your life. Can you think of people who typically use the same listening style? List them below with a brief description of your last encounter:

Judgmental: _____

Directing: _____

Empathetic: _____

Questioning: _____

Interpreting: _____

Active: _____

Looking at the six people you list above, whom do you most enjoy going to when you need to vent? Why? Whom do you least like? Why?

_____

_____

_____

How many listeners do you know who can adapt their styles and select an appropriate style effectively? Describe your last encounter.

_____

_____

_____

What type of listener are you? Are you satisfied with that style? Are you an effective listener for your friends? What could you do to make changes?

_____

_____

_____

Think of the last time a good friend came to you with a problem. Write a brief description about the situation.

_____

_____

What was the problem? _____

What listening style did you use? _____

Would another listening style have been more effective? _____

Describe a response to the problem in at least two of the listening styles.

_____

_____

_____

Reality ✔

Felippe and Marci have been married for 10 years. When they first got married, they fell into stereotypical gender communication roles. Marci preferred an empathetic listener when she had a problem. Felippe preferred a directive listener who could help him solve his problem quickly. When listening to each other, they responded with the listening style each preferred. When Marci came home from work one night, she said, "Felippe, I can't believe how awful my day was. My supervisor assigned four more cases to my workload, my coworker Barbara took my lunch from the refrigerator, my computer crashed, and I'm so tired, I could just cry." In his reply, Felippe used the directive listening style because he wanted to help her. He said, "Well, tomorrow when you go into work, go to your boss and tell him you can only do two additional cases. Then you need to have a conversation with Barbara and let her know to keep her mitts off of your food unless she's going to pay for it. Then you need to call the IT department and have a chat about getting a new computer. And tonight, I'll do the dishes so you can get to bed at 8:00." Felippe was very proud of himself when he offered this useful advice. He was shocked when Marci screamed at him, "You never listen to me. I don't know why I even talk to you!!!"

Imagine the same scenario with roles reversed. If Felippe described a similar day to Marci, she would probably respond, "I'm so sorry, dear. Tomorrow will surely be a better day. Why don't you sit down, and I'll order some food." Felippe would also feel Marci is not listening to him; her comments don't do anything to solve his problem. So Felippe says, "I'm going out for a while," and he leaves the house.

Felippe and Marci solved their communication difficulties by recognizing they weren't meeting each other's communication needs. They realized they each needed something different in the listening response if their relationship was going to work. Marci explained she needed supportive statements. Felippe told her he needed directive statements. Neither Marci nor Felippe really understood why the other person was helped by a specific listening style, but because they were committed to one another, they worked on practicing the listening style their partner needed.

COMMUNICATING WITH TECHNOLOGY

Our effectiveness in interpersonal communication continues to evolve with the rapidly changing channels of technology. We must now be adept at *technical communication*. At one time, people who were not communicating face-to-face generally spoke to each other on the phone. Paralanguage gave subtle meaning to the words being used in the conversation. However, we increasingly use computers to communicate. We now have e-mail and IM as a significant channel for our interpersonal communication. Paralanguage does not exist in the written form (except through emoticons). When communicating via the computer, it is imperative to recognize the difference between communicating with your friends and communicating with business associates, professors, or other professionals.

IM is becoming a new language. People write very quickly and with numerous abbreviations. A simple "Hello Professor, how are you?" is written "how R U?" While this may be an appropriate way to communicate with friends, it is not appropriate with teachers or business associates. The specialized jargon used in IM has the potential to isolate people and also may reflect negatively on your communication skills and credibility. Using these abbreviations in the wrong situation can make you appear to be illiterate. You may think you are clever, but most business people would assume you are sloppy, too casual, and a poor speller. The tone sent with these informal messages is appropriate for friends, but not for working associates. Would you walk into a boss's office and start the conversation with "Hey, wuzzup baby?" We hope not. Just remember where you are and to whom you are speaking at all times.

— Professional Perspective —

A clear writing style and a good grasp of grammar are essential! In every day of my working career, I have found being able to express myself in a clear, concise manner to be invaluable. I would strongly suggest that anyone preparing for a career in business take the time to brush up on the elements of English grammar. There is nothing more embarrassing than writing your first memo to your brand new boss with a terrific idea you've had and getting it back with grammatical or spelling errors circled in red! Yes, this has happened, and to more than one acquaintance of mine; so I know my eccentric employer is not the only stickler out there. The reality is that people will be distracted from the content of your writing, whether it is e-mail, general correspondence, or a major report, if there are glaring errors. Whatever you write, take the time to proofread. Before you send out anything with your name attached, be sure to print it out and read it as though you were the recipient. If you know yourself to be a poor speller, invest in a good dictionary and remember that spell-check button!

—Christina DeVries
Senior Account Manager
Spotlight Payroll Inc.

When you are e-mailing family and friends, you may not bother to proofread for spelling and grammar. But with anyone who is not a member of your inner circle, you must proofread e-mail as carefully as you would a composition. When other people read your e-mail and words are misspelled, they will perceive you to be careless or, worse, incompetent. Don't forget, it is extremely easy to type your note in a word processing program that can check for spelling and grammar. You can then copy and paste it into the body of your e-mail. But don't rely on these programs exclusively. You must reread everything before you hit the send key. Although this may seem like a waste of time, you will find that written mistakes can affect a promotion opportunity or advancement in any company.

Remember, nothing you write or post on the Internet for friends or business associates is private. What you write may be read by others. In fact, some communication on the Internet is intended to be read by others. A number of people now are using blogs (Internet journals) to record their private thoughts. However, these journals are available for anyone to read. If you do this in your spare time, it is possible for a coworker, a potential employer, or a boss to find your private journal. Depending on what you have written, there could be serious repercussions. Choose wisely.

Businesses may monitor internal and external communication. Your office computer is corporately owned. It isn't your play toy. Numerous corporations have rules forbidding personal software to be loaded onto an office computer. Companies also have policies about personal e-mail while at work. Some companies electronically store all communication. When you send an e-mail to someone, it doesn't mean that person won't send your comment to others. All electronic communication can be altered. Think of the implications every typed message might have. We are not trying to paint a gloomy "Big Brother is watching over you" picture, but you should be aware of the realities of the Internet. Privacy doesn't exist. Carefully consider the content of your e-mails and to whom they are sent. Making an immature or uninformed choice can bring unexpected consequences.

Answering Machines

There are two things to understand about answering machines. The message you put on your machine for others to hear needs to be concise and articulate. You never know who will be calling your answering machine, and the caller will judge you by the sound of your message.

Let's say you and your roommate are in your senior year of college. You are having fun and enjoying your last year of freedom before graduating. You've found a new rock group you really like. You decide to record a fun message on the answering machine with you yelling and the music blaring in the background. In addition, you recently sent resumes to potential employers. One day while you are in class, someone from human resources (HR) in a Fortune 500 company calls the number you've listed on your resume. The person hears the message you've recorded. Before the message is even finished, the person from HR hangs up and shreds your resume.

When you are the caller leaving a message on an answering machine, you need to be concise and provide the following information: name, time, reason for calling, phone number where you can be reached, and whether you expect to be called back. If you are hesitant, the answering machine will cut you off, and you will sound incompetent when your message is played.

Critical Thinking

An employer calls your phone number and gets your answering machine. What impression does your message create?

_____

_____

E-mail Addresses

E-mail addresses also communicate on an interpersonal level. Think about the e-mail names you have seen. Some people use profanity, sexual innuendo, cultural insensitivity, nationalistic overtones, or religious meanings that are easy to misinterpret and could be offensive to some receivers. Because your e-mail address is on your resume, it sends a strong nonverbal interpersonal message. It is a good idea to have two e-mail addresses—one for business and another address for friends. The one you select for business should have your name in it. You may say, "Good grief, doesn't anyone have a sense of humor?" The answer is "no." One simple, inappropriate choice says volumes about your lack of sensitivity, judgment, respect, and credibility. The perception of the receiver could have consequences you never imagined when you made your choice.

Choices and Consequences

List your own personal e-mail address and those of 10 friends. What messages do they send? What are the consequences of using these addresses on a resume?

_____

_____

_____

_____

_____

Frustrations

Because technology allows channels for communication to be open constantly, there are increasing intrusions on interpersonal communication. How often have you been annoyed by a cell phone going off during a meeting or presentation, or by a person who is not paying attention because she is working on a PalmPilot, BlackBerry, or checking a pager? Some people do need to be available at all times, but these people are rare. Others feel a need to be connected constantly, even at the expense of being annoying to others or tuning out the people with whom they are talking face-to-face. Interpersonally, what message are you sending when you answer your cell phone in the middle of a conversation with another person at dinner? What message are you sending when you are more concerned with your PalmPilot than with paying attention to the people in the group around you? You need to make appropriate choices for your communication in public. Some cities have already imposed bans on cell phones and pagers in restaurants and theatres. We seem to think we are invisible when using technology in public, but we need to remember: every communication action sends a message to other people.

Frustrations also occur when the sender and receiver disagree on using a particular technology to communicate an important message. For instance, in today's society, more people are using wedding Web sites to announce their engagements, to send invitations, to respond to invitations, to register for gifts, and to distribute photos of the event. This is an inexpensive and easy way for the happy couple to share their joy quickly. However, it breaks a long-standing social tradition of sending a printed invitation with a response card. Many people are offended by the impersonal nature of an electronic invitation. The perception is that the couple is trying to add as many people as possible to the guest list at very little cost. We have listened to just as many people voice extreme distaste over receiving an electronic invitation as we have listened to people happy to use them.

Another area where frustrations may occur is when information via technology is mass mailed rather than personal. If you are changing your job or have a "life update" do you send individual e-mails to people or just one message to everyone in your address box? Sometimes the information that is mailed to one person is not in a format that seems personal to the next per-

Critical Thinking

You just started a job to make some extra money in a local store near your university. Lars, your coworker, seems to be interesting, and at first you enjoy talking to him. As the relationship builds, you notice Lars only talks about his interests and what he is doing. He never asks you for your opinion or what you think. Even when you offer an idea, he turns it into something about himself. In fact, there are times he only asks you questions so he can talk about himself. (Did you get a haircut? When the answer is no, he launches into the haircut experience he just had.) You end up being a dumping ground for him. He tells you everything, but the relationship seems more like a self-help situation than a friendship. You feel a little sorry for Lars and would like the relationship to develop differently. What can you say to Lars to let him know you would like to be included in the conversation?

_____

_____

_____

_____

_____

You start dating Kelly on a full-time basis. Gradually you begin to think about the kinds of places you are going and the activities you are attending. You begin to realize you are doing everything that Kelly wants to do and rarely doing what you want to do. You don't say anything. In fact, Kelly talks you into changing your mind any time you resist doing anything. You are the kind of person who buys into the arguments and accommodates so there is harmony in the relationship. Kelly, however, is never convinced to try the things you want to do. You go to Kelly's family events and out with Kelly's friends, but Kelly refuses to see yours. Kelly proposes to you. By this point, you feel you are in love with Kelly, but you dislike yourself for the fact you are giving up what is important to you. What should you do?

_____

_____

_____

_____

_____

Reality ✔

I am barely sitting down when I hear a voice from the other stall saying, "Hi! How are you?" I'm not the type to start a conversation or fraternize in men's rooms at a rest stop, but I don't know what got into me, so I answered rather sheepishly, "Not bad."

The other guy said, "So what's up with you?" What a question! At that point, I thought this was the most bizarre situation I've ever been in. I said, "I'm like you, just traveling south."

Then I heard the guy say nervously, "LISTEN!!! I'll have to call you back. There's an idiot in the next stall who keeps answering all my questions, bye!" (Adapted from an anonymous e-mail.)

Keep in mind you always communicate! Every choice with technology leads to a consequence.

son. While society is accepting of the fact that people are busy, friends and colleagues may desire a more personal message from time to time to keep up the interpersonal nature of the relationship. If you rely only on mass mailings, you may find that your close friends become fewer.

Reality ✔

Increasing use of technology cuts down on the interpersonal exchanges that can happen between two people. The ten-minute time period between classes used to be a time when teachers could chat casually with their students. Now, more and more students are plugged into iPods and other listening devices. They sit at their desks with their heads down listening to music rather than interacting with the teacher or other students. What might a student miss out on by making this choice?

_____

_____

_____

Ethical Considerations

What do you do if you hear a message that was not intended for you? Let's say that you are in a bathroom stall when your boss comes in with another coworker. The boss says something about the job opening that your good friend is applying for. Do you tell your boss that you overheard the information? Do you tell your friend about the information that you really shouldn't know? Do you select another option?

_____

_____

_____

_____

_____

Pulling together the concepts in this chapter try to come up with some answers for the scenarios on the following page. There is no right answer. It may be useful for you to share your thoughts with others in your classroom and explore the most effective answers together.

Critical Thinking

Lucinda sits next to you in class. She seems to enjoy your company, and you like her as well. She begins to show up at places where you are. She meets you at the cafeteria or shows up in the library. She always has attentive nonverbal communication. She seems to like you so much she even imitates some of your mannerisms and reads the same books you do. However, every time you try to have a conversation with her, she only uses one-word answers. You realize you are sharing personal information, but she never self-discloses. She seems like a nice person, but you feel very uncomfortable with the one-sided self-disclosure. You have asked her to share more feelings and thoughts with you and she promises she will, but she never does. What should you do?

_____

_____

_____

_____

_____

Randy is an RA on your dorm floor. He never lets you finish a sentence. He always tells you exactly what you should do and how you should do it. He is a true problem solver. You don't even get a chance to explain a situation that is problematic. By the time you have just started to explain a problem, he is spouting off directions for how you should handle it. He never allows you to process information. In addition, he comes up to you the next day and asks whether you have done what he told you to do. He gets on your case immediately if you didn't. You perceive that he only cares about himself, and you don't feel he is acting as the resource person he should be as an RA. What should you say?

_____

_____

_____

_____

_____

Delia is a good friend of yours. After high school, you go in different directions. You go to college, and she gets a job in a local company. You keep in touch by e-mail for a while, but you find you have little in common as the years pass. Delia begins forwarding to you every e-mail she receives plus all of the jokes she thinks are funny. Her updates on her life are sent to a list of over 50 people. You are not interested in the little details she is including in these e-mails. Even though you still like her, you realize you've changed dramatically over the years. You are disappointed by the fact you don't get any personal e-mail from her. You are now receiving information you no longer desire at least two to three times a day. What should you say to Delia?

_____

_____

_____

_____

_____

SUMMARY

Solid interpersonal skills are an essential ingredient for successful relationships in your personal and professional lives. It takes time to develop critical listening skills, acceptable verbal and nonverbal techniques, and to discover how to self-disclose personal thoughts with new acquaintances and build trusting relationships. Self-disclosure at some level is the key ingredient in making every relationship work—from the casual acquaintance to the true friend.

As you become more comfortable with technology, it is also important to think about how technology removes warmth from the interpersonal process. How important is it to you to hear the voice of another person? See the person's face? Simply be in the presence of others to discuss important issues? Your answer to these questions helps you to focus on the definition and meaning of interpersonal communication. How you balance verbal and nonverbal communication through various channels tells other people how you feel about them.

Interpersonal skills can be improved with a little effort on your part. Each improvement in your ability to communicate with others makes you more confident as you integrate into a diverse society. In turn, your confidence and skills allow you to be perceived by others as competent.

Key Words

active style

blind area

body

closing

conversation

conversational process

conversational setup

directive style

empathetic style

hearing

hidden area

interpersonal communication

interpreting style

Johari Window

judgmental style

listening

listening/feedback styles

open area

opening

questioning style

self-disclosure

technical communication

unknown area

Crossword 5: Communicating Interpersonally

Across

1. A new channel providing great challenges for interpersonal communicators.
3. A tool used to analyze self-disclosure and conversation in building relationships.
5. The listening style where the person asks sincere questions and paraphrases to keep the communication going is called _____.
9. People who tell you what to do when you talk to them about a problem are using the _____ listening style.
11. The act of giving personal information to another person.
12. When someone prefaces their conversational remarks with, "I have some really bad news," they are using conversational _____.
14. In the _____ part of the conversation, you exchange jokes, information, or attempts at persuasion.
16. _____ is the process of assigning meaning to what we hear.
18. An extemporaneous, interpersonal exchange is called _____.
19. When a listener uses perception checking to see if they got the message, they are using a _____ paraphrase.
20. When a listener asks, "Does that mean that you are really happy?" they are checking on the _____ state of the speaker.

Down

2. When Roberta says, "So what did you do to cause that?" she is using the _____ listening style.
4. Communication between two or more people in a personal or professional relationship.
6. When people offer an alternate explanation for an event, they are using the _____ listening style.
7. In the _____ part of the conversation, you say, "See you later!"
8. A person who says, "You never should have been that stupid," is using the _____ listening style.
10. When Ray says, "Oh, I'm so sorry to hear that; you must feel awful!" he is using the _____ listening style.
13. In the _____ part of conversation, we identify we are willing to converse.
15. _____ is the process of sound hitting our eardrums.
17. A telephone, IM, e-mail, or an answering machine are all examples of _____ channels.

CHAPTER 6

Conflict and Relationship Stages

OBJECTIVES

After reading this chapter, you should be able to:

- Understand the nature of conflict
- Identify the five conflict-resolution styles and analyze their use
- List the five stages in relationship development
- Identify appropriate behaviors for each stage
- Explain the concept of "I" messages and practice incorporating them into your communication

---

Interpersonal communication is comprised of the elements we discussed in the previous chapter. However, interpersonal communication doesn't always go smoothly even when you are skilled. When you are listening, making language choices, self-disclosing, or engaging in conversation, conflict can often arise. Understanding the nature of conflict and how it affects interpersonal relationships will help you to be successful in your personal and business life.

Conflict occurs any time there is a disagreement between two or more people. While many people think conflict is undesirable, it is actually essential to any growing relationship. What is important is how you resolve the conflict that occurs. Resolving conflict can be ineffective or effective. In interpersonal communication, ineffective conflict resolution involves yelling and screaming, manipulating, issuing ultimatums, silence, or refusal to discuss issues. These strategies leave people feeling angry, used, scared, and/or frustrated. Do you know a parent who resolves conflict in the home by yelling ultimatums? Have you experienced a person who claims to have no opinion about anything? Has a significant other ever refused to discuss an important issue?

Effective conflict resolution employs a variety of styles, which we discuss below. Spirited discussion, active inquiry, effective listening skills, critical thinking, and problem solving are all components in effective conflict resolution. If two people care about each other, they want to find a solution to the

⇨ **Try It!** ⇦

Describe an instance where someone you know resolved conflict ineffectively. What was your reaction?

_____

_____

_____

_____

_____

disagreement without creating animosity in the relationship. If you are afraid of conflict, chances are that the outcomes of disagreements you have faced were negative and uncomfortable. People who have engaged in effective conflict resolution tend to enjoy working out differences and coming to an acceptable resolution. A healthy working relationship between two people must include an environment where both participants feel they can share opinions and participate in resolving disagreement. Both people need to feel that they will be heard and that both parties will share equally in the resolution, rather than one person winning and the other person feeling ignored.

The potential for conflict exists everywhere in daily communication, from small choices like how to clean your apartment or where to eat dinner to big decisions like whether to spend thousands of dollars on a car or house. You will find conflict around every corner. So will you employ the skills to resolve conflict effectively? Or will you use ineffective strategies? All conflicts, once they are recognized, can escalate or de-escalate. When we use ineffective strategies, we cause escalation. For example, if you mouth off to a parent, superior, or sometimes a partner, you may escalate a conflict tenfold. What other choices do you have? Thinking carefully about how to respond to someone. If you choose the right words and tone, you can de-escalate a conflict immediately.

CONFLICT-RESOLUTION STYLES

In any relationship, conflict is inevitable. Many students have a very negative connotation for the word conflict. Conflict itself, however, is not bad. It simply means disagreement. However, if conflict or disagreement is handled poorly, the result will be negative feelings. In their classic work on **conflict-resolution** styles, Ralph Kilmann and Kenneth Thomas (1977) identify five different styles and suggest you should have all five styles in your repertoire so you can select the most appropriate resolution style for any given argument.

- Competing
- Avoiding
- Accommodating
- Compromising
- Collaborating

You should become familiar with each style and use the one that will be most effective in a given interaction. Most of us tend to use the style with which we are most comfortable rather than selecting the style that best enables us to handle specific disagreements. The most effective communicators are able to apply all of the five styles depending on the situation. Learn to assess the needs of all parties, so you can use the style most likely to result in everyone having a positive experience.

Competing Style

When it is important to "win" the conflict at all costs, the **competing style** is appropriate. This style is effective when you truly believe in something or in a crisis situation where the conflict must be resolved immediately. One aspect of this style is a refusal to listen to the arguments of others; the goal is to prevail, not to share decision making. For example, when a 5-year-old says he doesn't want a coat and the temperature is 12 degrees outside, some parents say, "You'll do it because I'm the parent, and I said so!" This style is, however, ineffective in most interpersonal relationships. Most people do not want to be dominated, and competitive responses close the door to further discussion. A competitor does not listen to others and is not concerned with their thoughts or needs. Even children absorb this message when parents always use the competing style.

While you may have to deal with a parent who is a competitor, what happens when you are grown and have a friend or partner who uses this style all the time? Would you be happy being in a relationship with someone who always has to win or be right? Sometimes in interpersonal relationships, the competitive style can turn into the subcategory of bullying. **Bullying** occurs when a person must be right no matter what, and they railroad you into doing or believing as they do. You may go along with the bully or end the relationship. On the other hand, if someone has told you to "choose your battles," they might be indicating that you are unreasonably aggressive. Be sure you don't turn into an interpersonal bully who has to win every argument at any cost. Recognizing when others are using a bullying style can help you determine the best response to this type of tactic.

On the positive side, two people who are enjoying a spirited discussion of an issue can also be using the competitive mode of resolution. They may both be asserting themselves, wanting to win the discussion, and having fun with trying to make the other person give in and let them win.

Avoiding Style

When people walk away from conflict, they are using an **avoiding style.** People who use avoidance say, "I'm outta here" when a heated argument begins. They physically remove themselves from the situation. Think about our example of Felippe and Marci in chapter 5. When Felippe didn't think Marci was listening to him, he left the house. He did this rather than attempt to resolve the disagreement. This style is important to use whenever there is any threat of physical or verbal abuse either to you or from you. Unless abuse is an issue, the avoidance style is one of the least useful styles because nothing is resolved. One person leaves, but the problem remains.

There are two subsets of avoidance. Someone might **withdraw** from a conflict for one of two reasons: (1) He or she has no opinion on the topic or no vital interest in the outcome. If so, there is no reason for them to engage in the conflict. (2) The person is truly afraid of conflict. If he or she can't handle the negative emotions they feel when people start raising their voices and arguing, withdrawal is a means to avoid those uncomfortable feelings.

Another subset of avoidance is ***delaying***. Delaying happens when someone is too upset to continue with the conflict at that moment. Whenever you feel that you might say or do something that you'll regret later, it may be best to delay the conflict until you calm down and can express yourself appropriately. In this case, it is best to let your partner or friend know what is going on. Saying something like, "I need to talk about this tomorrow," or "I'll come back in an hour to discuss it," lets the other person know that you aren't simply walking out.

Accommodating Style

When people give in to someone else to promote harmony in the relationship, they are using an ***accommodating style.*** This occurs if people are afraid of conflict, afraid to voice an opinion, or are so easygoing that they do not have a strong opinion one way or the other. However, if you have an opinion, you should not rely on this style. People who repress their own opinions in relationships may become hostile or depressed. Sometimes they even play the martyr role, which can be annoying to others.

Your opinions should always be articulated when you have them. For example, if Maureen asks Erik where he wants to go for dinner and he says he doesn't care, he should not say "Oh I hate that place" when she picks the diner in town. If he has only one dislike, he can say, "Let's go anywhere except the diner." If he has a list of places he dislikes, then he should not use the accommodating style. You should only use this style if you truly don't have an opinion and are willing to do what the other person wants to do without question or comment.

Compromising Style

When both people give in slightly, they are using a ***compromising style.*** Let's say you and your friend want to go out to dinner together. Your friend craves Kentucky Fried Chicken, but you crave a Big Mac. Neither of you is willing to budge. As a compromise solution, you might go to a local diner where your friend could get a three-piece chicken dinner, and you could order a huge hamburger. In this case, neither of you is getting what you really want, but you are both getting a little of what you want. A compromise can work well in some situations where there is no other resolution, but in this example, both individuals would probably feel cheated.

Collaborating Style

When people work through the problem-solving process to come to the best solution for each of them, they are engaging in a ***collaborating style.*** The collaborating style mirrors a problem-solving model called the standard agenda (Young, Wood, Phillips, & Pedersen, 2007) that we cover in chapter 13. By slightly changing the terminology of that model and applying it to conflict resolution, we get a six-step collaboration process:

1. *Define the problem.* In this step each party needs to identify that there is indeed a problem requiring attention.
2. *Explore the facts.* Each party identifies their needs. Even more importantly, they must listen carefully to learn the needs of the other party. If you cannot get through this step, collaboration cannot take place. Both parties must self-disclose honestly and completely.
3. *Brainstorm for possible solutions.* In this phase people, generate a list of solutions off the top of their heads—as many as possible without stopping to analyze.

— **Professional Perspective** —

A flexible attitude is a great asset for almost every challenge. When starting out as an agent, I would often go into a negotiation with my desired outcome clearly in mind. These encounters would often deteriorate into a battle of wills—with no one satisfied. As my skill improved, I listened carefully to the other person's remarks and always took notes. I tried to reveal as little as possible of my reactions until I had time to reflect and review. Using this approach often led me to discover things that the other person needed that I hadn't yet considered. This would give me the opportunity to present my clients' needs in return. These negotiations resulted in above-average deals for my clients, but with the producers feeling that the transaction had been fair and reasonable.

—Christina DeVries
Senior Account Manager
Spotlight Payroll Inc.

4. *Set criteria to determine the best solution.* Generating a list of what satisfies each person helps to determine the best solution. The first criterion should always be, "Any solution must be acceptable to both of us." There is more in-depth discussion of this concept in chapter 13.

5. *Evaluate and select a solution.* Here each solution is evaluated against the list of criteria to determine which solution might work best.

6. *Finally, test the solution to see whether it will work.* Put the solution into action and see if it is effective.

Collaboration is very effective when each person needs to feel involved in resolving an issue. It does, however, take more time and communication than the other conflict-resolution styles. See the Reality Check box for an example of collaboration.

— **Professional Perspective** —

As a police officer, conflict resolution is a constant challenge. My communication skills, verbal and nonverbal, are very important tools in facing a variety of situations. Responding to a domestic violence call requires instant decision making to restore order and to get both parties listening and talking to each other again. Separation of the arguing parties is the first priority, and then problem-solving discussions begin. This scenario assumes the police arrived during the verbal argument stage.

The two most important skills to possess in resolving conflict are patience and an outsider's eye. Patience gives you the ability to understand what other people are saying and to respond to them in a calm, thoughtful manner. And, the outsider's eye gives you perspective to assess the needs and goals of people in conflict so you can present reasonable options for conflict resolution.

My job is to protect and serve the community. Conflict is part of the interpersonal process I am expected to resolve. I think with patience and an outsider's eye before I speak. Try to develop these critical skills.

—David P. Strus
Law Enforcement Officer
Nutley, New Jersey

Reality ✔

We know many married couples end up fighting about the little things in daily life.

For example, Shawn and Brenda have been married for five years. One of their daily fights occurs over the cap on the toothpaste. Brenda works as an advertising executive and is on a tremendously busy schedule. She leaves the cap off. Shawn is a stay-at-home dad who takes care of the kids and the house. He prefers the cap on. They recognize the toothpaste is a constant source of discussion.

In a true collaboration, they would:

(1) Define the Problem. "Hey honey, we have a problem with this toothpaste cap, can we talk?" "Sure, I agree."

(2) Explore the Facts. What is the issue over which they are having conflict? As they talk about it, Shawn discovers Brenda feels extremely stressed every morning trying to leave the house on time. She feels that every five seconds saved helps her to relax. She hates screwing the cap back onto the tube. Brenda discovers that since Shawn is responsible for cleaning the sinks, he hates having dripping toothpaste stuck on the sink like cement. He is also concerned about the germs associated with having opened toothpaste so close to a flushing toilet. He's heard that germs can travel six feet when a toilet is flushed. He feels the opened toothpaste could be a health issue for the kids. Once they hear each other's concerns, they have a better understanding of why they can't simply accommodate each other on this issue. They don't have to agree with each other (Shawn still thinks it is stupid that Brenda thinks this is a time-consuming effort), but at least the communication helps them understand each other's perspective.

(3) Brainstorm Possible Solutions. Shawn and Brenda brainstorm: (a) They could get separate toothpastes; (b) They could coordinate their schedules so that Brenda brushes her teeth then hands off the toothpaste to Shawn who would replace the cap when he finished brushing his teeth; (c) They could get the pump toothpaste so that no cap existed; (d) They could get a flip-top cap; or (e) They could remodel the bathroom and have separate sinks.

(4) Set Criteria to Determine the Best Solution. Shawn and Brenda establish the following criteria in order of importance:

1. Any solution must be acceptable to both of us.

2. Any solution must minimize the mess and health hazards.

3. Any solution must accommodate Brenda's schedule.

4. Any solution must be affordable.

(5) Evaluate and Select a Solution. Shawn and Brenda evaluate each solution against their criteria. Getting separate toothpaste tubes is acceptable to both; however, it wouldn't minimize the mess and health hazards. This solution does meet criteria 3 and 4. Coordinating when they brush their teeth is such a hassle that it doesn't really meet criterion 1, and it might slow Brenda down in the morning if she has to wait until Shawn is available. But, it does meet criteria 2 and 4. Getting the pump toothpaste meets criteria 1, 2, and 3. They are on a tight budget, however, and the pump toothpaste is very expensive. The flip-top toothpaste doesn't cost a lot and will meet criteria 1 and 3. It still gets a little messy, but not as bad as the regular tube, which is left open. Remodeling the bathroom is so far beyond their budget that it cannot even be considered even though it would meet the other three criteria.

	Separate	Hand off	Pump	Flip top	Remodel
Acceptable	Yes	No	Yes	Yes	Yes
Mess/Hazard	No	Yes	Yes	Yes	Yes
Accommodate	Yes	No	Yes	Yes	Yes
Affordable	Yes	Yes	No	Yes	NO!!!!!!

They determine that the flip-top toothpaste is the best solution at this point. Even though it costs a little more, it meets the other three criteria better than any of their other solutions.

(6) Test the Solution. Finally, they try it to determine if it will work.

Critical Thinking

Think about various couples or friends you know. What are their conflict-resolution styles?

1. Couple #1 _____

2. Couple #2 _____

3. Couple #3 _____

INTERACTING WITH PEOPLE WHO USE DIFFERENT STYLES

Think about the number of people who must try to resolve conflicts with one another. How will they get along? There is no simple answer. Sometimes, two competitors will hate each other because no one can "win" the argument. We know two competitors, however, who get along well because they love to argue. In fact, this couple has had four-hour discussions on the following topic: "If you had to give up cake or ice cream for the rest of your life, which would it be?" Integral to their discussion was whether ice-cream cake is defined as a cake or ice cream because that would influence their decision. To most of us, this kind of discussion is unimaginable. But this couple really enjoys these discussions.

Putting a competitor in a relationship with an avoider may sound promising as a way to solve problems, but in reality it isn't. Think about people you know who use the competitive conflict-resolution style. How do they react when someone walks away from them? Most of them probably demand as loudly as possible, "DON'T YOU WALK AWAY FROM ME!"

Two accommodators would get nowhere—"Where do you want to eat?" "I don't care. Where do you want to go?" "I don't care." These people will starve to death before they resolve their conflict. They are also comical to everyone who overhears their apathetic exchanges. Can you think of other examples?

Ethical Considerations

You told something to your significant other in confidence, asking them to never tell another person. You find out later that they told someone. What conflict-resolution style will you use to resolve this?

_____

_____

_____

_____

_____

Reasons for Styles

It is important for you to think about your own style. Are you happy with it? Do you feel confident in your own conflict-resolution skills or would you like to change? Anyone can learn these styles and use them, if they want to. But you also need to think a little about why you use your current style. Most traditional-age college students have spent the last 20 years developing their styles through interactions with their families and friends. Those of you who are nontraditional students have spent even more time developing your style in many contexts—in business and with families and friends.

If your usual style is to accommodate others, ask yourself whether you are doing this because you honestly don't have an opinion, you are very easygoing, or you were conditioned to use that style because that was how your family approached conflict. Children who grow up with authoritarian, alcoholic, drug-addicted, or verbally abusive parents learn very quickly to be accommodators so they can stay out of harm's way. You can change your style once you understand the reasons for your behavior.

Chances are if you are a competitor, you grew up in a family where arguments and discussions were openly encouraged. You were allowed to speak your mind, and sometimes you were encouraged to do so. If you think back to the discussion about the communication process, it is essential for you to understand the other person's circumstances in interpersonal communication as well as your own. Let's say Nicole and Tiffany are good friends at school. Nicole grew up in an abusive family. Tiffany did not. When Tiffany wants to talk through a disagreement, Nicole just gives in to her. Tiffany perceives Nicole as spineless with no opinion. With Tiffany's background, these characteristics are not desirable. Nicole, on the other hand, is reminded of her domineering mother whenever Tiffany raises her voice and gets excited during a good discussion. Once these friends can talk about their circumstances (for example, their backgrounds), each of them should begin to alter their communication style to keep the relationship going. If they do not, the relationship may gradually fall apart. Even if Nicole and Tiffany are unwilling to change, their discussions illuminate their differences and allow a greater understanding of each other's style.

An effective use of the five styles of conflict resolution will help you to smooth over rifts in interpersonal relationships. Since no style is appropriate in all situations, building your skills is necessary. You should practice using styles in different situations. Having the knowledge and adaptability to use the appropriate style in each interpersonal situation helps you to become an effective communicator.

Even if you learn to use all of these styles effectively, it is important to remember there are some conflicts that can never be resolved completely. Two friends may decide that certain topics are "off-limits" and yet remain friends. Their taboo topics are never raised when they are together, and they get along fine. Or, the friends may decide the disagreements are too important to suppress, and they may end the relationship.

— Professional Perspective —

After learning about the five conflict-resolution styles in college, I thought my conflicts could always be resolved. I never imagined that I would run into a real-life problem that was simply not resolvable.

After graduating college, I finally met the man that I wanted to marry. Everything in our relationship was fine, however, some members of my family didn't think so. They didn't accept the fact that my future husband and I were different races. My dad especially had the idea that interracial marriages were wrong. I did my best to sit down and talk to my family about where I was coming from, but nothing was ever resolved. There were multiple times that I thought I had gotten my point across, just to find out that my dad had another point to strike against what I had said. My father refused to attend the wedding.

My husband and I waited over a year and a half hoping that my dad, and some other family members, would come around, but they never did. On my wedding day I walked myself down the aisle, had the most picture-perfect day of my life, and realized that not all conflicts are able to be resolved. My mother was there for my support and I danced with my grandfather at the reception when traditionally most women dance with their dad. Although I was missing a few members of my family, I didn't focus on that for one second that day. Sometimes you just have to make your decisions and understand that everybody will not always come to an agreement.

My father and I still talk; however, he is still holding to his claim that he doesn't "accept" our marriage. Maybe one day he will change his mind, but until then, we all live our lives through the decisions that we have made and adjust to respect what others believe is right.

Mandy Aikens
NCAA Compliance Coordinator & Head Softball Coach
Nyack College

STAGES OF RELATIONSHIPS

Interpersonal communication becomes more complex as relationships mature. Family, colleagues, close friends, and significant others depend on competent communication to sustain and/or increase the closeness of the relationship. Some people allow the daily routine of life to alter their connection to others. They may concentrate on their careers and assume that relationships can wait until they have more time. Or, they may move and spend more time making new friends than communicating with those left behind. Physical distance is not an excuse to end communication with people who matter to you. Emotional ties with your friends can continue, but there must be a personal willingness on your part to show others they mean something to you. Keep in touch with people who make a difference in your life.

Specific difficulties occur when you communicate via a technology channel rather than face-to-face meetings. These difficulties can be overcome, however, if you are truly committed to a friend. How many people have you let drift away who had been close friends at one time? How many people have allowed you to drift away? These decisions can trouble you in the years ahead, so start to think now about the complex nature of interpersonal communication. Try to make appropriate decisions about relationships that really matter to you. U.S. culture values loyalty and credibility. Whenever you make a decision to call someone a friend, you should be committed to the relationship. Use words wisely as you build relationships. If you don't want to be hurt or disappointed by another person, be sensitive to any behavior on your part that might hurt others.

All of you have been involved in friendships, and some of you have been in romantic relationships. Unfortunately, you may not be aware there are various behavioral stages throughout a relationship. This lack of awareness makes it difficult for you to realize what is going on in a relationship, how to progress, or how to effectively end one. There are many models for ***relationship stages,*** but we think Mark Knapp and Anita Vangelisti (2000) provide the most meaningful one for college students.

- Contact
- Involvement
- Intimacy
- Deterioration
- Repair or Dissolution

Contact

Stage one is the ***contact stage***. This is where you meet someone for the first time. You usually decide right away whether a person meets your criteria for someone you would want to get to know better. Sometimes we miss good potential relationships because our initial perception of another person dissuades us from pursuing a conversation. If we are in a hurry, we might not take the time necessary to learn if we have correctly assessed whether someone would be likely to develop into a friend. Or we could be too judgmental about artifacts, deciding someone isn't wearing the right clothes or driving the right car.

Once you see the other person and decide you'd like to communicate, a conversation ensues. We make a lot of decisions based on an initial conversation. If you haven't learned the conversational skills detailed in the previous chapter, you may have a hard time building relationships.

Choices and Consequences

Describe someone you met, and you immediately decided the two of you weren't on the same wavelength. Why did you make this decision? Were there any consequences?

_____

_____

_____

Involvement

Stage two is called ***involvement.*** In this stage, we continue to get to know another person. We may start to see or call him or her on a regular basis. We start to do some initial self-disclosure about our likes and dislikes, our hobbies, and our backgrounds. Remember our discussion about appropriate self-disclosure during this phase. It is important to move at a reciprocal rate. We may also experiment a little in this stage to see how the other person reacts to certain behaviors. For instance, we may not call when we say we will, or we may show up late to an event or try a public display of affection to see how the other person reacts. As we become closer through the self-disclosure process, we begin to move forward to the next phase.

Choices and Consequences

Describe the type of "testing" you have done in interpersonal relationships. Why did you try out this behavior?

_____

_____

_____

Were there any consequences to this choice?

_____

_____

_____

Intimacy

Stage three is ***intimacy.*** This can be either romantic intimacy or friendship intimacy. People commit to each other in different ways depending on their circumstances. Many people model themselves on the relationships in their family history. Some people commit through verbal exchange, expressing thoughts about what the other person means to them. Others commit by doing things for the other person. This is another area where males and females often misunderstand one another. In gender theory, the research demonstrates that the majority of females generally feel closer when they talk about a relationship, whereas males demonstrate closeness by doing things for others (Wood, 2001, pp. 199–203). For example, Tom and Annika are friends. Tom checks Annika's car on a regular basis to make sure her tires are safe and her oil level is fine to show he cares about her. Annika doesn't really notice his actions. She wants to talk about their feelings for each other. Without understanding the communication rules the other person is using, they may totally misunderstand each other. Their friendship could easily fall apart rather than grow and develop.

In addition to the commitment you make privately to one another in this stage, you may also do it publicly. You might wear rings to signify your devotion to one another. You might get married. You might introduce your partner as a dear friend or significant other. Once again, our background plays a major role in our communication style. Some people float easily into the intimacy stage. These individuals become intimate with a variety of people in a very short time. Other individuals will avoid intimacy at all costs and leave the relationship when the first talk of commitment is mentioned.

Critical Thinking

Describe a relationship where you had misunderstandings about the intimacy stage based on gender differences.

_____

_____

_____

_____

— Professional Perspective —

The intimacy stage of interpersonal relationships varies greatly by culture. Growing up in a small town, I'm accustomed to the philosophy of helping out your "neighbor in need." My first week in Korea, I was overjoyed to find that one of my coworkers was eager to give me a ride to and from work every night. Not only did this save me money every week, but I had the opportunity to get to know one of my Korean coworkers better. However, after a few weeks, our mutual ride to and from work turned into the talk of the office. I had students leaving anonymous notes on my desk asking if I was "interested" in Seen Jyon Jee.

A couple of weeks later, I was approached by another Korean teacher, asking me if they could join us on a date. I was confused, thinking that our ride together to and from work was merely a mutual traffic pattern. Only later did I realize that I was beginning to commit to a serious relationship. I discovered that in Korea, men approach women, and then pursue them, if they feel that the woman has something to offer them.

Unknown to me, I was participating in a mating ritual, without my knowledge. Whereas I thought I was simply accepting a ride, I was actually committing to a long-term relationship!

Raymond Weaver
Residential Care Supervisor, The Sage House
Former Secondary English Teacher
Ilsan, South Korea

Deterioration

Stage four is *deterioration.* It is important to understand that most people try not to enter this stage if they truly care about the other person. Furthermore, it is possible to repair a relationship and move back to the intimacy stage. All relationships will fluctuate through the stages at various times. There are two types of deterioration: intrapersonal dissatisfaction and interpersonal dissatisfaction.

Intrapersonal dissatisfaction occurs whenever we feel dissatisfied with a relationship. This can happen for a variety of reasons. For example, one of your friends tells you their significant other is planning a surprise trip for them. Suddenly, you feel your significant other should do the same thing for you even though surprises have never been a part of your relationship. You begin to feel some dissatisfaction with your partner. You must try to determine if your dissatisfaction is real or imaginary. Sometimes we fall into the "grass is greener" syndrome when we look at other people's relationships or fantasize about others with whom we might have been involved.

Critical Thinking

Describe a time when you felt disappointed in a relationship of your own after hearing about someone else's relationship.

_____

_____

_____

_____

Interpersonal deterioration occurs when personal dissatisfactions affect both parties. Partners make decisions to isolate or distance themselves. Little habits or quirks that we previously overlooked suddenly become annoying. Comparisons with other people, usually reflecting negatively on the partner, become more frequent. Conflict situations become more numerous. It is important to remember that even at this stage of deterioration, if there is commitment from both individuals to save the relationship, it can be repaired.

Repair or Dissolution

Following stage four there are two options: *repair* or *dissolution.* If you choose to move to the repair stage, then you have intrapersonal or interpersonal repair options. For example, Deidre and Arkiem have been married for a year. When Deidre was growing up, part of her family life involved playing board games every Friday night for entertainment. She always felt this activity provided a bond within the family, and she always assumed she would carry this tradition into her own marriage. Arkiem, however, dislikes games and did not enjoy playing them when he was young. Deidre began to feel dissatisfied, missing what she perceives as an opportunity for bonding. If she wanted to repair her own dissatisfaction, she could do it either intrapersonally or interpersonally. Intrapersonally, she could give up the activity completely. She could convince herself that playing board games is not an important activity for their relationship. She could decide that her need for games was too trivial for her relationship with Arkiem to suffer. In this case, the relationship would move back to the intimacy stage. You'll notice the parallel here to the accommodating or consensus style of conflict resolution. The same rules apply. If you are going to do intrapersonal repair and adjust your own expectations, it is imperative that you truly feel that way. Otherwise, your decision may come back to haunt you.

Another option would be for Deidre to try some interpersonal repair. She might explain to Arkiem how important game playing is to her. She could try to get him to understand it isn't just a game—it's an activity that makes her feel very close to the important people in her life. She might ask him if there

---

Critical Thinking

Describe a relationship where you did intrapersonal repair. Was it effective? How do you now feel about the decision you made?

_____

_____

_____

_____

---

was some way he could try to incorporate this activity into their relationship on a semiregular basis. They might negotiate which games are acceptable and how often they would play them. In this case, both people are working to resolve the problem.

If you don't choose to repair the relationship, the only other option is to dissolve it. This is the moment in a relationship where you move away from each other physically and emotionally. You may occupy different spaces. You may dissolve the relationship legally. Dissolution should be a conscious choice. If you truly feel you no longer want to be in a relationship with someone, be honest with yourself first. Then, you need to be honest with the other person so he or she knows there is no possibility of repair. Be sure to use the appropriate channel for this communication. Many people choose the option of becoming antagonistic, hoping the other person will do the dirty work of breaking off the relationship. As an effective communicator, you should always take responsibility for your feelings and act appropriately.

"I" MESSAGES

As we communicate with other people through the stages of relationships, it is too easy to use accusatory statements. Because many people are not comfortable talking about their own needs, they sometimes resort to the use of comments that attack or put down other people. For example, after three years of marriage, Nina tells Perry, "You never tell me you love me." Perry is stunned because he knows he has said those words many times. He feels he needs to defend himself, and quickly says, "I just told you that yesterday!" Now an argument begins. Nina would have been more effective if she had phrased her initial comment to highlight her personal communication needs.

"I" messages are designed to enable communicators to state their personal needs clearly in a nonaccusatory manner. "I" messages can be valuable in any of the stages of relationships, and you can easily see how they could help de-escalate the types of conflict we talked about in the beginning of the chapter. Imagine that one of the students in your classroom comes to class late every day. The professor is obviously annoyed at this behavior. Instead of saying, "What is your problem?" or "You need to get to class on time" (both create negative feelings and can escalate the conflict), an "I" message indicates what the person wants to have happen by explaining why it is important

to them. In this example, the teacher can say, "I need you to arrive on time, because when a student comes in late, it disrupts me and the class." The student should feel less defensive toward this statement. The teacher is simply articulating a need and an explanation for it, and the student can say, "Tough, I'm not doing it," or "Sure, no problem," or "I'm sorry, but the teacher in my last class constantly runs overtime. What can we do about this?"

⇨ **Try It!** ⇦

There are many ways to incorporate "I" messages into your speaking style. Keep in mind the key concept is to identify your feelings or needs without accusing the other person. Go back to the example at the beginning of this section. What are some other ways that Nina might express her feelings as "I" messages? How might Perry respond with "I" messages?

_____

_____

_____

_____

_____

In business it may be helpful to tell your colleagues what your needs are. If you need to have information 24 hours ahead of time to do a good job, then let people know your timetable. If you don't clearly describe your schedule, you could be tempted to yell at someone, "You always wait until the last minute!" Such a remark could immediately ignite a conflict. The statement is accusatory. The only thing you really want your colleagues to do is to give you enough lead time to allow you to do a good job. What would be the most effective means of reaching that goal? Remember to include a reasonable explanation for what you need.

Some of the biggest complaints in the business world are that people feel unappreciated. If you feel this way, you need to speak up. Depending on your work situation, you may be able to say to your boss, "I need to hear I've done a good job occasionally and know the reason why." There are some managers who don't recognize the importance of communicating praise to their employees. If your work is better when you receive appropriate praise, consider using an "I" message. You may also need to say to your colleagues, "The words 'thank you' mean a lot to me, and it would help me to hear that once in a while." These are all valid personal needs. Communicate them in a positive manner.

While "I" messages can definitely de-escalate conflicts, not everyone feels comfortable with them. For some people it is difficult or downright painful to phrase communication this way. However, if you work on eliminating accusatory language and developing this skill, you may find yourself in fewer argumentative situations.

As a word of caution, if you have so many needs that you are constantly bombarding others with them, you will soon find yourself isolated from the interpersonal relationships you were trying to build. No one wants to be around someone they think is needy (unless of course they want to be needed). However, if something is really bothering you in a long-term, committed relationship, it is probably useful to explore the issue with your partner using "I" messages.

Obviously, not everyone can meet all of your needs, even if you use "I" messages. You occasionally have to accept the way other people work and think. If you can't accept them, then you may want to reevaluate the relationship. The purpose of an "I" message is to avoid an escalated conflict as you explore communication options in the varying stages of interpersonal relationships.

Choices and Consequences

Describe the choices you made to end an interpersonal relationship. What were the consequences?

_____

_____

_____

_____

What would you do differently now?

_____

_____

_____

_____

⇨ Try It! ⇦

Convert the following examples to "I" messages:

You always leave your clothes laying around. (to a roommate) _____

_____

You always use my things without asking. (to a roommate) _____

_____

You graded this assignment unfairly. (to a professor) _____

_____

Note: Changing the first sentence to "I feel that you always leave your clothes laying around" is not an "I" message! It's still an accusation.

SUMMARY

Relationships are an essential part of social existence. Developing relationships and maintaining them are personal challenges for every communicator. If you find people who are worth knowing, the effort of maintaining good communication can enrich your life in many ways. It is important to know that relationships normally fluctuate through stages. There are good times and bad times. But, effective communication keeps a relationship healthy and successful. Set your own limits on how much you are willing to adapt to the needs of others, and make your relationship decisions based on that answer. Treat other people the way you want to be treated in a relationship. You face yourself in a mirror every morning; make sure you honestly like what you see.

Key Words

accommodating style
avoiding style
avoiding style
accommodating style
bullying
collaborating style
competing style
compromising style
conflict
contact stage

delaying
deterioration stage
dissolution stage
"I" messages
intimacy stage
involvement stage
relationship stages
repair stage
withdrawing

Crossword 6: Conflict and Relationship Stages

Across

5. The conflict-resolution style that yields the most satisfaction for both parties, but also takes the most amount of time, is called ____.

6. Many people occasionally experience some kind of deterioration in their relationships. In this stage of the relationship, communicators can work intrapersonally or interpersonally to ____ the relationship.

9. A person who walks away from a conflict situation is using the ____ resolution skill.

11. The relationship stage where one or both partners begin to feel dissatisfied with the relationship.

12. Once two people commit to one another as friends or romantic partners, they have entered the ____ stage of relationships.

13. When you meet someone for the first time, you will determine whether you want to see him or her again. This is the ____ stage of relationships.

Down

1. Saying, "I really need to have you help me around the house," rather than, "You are lazy!" is an example of ____.

2. The ending of the relationship is called ____.

3. This is the relationship stage where two people begin to self-disclose more information about likes/dislikes or backgrounds.

4. As we meet someone for the first time, we must decide if this person will become a friend. Any relationship goes through six ____.

7. A person who says, "I don't care. Whatever you want to do is fine with me," is using the ____ conflict-resolution skill.

8. When two people defend their point of view as correct and neither will yield, they are using the ____ conflict-resolution skill.

10. Disagreements between two people result in ____.

13. If two people in a conflict both decide to give up part of what they want to reach a mutual goal, they are using the ____ conflict-resolution style.

Crossword 6: Conflict and Relationship Stages

CHAPTER 7

Initial Speech Preparation

OBJECTIVES

After reading this chapter, you should be able to:

- Identify the first seven steps of the speech design process. There are a total of 11 steps. Steps 8–11 appear in chapters 8 and 9.
- Select an appropriate topic
- Narrow a topic to fit into a time limit
- Find an effective key for a presentation
- Write a specific goal statement
- Write an effective thesis statement
- Explain the concept of audience analysis

Students often dread making an oral presentation. One of the reasons for the nervousness they feel is that they do not know how to construct a presentation. If you aren't confident about how to do something, you become very apprehensive. This chapter will help you learn to prepare for your speech. While these new skills won't make all of your nervousness go away, solid preparation will soothe some of the butterflies.

THE SPEECH DESIGN PROCESS

First, you need to get into the proper frame of mind. One of the authors once heard someone say, "It is important to say 'I have a speech to give,' not 'I have to give a speech.'" What is the difference between these two statements? The first one is a positive statement. It says you have a topic you think is interesting and important, and you want to share it with your audience. The second one implies an obligation, a dreaded task. Which statement helps your attitude and the psychological frame of mind to do your best? The first one, of course!

The next preliminary step is to understand the purpose for giving a speech. If speakers think they are giving speeches just to talk, they are missing the entire point of the speaking opportunity. Think about speakers you've observed who simply talk *at* the audience. They are there for the sole purpose of showing off, spewing knowledge at the audience, or listening to their own voice. An audience soon grows bored with these presentations—and should! To be a good speaker, you must always remember you are there for the audience. The sole purpose of a speech should be to get the audience to understand your topic. It is extremely important to keep the listeners in mind at all times.

Once you are in the right frame of mind and understand you are creating something for your audience, you can begin the ***speech design process.*** While there are a number of ways to approach designing a speech, we find the following steps to be the most valuable.

1. Select a general purpose
2. Select a topic
3. Narrow the topic
4. Find the key organizing feature
5. Write the specific goal statement
6. Write the thesis statement
7. Analyze the audience
8. Research
9. Organize
10. Outline
11. Select delivery style, visual aids, and practice

Why do we call this a speech design process instead of writing a speech? An effective speech is one that is assembled one piece at a time. The speech design process takes you through 11 steps. These steps keep you focused on your final product. The first seven of these steps are discussed in this chapter. You'll notice these steps take you through the planning stages of speech design. You don't actually begin researching until step 8. Steps 8–10 are included in chapter 8 and step 11 is presented in chapter 9.

STEP 1: SELECT A GENERAL PURPOSE

A ***general purpose*** is the overall goal of your speech. There are three main purposes for public speaking: to ***inform***, to ***persuade***, and to ***entertain***. There is some overlap in these purposes because informative and persuasive speeches can also be entertaining. With an entertainment speech, the main purpose is to make people enjoy the subject and your performance.

What is the difference between informing and persuading? An informative speech is a factual speech. You might describe, explain, or give the details about something. For instance, you could inform an audience about three cultural sites in New Orleans. However, if you try to explain why New Orleans is a great place to visit, you have crossed the line into a persuasive speech. You have added opinion to your purpose. "Great" is an opinion word. Someone might argue it's a fact that New Orleans is a great place to visit. The use of "great," however, makes this sentence an opinion statement and the speech becomes persuasive. As another example, someone may try to inform you that Tool is the best band ever. The use of "best" makes the speech persuasive. It is important to stick to the facts in an informative speech. If you begin to evaluate or express a judgment, the speech becomes persuasive.

STEP 2: SELECT A TOPIC

The next part of the design process is to *select a topic.* This is generally the hardest part of the public speaking endeavor. What should you talk about? The first thing to do is begin *brainstorming*: write down as many ideas as you can think of without evaluating them. For example, start with a simple topic— pets. Pets remind you of cats, cats remind you of litter boxes, litter boxes remind you of sand, sand reminds you of the beach, the beach reminds you of the sun, the sun reminds you of tanning, tanning reminds you of burning, and burning reminds you of cancer. You remember your aunt was just diagnosed with breast cancer, and you think that it would be important and interesting to give an informative speech on the three warning signs of breast cancer.

This may seem illogical, but that's how brainstorming works. If you had stopped brainstorming when you hit the word litter box, you would never have arrived at breast cancer. Brainstorming is a nonjudgmental, creative process where thoughts are not necessarily regulated by logic.

⇨ **Try It!** ⇦

Write as much as you can next to each question without evaluating it.

1. What topics do you like to read about? _____

2. What current events interest you? _____

3. Where have you traveled? _____

4. What hobbies do you have? _____

5. What activities do you do in your spare time? _____

6. What is interesting to you about your major? _____

7. What campus or world issues do you care strongly about? _____

Now look back over your list and think about which of these items could be a potential speech topic.

As you try to decide which topics would be acceptable for your audience, there are a number of criteria you should consider.

1. Choose a topic that accomplishes your general purpose (inform, persuade, or entertain). If you are doing an informative speech, you should not pick a topic you feel very strongly about. For example, it is possible to give an informative speech about being CPR certified. However, if you are passionate about this topic and feel everyone must be certified, it will be extremely difficult for you to stay in an informative mode without persuasive comments/words entering your remarks. You may do better to save that topic for a persuasive speech.

2. Choose a topic that fits within the time limit. A speech about the history of Asia will not fit into five minutes. You must begin with a reasonably narrowed topic.

3. Choose a topic that is appropriate for the audience. It should not be too technical or too trivial. It needs to be something that will interest them. Audience analysis is discussed later in the process. But, now is a great time to place your focus on the receiver, not yourself.

4. Choose a topic the audience does not know much about (if the speech is to be informative) or a topic the audience does not agree with or needs to have reinforced (if the speech is to be persuasive).

5. Choose a topic that interests you. If you are not interested in the topic, there is virtually no way to make it interesting for an audience.

Ethical Considerations

Is it ethical to select a topic that you know nothing about? What if you plan to research it?

_____

_____

Step 3: Narrow the Topic

The next step is to **narrow the topic.** Beginning speakers often make the mistake of using a topic that is much too broad, such as the symptoms, causes, and cures of depression. When speakers have this much material to cover, the only thing they can do is to provide a list of facts: here are the six symptoms, these are the eight causes, and here are the three cures for depression. What does the audience remember? Nothing. If you narrow this subject and discuss only three of the symptoms of depression, the audience will remember more information from your speech. You can explain what each symptom is and give examples. Focusing on fewer specifics and presenting them in-depth enhances understanding. Here are a few examples of narrowing a topic:

Ineffective: The band Blink-182
Effective: The drummer from Blink-182 uses three unique types of instruments
Ineffective: Edwardian furniture styles in antique stores
Effective: Edwardian-style furniture has three distinct characteristics

Your word choices are extremely important as you narrow your topic. By simply changing your wording slightly, you alter the message of your speech. For instance, the statement above could just as easily read "Blink-182 has three hit songs." It is in your best interest to spend time at this point in the design process to make sure your word choices are focused properly to accomplish your speaking goal. Let's look at another example.

Let's return to the possibility of a speech on depression. Although the topic could be an interesting one to share with your audience, a speech on "depression" is too broad. What can you cover in an eight- to ten-minute speech that allows you to introduce a new understanding of depression to the audience? You could narrow the focus to three symptoms, three steps in a treatment program, *or* three types of drugs used to treat depression. You may find yourself saying, "But I want to talk about so much more!" Alas, there is a time limit. A brief overview of symptoms, causes, and cures leaves the audience with nothing new. With a focus, the audience learns something about depression, and you've done your job as an informative speaker.

⇨ Try It! ⇦

Take the topic of "music" and narrow it to an appropriate topic for a five-minute speech.

_____

_____

_____

You'll notice our examples all include "three" of something. Three is considered to be a magical number in public speaking. Remember the second step of the perceptual process? We all organize information before we assign meaning to it. Our minds organize information better when there are chunks of three and four items. This is why a phone number is not a seven-digit number. It is a chunk of three and a chunk of four numbers. Your social security number and other pieces of information in our society are broken up the same way.

Imagine a student who attempts to give a speech on 14 places to visit in Boston. By the time she is finished with this "list" speech, the audience does not remember a thing or is sound asleep. If she had broken the speech into chunks of three: three historical places, three universities, three major ethnic groups, three major waterfront attractions, three cultural activities, *or* three major restaurants, the audience would walk away with a clear understanding

---

Choices and Consequences

You really want to talk about the artist Matisse. You are enthralled by his work. You want to cover his life history and artistic theories, the medium he used, and his relationship with Picasso. What are the consequences of talking about all of this for your classroom speech?

_____

_____

_____

What logical choices could you make?

_____

_____

_____

and appreciation of something they didn't know previously. That is good communication. If you are still having trouble narrowing your topic, you may find the next section on finding the key to be useful.

STEP 4: FINDING THE KEY

The next step in the speech design process is to find a key. The **key** is the organizing feature that describes the similarity among your main points. Examples of a key are: steps, aspects, characteristics, parts, areas, or reasons (Brickman & Fuller, 1986, p. 42). If you choose to cover three different types of medications, the key is "types" and for a speech on depression the three main points could be Zoloft, Paxil, and Prozac. If you choose three reasons to treat depression, the key is "reasons," and the main points might be "better intrapersonal communication, better interpersonal communication, and better social communication."

Speakers sometimes choose three unrelated points—or loosely related points—instead of a key. This makes their speech difficult to remember. If a speaker decides to talk about Bon Jovi and says, "I want to cover the band members, the music, and how they became famous," there is no key in this speech other than "stuff" about Bon Jovi. The three points are unrelated and difficult for an audience to follow and remember. If this student narrowed the topic and selected an appropriate key, he could choose among the following speeches:

The three main band members.   (key: band members)
The three best-selling songs.   (key: songs)
The three events that led to their fame.   (key: events)
The three characteristics of their music.   (key: characteristics)
The three characteristics of their instruments. (key: characteristics)

You'll notice how much tighter the speech is once the speaker chooses an appropriate key. You don't want to have an "everything-you-ever-wanted-to-know-about-X" speech.

If you are having trouble finding a key, you may want to try some diagramming. By brainstorming visually on paper, you can see which keys are strong and which are weak. Let's say Alice wants to talk about tomatoes. But she's not sure of a key. She knows she wants to talk about how to plant them, the types, and the uses. If she chooses those three main points, the only key is "stuff." If she continues to diagram, she comes up with the following.

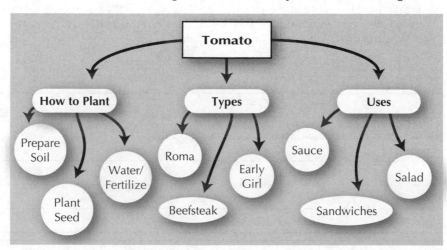

Looking at her diagram, she notices that "how to plant," "types," and "uses" all are strong keys. Each key yields three related main points. If she continued the diagram with "Roma" and listed "origin," "sauce," and "advantages," Roma would not be a strong key because the three main points are unrelated. This means she would have a "stuff" speech about Roma tomatoes. But if she continued the diagram with three advantages of Roma tomatoes, then she would have a strong key because the points all relate to one another. This type of brainstorming can be useful for finding a topic, narrowing a topic, or finding the key and main points.

⇨ **Try It!** ⇦

Use this diagram to brainstorm for three good keys for a speech about "music." Add more boxes where you need them or use a blank sheet of paper so you can put boxes wherever you like.

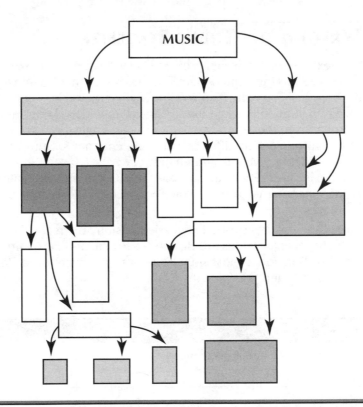

STEP 5: WRITING THE SPECIFIC GOAL STATEMENT

Instructors will call this a purpose statement, a specific purpose statement, or a **specific goal statement.** The specific goal statement is for design purposes only. You write it so you know exactly what you want your audience to remember or learn. This statement places listeners in the central position; you want the audience to come away with an understanding of the topic.

A specific goal statement should be a full sentence. It should be limited to one idea. Generally, the statement will read:

After my speech, I want my audience to understand that
there are three different drugs that are used to combat depression.
there are three steps in planting a tomato.
there are three reasons why Bon Jovi became famous.

Notice that if you use the phrase "to tell the audience about . . ." in your statement, you are no longer receiver oriented. Focus on the receiver.

⇨   **Try It!**   ⇦

Write a specific goal statement for your speech about music.

STEP 6: WRITING THE THESIS STATEMENT

The next step of the design process is to write the ***thesis statement.*** Some instructors call this the central idea. The thesis statement is integral for speech design purposes. You write it so you know what the main points of the speech will be. Keep in mind that the thesis/central idea in oral communication may be dissimilar from those you learn about in an English class. Oral and written forms of communication differ because the channel for information is different—spoken delivery versus written delivery.

The thesis statement is an extension of the specific goal statement. It clarifies what "three items" you are going to discuss. Thesis statements are written as follows:

Three different drugs used to fight depression are Prozac, Zoloft, and Paxil.
Three types of tomatoes are Beefsteak, Roma, and Early Girl.
Three of Bon Jovi's most popular songs are "Livin' on a Prayer," "Raise Your Hands," and "Keeping the Faith."

⇨   **Try It!**   ⇦

Write a thesis statement for your speech about music.

Once you've written your specific goal statement and thesis statement correctly, the rest of the speech falls into place nicely. As you begin to research your topic, collect only information that relates to the goal and thesis statements, and reject any unrelated material. The clear guidelines of the goal and thesis statements help you avoid the mistake of including information that isn't appropriate for the topic. All of the material in a speech must relate to your goal and thesis statement.

STEP 7: AUDIENCE ANALYSIS

Since speaking is a receiver-oriented phenomenon, adapting your speech to the audience is essential. There are numerous choices to make as you design your speech: structure, language, the performance space, and time of day, just to name a few. When you think about your audience in each step of the design process, you create the most effective presentation. The two main considerations in *audience analysis* are the characteristics of the people and the characteristics of the situation.

Characteristics of People

Demographic analysis is an analytical look at the age, sex, socioeconomic status, educational level, and professional experience of the audience. However, if you collect this information, what do you really know about the audience? In the 1950s, speech textbooks stated women preferred speeches on babies, art, and music. Men preferred speeches on business, science, and sports. Is this true today? Well, it may not have been true in the 1950s either. Here's a related example. If you are giving a speech to a group of women in their forties who have PhDs, and all make over $50,000 a year, what do you know about them that would help you to adapt your topic for them? Nothing really. Let's say you want to give a speech on how to crochet a blanket. Is that appropriate for this audience? Many students automatically say no. However, this group may be in high-stress jobs. Crocheting is an excellent stress reducer. The topic could actually work.

Certainly demographics are useful. We shouldn't talk about safe sex to a group of first graders, pro-choice to various religious groups, and retirement planning to high school students. But beyond those obvious conclusions, demographics alone just don't give us the information we need to shape our remarks. Should we give a speech about skydiving to a group of people age 60+? Well, it depends on the group. If we say they are too old, we are stereotyping. We know people who took their first jump from a plane after the age of 60. Should we exclude a speech on checking for breast cancer when we find out there are males in our audience? Perhaps not. Males should also check their chest tissue for cancer since 10 percent of breast cancer cases occur in men. And certainly speeches on breast or testicular cancer can be informative to the opposite sex because they may share the information with loved ones. When you make assumptions about the audience by looking only at demographics, it is easy to stereotype. An inaccurate assumption about the audience could ruin your speech.

So what do you need to know about your audience that would be useful in designing your speech? Some of the following questions could provide useful insight: (1) How familiar is the audience with the topic? (2) How interested is the audience in the topic? (3) Why is the audience there? and (4) How much experience does the audience have with the topic?

We need to know the extent of the audience's knowledge about the topic so we can present new information. If we open a speech with a statement that repeats information the audience already knows, we will bore them and lose their attention immediately. On the flip side, if a speaker is using terminology the audience doesn't understand, communication stops instantly. Think about a teacher who spoke in specialized language without defining terms. What was your impression of the teacher? It's likely you were lost, bored, frustrated, and did poorly on exams in this teacher's class. Make a conscious choice not to put your audience in that same situation.

It is often very difficult to recognize what the "general population" does or doesn't know about a topic. We have listened to students give speeches about their academic majors that were so far beyond the audience's knowledge of the subject that the speeches failed. For example, a student who wanted to give a speech on message encryption finally had to admit the audience did not have the background for the speech (or the interest), and the student changed to a much simpler computer-related topic. While this speaker was really interested in talking about message encryption, he realized that speaking is about the audience, not the communicator.

Is the audience interested in the topic? While the speaker should consider whether the topic will be engaging for the audience, it is also the job of the speaker to make the topic interesting. We always tell our students that we think oral communication is a fascinating topic. Do you think students agree with us? Is this the most riveting class you have at school? If we assumed you are as interested in this material as we are, we would be making a big mistake. We know we need to find ways to make the material interesting and applicable to you because speaking is critical for your future success.

Also, in analyzing your audience, you need to know why the audience is there. A captive audience is much different from one that comes to hear a speaker because they think the topic is interesting, or they've heard that the speaker is really good. But think how many times you've been disappointed when making assumptions about speakers prior to actually hearing them. As a speaker, you may have to work harder to interest a captive audience than an audience who chose to hear your presentation, but in both cases you must make an effort to maintain their interest.

How much experience does the audience have with the topic? This is another piece of information you can use to help design your presentation for the audience. Some speakers would only analyze the demographic of age. For example, in giving a speech to first graders on how to cook breakfast, the demographic of age would suggest you should only cover simple items such as peanut butter toast with raisin smiley faces or pouring a bowl of cereal. However, experience is a better indicator of what is appropriate. In some preschool environments, little children learn the art of pouring milk, washing dishes, and doing creative baking, while in others, children may never have poured a cup of milk. The experience levels of these children could be quite different, and yet, the children are all the same age.

⇨ Try It! ⇦

How would you make your topic of music relevant and interesting for your classroom audience?

Note that some topics are much easier for an audience to relate to than others. A speech about a popular band may not take much effort if your audience analysis reveals students are excited about that particular band. A speech delivered by a music major about the bassoon might be more difficult.

In fact, in one class where a student did a speech about a bassoon one of the classmates had never heard of the instrument—she thought it was an animal!

Characteristics of the Physical Setting

Good speakers should always be familiar with the ***physical setting*** of the speaking situation. The arrangement of a room is important. You need to know where the audience is seated in relation to your speaking area. This allows you to develop a mental picture of how to make eye contact with each section of the audience when you practice giving your speech. If the space has a balcony, you need to look up in addition to scanning the main audience level. A speaker should be aware of the seating arrangement to be prepared for audience interaction. If an audience is seated in rows, members of the audience are less likely to interact with each other during a speech. If the audience is in a circle or in small seating groups, they may talk to each other more easily while you are delivering your speech. These more intimate settings can be challenging for a speaker.

— Professional Perspective —

Anyone over the age of four knows that words can be hurtful or offensive. That's a fact of life—both personally and professionally. Just as you're told to "think before you speak," it's equally important to "think before you write." I write commercials for a living. I help advertisers sell their products to millions of radio listeners. When you write copy for an audience, it's crucial to know who your audience is. You wouldn't market a drug for arthritis pain by using MTV-style slang because your target audience is people over the age of 50. If you're trying to sell a DVD player, you don't have to trash VCRs. There are still plenty of people out there who don't embrace new technology as easily as you do. There are ways to persuade people to try a product and to capture their attention without being "in your face." Be conversational. Don't insult your audience or "talk down" to them. And be honest. Don't promise what you can't deliver. In addition to creating possible legal complications for you and your employer, it will erase all levels of trust that a consumer might have for a particular brand.

—Jana Polsky Deneroff
Writer/Producer, Creative Services
CBS/Westwood One Radio Networks

You need to know what furniture is available for your use. Are you planning to use a lectern? What will you do if there isn't one available? Many instructors ask you to deliver your speech without a lectern to give you practice standing in front of an audience. It is much easier to adapt to using a lectern than it is to stand in front of the audience. Do you need to have any special equipment? Do you need a microphone? Is a microphone necessary in a small space? An experienced speaker should know how to use a microphone and in what circumstances it is necessary. Always check your audio levels prior to speaking.

Is there a space to place your visuals? Work with your visual aids as you prepare your speech, so you are comfortable handling them. For instance, if you have a three-dimensional, round object, putting it on a flat surface won't work. It will undoubtedly roll off, distracting you and the audience. Some people arrive with a PowerPoint aid when there is no computer system available. Whatever visual you use, you must arrange in advance for all of the equipment you will need. We will return to this topic in chapter 9 on visuals.

Another aspect of the physical situation is the time of day. Time of day can affect the mood of your audience. The audience is in a captive situation. Audiences who have just had lunch will be sleepy; those who haven't will be hungry. Audiences who are there early in the day may be tired; those who are at the end of their day may be anxious and ready to leave. Know the potential mood of the audience, so you can adapt your speech accordingly.

You may also want to investigate whether there are fluorescent lights in the room that make a buzzing noise. If there is an alternative light source, you may choose to use it. Some audience members are so annoyed by buzzing lights they will be unable to listen to your message.

Electrical outlets are another item you need to check. If you are using any kind of electrical equipment, you need to know where the outlets are. Remember, electrical outlets may be there, but the outlets may not work. Do you need an extension cord? We've watched many audiences lose interest quickly because the speaker couldn't figure out the technology. Be prepared. It's your speech, and you want to do well.

Regulating the temperature of a space is also important. A colleague reported that in a congregation where he used to be a member, the building was kept so warm that many in the audience were more likely to sleep than listen. The issue of temperature may seem to be trivial, but how hot or cold a room is can contribute to audience attitudes and behaviors. As a speaker you need to be sensitive to the physical comfort of the audience.

Finally, just seeing the layout of a room prior to a presentation can alleviate some of the nervous feelings associated with speaking in public. The more you know about the space, the more you can control the jitters as you prepare to speak.

Summary

The speech design process is methodical and logical. Don't neglect any of the steps in your planning, because it will come back to haunt you on the day you deliver the topic. Once you adjust to the fact you are going to deliver speeches most of your adult life, it becomes easier to remember this process and follow the procedure without having to think about it.

Preparing to speak is like training for a sporting event. The process is repetitive. As your mind adjusts to the routine of learning, the next speech is planned more quickly and more effectively than the one before it. Speaking improves with practice just as your endurance improves with weight training and running. Your mind and your body need to remain healthy throughout your life. Work and patience now can lead to tremendous professional rewards in the years ahead of you.

Key Words

audience analysis	narrow the topic
brainstorming	persuade
demographic analysis	physical setting
entertain	specific goal statement
general purpose	speech design process
inform	thesis statement
key	topic selection

Across

7. What we call the procedure used to create a speech.

11. The overall goal of your speech.

Down

1. During audience analysis, you also need to analyze the _____ so you know about placement of furniture, equipment availability, and electrical outlets.

2. This process can help you to find a topic if you get stuck.

3. The two most important facts to find out about your audience are their _____ and _____.

4. A _____ statement tells you what main points your speech will focus on.

5. Once you have chosen your topic, you need to figure out what you want your audience to remember. A _____ statement will keep you focused on your receiver.

6. This is a word like steps, characteristics, aspects, or parts. It is the similarity among your main points.

8. An analysis of the audience relying on characteristics of people, such as age, race, and sex.

9. It is important to do this so your speech fits in the time limit.

10. The second step of the speech design process. You must choose it with your audience in mind.

CHAPTER 8

Constructing the Speech

OBJECTIVES

After reading this chapter, you should be able to:

- Explain the difference between facts, opinions, statistics, and examples
- Identify five organizational patterns
- Identify the parts of an introduction and conclusion
- Construct an effective outline

Chapter 7 introduced the planning stages of speech design and concluded with a discussion of the importance of knowing about the audience and the physical setting when you prepare your speech. Now we return to the next steps in the speech design process: research, organization, and outlining. Each step helps you focus clearly on the presentation you are about to give. That is the real benefit of following this process. As you design a speech, each step in the process becomes a piece of the greater puzzle—your presentation. You are the only person who will know how much hard work it took to organize the information. A good speech is a personal reward. Yes, the audience will enjoy it, but you are the one who has the greatest satisfaction in a job well done.

STEP 8: RESEARCH

Once you determine the design elements of the speech, it is time to do your ***research***. Some students want to speak from personal experience. Other students believe themselves to be experts on numerous topics. Although you may be your own greatest resource, you still need research to bolster your credibility and to ensure the accuracy of your remarks. You'll notice we have citations in this book. We have over fifty combined years of teaching experience. We consider ourselves to be experts in this field. However, we still use other resources and cite our sources. Even if you have been fly-fishing since

— **Professional Perspective** —

[*Which of the elements of speech design is the most important? Judging from this student's explanation, they all may be necessary and equal in importance. This piece was written in an undergraduate speaking class years ago, but still holds true today and pulls together the concepts from this chapter and the previous chapter.*]

So far in class you have covered some very interesting topics. I suppose the main point of your class has been **know your audience.** I mean, if you don't know your audience, then you could end up trying to tell your audience something they won't understand. I know I've had teachers that forget that you're an undergrad student and not some research scientist or something like that. And they were really boring, too. You have to use some energy when you speak. That's what I'm really trying to say here. **You have to use energy and emotion when you speak.**

Forget that stuff about knowing your audience—that was stupid. So, you've got to show energy and emotion. That way you'll be interesting to listen to. Some people get so caught up in their emotion during a speech that they even lose sight of their purpose when they are speaking. Never do that. Always keep your purpose in mind. That's it. Forget that baloney about using energy and emotion.

You have to **keep your purpose in mind.** I think that is my main point here. Because if you stick to your purpose, then everything will fall together. Sometimes I'll just go on and on and everything I say will be directed toward my purpose. I may jump around a little, but I usually manage to stick to my outline. I can't stand it when people go from one thing to the next without any organization. You have to be organized.

So let me start with that. **Be organized.** I mean, what if your audience is a little uninformed and here you are trying to talk about nuclear physics or something and you're jumping from one thing to the next? They won't understand. Which is why you have to know your audience. I guess that's basically it then—**know your audience.** That's what I'm trying to say here.

Greg Chesterton
Former Undergraduate Student
The Pennsylvania State University

you were 3 years old and your dad is the host of a popular fly-fishing television show, you can still back up your facts with a citation from *Field and Stream* magazine. Try to attribute all of your assertions to documented research. A simple citation makes a powerful impression on an audience.

The Internet

Where do you get research material? Most students go immediately to the Internet. If you know where to look and carefully analyze the quality of the source, the Web is a tremendous resource for thousands of online journal articles. Many libraries have their resources online and newspapers are also available online. Because online versions sometimes differ from hardcopy versions, be sure to specify in your citation which resource you used.

How do you know a credible Internet site from a noncredible one? First, analyze the address. A .edu extension indicates an educational site; a .gov extension is a government site; the .org extension is an organizational site; and .com can be any number of groups or organizations. Many of these sites contain facts, but they also contain opinions. You might assume the information is accurate, but you need to verify the information before you use it in a speech. It would be reasonable to expect the national site for Special Olympics to be accurate. While product sites may have some facts, the information is shaped to persuade you to believe in the product or the company. If we, the authors, created a university Web site, we would have .edu as our extension. What if we included medical advice from Dr. Young and Dr. Travis? No one would regulate this information. It would be up to you to determine that we are not medical doctors even though we use the title "Dr." You must evaluate the credibility of the site and the reliability of the information provided there. Be responsible and check the information against other sources.

There are some other factors to be aware of as well. If there is a tilde (~) in the Web site address, it means a subgroup of the original domain has published the site. The original site may not control the information. You should determine the credibility of the person who authored the information. Evaluate whether the information is fact or opinion. How current is the information? Look for a disclaimer on the Web page and consider its significance.

Some students do not evaluate the credibility of site information. Recently, in an oral communication course taught by one of our colleagues, a speaker tried to convince her audience that hair dyes cause brain damage. When we examined her sources, we found there was indeed an article on the Internet about hair dyes causing brain damage. We read the article in disbelief. It used terms such as "dizzy blondes." When we clicked on the "about this Web page" icon, we found the entire news site was political satire. Not one statement on it was true! The student who used the information on this site in her speech was extremely careless. She presented information that was not true. If she had checked the information against other sources, she would not have made this mistake. Remember, it is your obligation as a speaker to make sure all information is accurate and reliable. Furthermore, as an audience member you must listen critically. You should research any remark that sounds unbelievable or out of line.

⇨   **Try It!**   ⇦

Name three of your favorite products. Now, find their Web sites and report briefly on the accuracy of the information provided there. How much material is informative and how much of it is persuasive? What other information could the site provide?

_____

_____

_____

_____

_____

_____

There are thousands of Web sites. Many are inaccurate. Just because information is on the Internet doesn't mean it's true. What are the credentials of the people running a Web site? What if you discovered that a relationship advice Web site you were frequenting for personal help was run by a first-year student at your own school? How accurate do you think the advice you've been following is now? Would you be embarrassed? Angry? You may not think this is possible, but this is a true story.

Library Research

Traditional research tools include hard copies of books, periodicals, magazines, journals, and newspapers. You should always supplement your Internet research with traditional research. By the time you enter college, you should be quite familiar with locating information in a library. If you cannot, it is time to take advantage of the resources your school offers and become familiar with these research tools. Most universities offer tours of their library facilities. Librarians are always glad to assist people who are looking for information. Ask for their help. A knowledgeable librarian is another great resource for finding information.

Ethical Considerations

As you do your research, it is important to keep accurate records of what information comes from each source. Imagine that you have an important piece of information, but you can't remember where it came from. What would you do?

_____

_____

_____

_____

Interviews

You can also gather information by making a connection with members of your community. Interviews can yield useful information. Examples of local sources include teachers, police officers, politicians, doctors, counselors, clergy, lawyers, business owners/managers, or people involved with nonprofit organizations such as the Lion's Club. Don't forget to consult with the professional people on your campus. Every local contact adds credibility to your remarks. A local resource allows the audience to recognize the value of your discussion because a local connection makes the topic personal for them.

In preparing for an interview, it is important to:

- Schedule the interview well in advance.
- Know the background of the person you are interviewing to make sure he or she has the expertise you need.
- Know what part of the speech you want to reinforce with your source's quotes, so you don't waste his or her time.
- Plan your questions carefully in advance. Do not ask questions you have not prepared.
- Make sure to be on time.
- Check with the person the day before the appointment to make sure his or her schedule hasn't changed.

- Take notes while the person is speaking.

- Check in advance if the person will allow you to record his or her answers. Never ask this question once you are there. Always turn the recorder off if someone says, "This remark is 'off the record.'" Don't question this statement. The remark can never be mentioned to anyone. This is a test of your ability to respect the wishes of the interviewee.

- If the interviewee agrees, a phone interview is another potential source. Do not, however, record a phone conversation without permission.

Choices and Consequences

You read an article about a crime in the local paper. It interests you, and you decide to do a speech on the topic. You research national publications and the Web for statistics and information. You do not interview any local community members. What are the consequences of this choice?

_____

_____

_____

Types of Supporting Material

Supporting material is the information you use to convey a point. Supporting material can include expert opinion, facts, statistics, definitions, and examples that describe, illustrate, or explain. *Expert opinion* can come from a local source or quotations in national publications. Expert opinion helps boost your credibility.

Facts include information known to be true, such as dates, names, titles, and numbers. Facts are often defined as observable phenomena. You can state a number of people who died in a local tragedy. That is a fact. *Statistics* are a descriptive use of numbers—and a good way to make numbers have meaning to a listener. For instance, on a campus of 3,000 people, 1,500 are male. Instead of reporting 1,500 males are on campus, it is more effective to say 50 percent of the population is male. A percentage is easier for the audience to remember. The speaker should, however, be prepared with the actual numbers in case an audience member asks a question. When using statistics, you must:

- cite the source;
- indicate the date the statistic was developed; and
- include the sample size if research was involved.

In addition to using statistics, however, sometimes just using the smallest form of a number will make the best impression on a listener. For instance, if someone falls 20 feet, you can use a smaller number by saying they fell two stories. Twenty feet may be more accurate, but it is also more abstract. The audience will connect better with the simpler form of the number.

As a critical listener, it is essential for you to process the meaning of numbers carefully. Paul Krugman (2003) uses an example of Bill Gates walking into a bar. The minute Gates enters, the average person in the bar becomes a billionaire. You know the status of the people in the bar hasn't changed; however, statistically speaking, the average net worth of each person is over a billion dollars. This story illustrates how easy it is to manipulate numbers to support your conclusion. So, listen critically and analyze messages carefully when numbers are used. As a speaker, you need to be ethical when using statistics to support your points. As another example, a news headline from 2004 announced "Child Antidepressant Use Skyrockets" (DeNoon, 2004). The story claim was that antidepressant use in children was up 100%. That sounds extremely alarming! However, the article goes on to state that "antidepressant use is up 100% to 0.16% of girls and up 62% to 0.23% of boys. Although the article included the actual statistics (each less than a quarter of a percent), it first summarized the increase as 100%—creating the impression that a shocking number of children were now using antidepressants.

Definitions are an explanation of a word, phrase, or concept. Definitions are important if the audience doesn't know the specialized vocabulary used in the speech. Be sure to think about your presentation as if you were an audience member. In order to avoid sounding condescending, you may want to introduce a definition with a phrase such as, "As you may know. . . ." What may be perfectly common language to you may sound foreign to some audience members.

Analogies are comparisons. They show how one thing is similar to another thing. When we learn new information, we often try to compare that information to something that we already know. This is an easier way for us to process the thought. For example, in the South, a student was giving a speech about a ski slope and tried to explain what a newly-groomed slope looked like. Since the other students in the room had no idea, she used an analogy. Rather than saying the snow looks "bumpy" or "had long lines through it," she said, "A groomed ski slope looks like a Ruffles potato chip." Immediately the students could grasp exactly what she was talking about.

Examples are phrases or stories used to describe, illustrate, or explain a concept. They can be real or hypothetical. You should use an example any time you make a statement that may need clarification. If Mary states, "Volunteering can be a rewarding activity," she needs to follow the statement with an example of a time when she volunteered and found it to be rewarding. The example she uses will help clarify the concept of volunteering for her audience.

To pull together relevant and up-to-date supporting material, make sure to listen to the news carefully for two weeks prior to your speech. Read the paper, listen to the radio, read magazines, and use the Internet (with caution). New information about your topic may appear in the news. Include it in your speech. This makes you sound totally up-to-date in your research and much more credible to the audience.

Another way to make your speech unique and memorable is to find information that the audience has never heard. Without new information, the audience doesn't need to listen to the speech. Most audience members are aware of basic information on a variety of topics. It is your job to pique their interest with new information, exciting examples, and interesting descriptions.

Critical Thinking

Look at Olga's use of supporting material in the following speech.

"Low self-esteem is one cause of depression. [Adds definition and attributes source.] According to Young and Travis, authors of *Oral Communication: Skills, Choices, and Consequences*, self-esteem refers to how you feel about yourself. It is tied to self-concept, but it places a value on characteristics. [Add example to illustrate definition.] Young and Travis continue by saying that if a person is 5'1" tall and values height, then the person's self-esteem lowers. You can see how the person could get depressed if he were to dwell on an unchangeable characteristic. [Adds a more in-depth hypothetical illustration.]

"Let's look at Khineesha for example. She is an 18-year-old college student. When she was in high school, she got straight As with very little studying. When she came to college, however, she studied the same amount of time believing classes would be the same. She was horrified to find out she earned a D on her first exam. [Explains how this relates to the topic.]

"What happens to Khineesha's self-esteem at this point? She has some choices. She can rationalize that the test was unfair, which would not lead to a change in self-esteem and/or depression. She can decide she did not prepare well enough for the exam. This probably wouldn't lead to a change in self-esteem either. However, if she decides she is not smart enough for college, then her self-esteem will drop [add statistic for effect]. If she continues to do poorly on exams, she may develop depression and join the 9.5 percent of U.S. adults age 18 and over who have a depressive disorder according to the National Institute of Mental Health."

STEP 9: ORGANIZING

One of the biggest mistakes public speakers make is to use a "slap-it-together" organizational structure. They simply place each point in random order. It is important for a speaker to choose an appropriate organizational pattern for her topic, audience, and speech. We will cover five *organizational patterns* for informative speeches; additional structures are included in chapter 11.

1. Time
2. Space
3. Topical/Classification
4. Comparison
5. Contrast

We will explore one topic and demonstrate how the focus changes within the structure. As you look at the structures, notice the integral relationship between the structure and the key. The key you choose will tell you which structure is most appropriate. Let's examine the topic: The City of Boston.

Time Structure

A *time structure* highlights steps in a process or a sequence of events. If you want to give a time-structure speech, you might do the following three steps in the process of making plans for a trip to Boston: (1) decide how to get there, (2) make reservations, and (3) pack (key: steps). Another time structure could highlight three events in the founding of Boston. You could include (1) Thomas Dudley called the new settlement, Boston, after its English namesake, (2) a 1630 meeting between William Blackstone, John Winthrop, and Isaac Johnson decided the location of the new settlement, and (3) the first homes were erected in 1630 (key: events).

Space Structure

A *space structure* emphasizes parts and how they fit together to form a whole. You could give a speech on the four geographic areas in Boston. These would include (1) North Boston/Cambridge, (2) South Boston, (3) West Boston/Chestnut Hill, and (4) East Boston/Waterfront (key: geographic areas).

Topical/Classification Structure

The *topical/classification structure* is used most frequently. This structure highlights keys such as the three types, aspects, characteristics, parts, or reasons. Here you could talk about three of the universities in Boston: (1) Harvard, (2) MIT, and (3) Boston University (key: universities). You could also discuss three facts about Bunker Hill: (1) June 17, 1775 battle, (2) about 1,500 American militia fought against 5,000 British, and (3) 40 percent of British forces were killed (key: facts).

Comparison Structure

A *comparison structure* demonstrates the similarities between two things. If we compare Harvard's and Boston University's program similarities, we could talk about the fact they both have degrees in (1) English, (2) science, and (3) math (key: similarities). As another example, we could also compare Boston, Massachusetts, and Little Rock, Arkansas, stating they have (1) historical monuments, (2) interesting people, and (3) fine dining (key: similarities).

Contrast Structure

A *contrast structure* highlights the differences between two items. If we contrast three differences between Harvard and Boston University, we could talk about (1) type of school (private/public), (2) founding dates (1636/1839), and (3) location (Cambridge/Boston) (key: differences). If we contrast the climate between Boston and Little Rock, we could discuss (1) temperatures, (2) precipitation, and (3) severe weather incidences (key: differences).

You can see how each of these structures gives you a different focus even with the same basic theme. If you choose a different structure you get a completely different speech. For example, a classification speech about three types of transportation is different from a speech comparing air travel to bus travel. For each example we gave you, you could create many more. Each structure demonstrates how the focus of a speech changes. The diagram on the next page gives you a visual example (Gormley, 1987). See how we visually represented organizing the topic of apples.

Interestingly, if you construct your key appropriately, you will automatically realize which organizational structure is appropriate for your speech. For example, if your key is "steps," then your organizational structure is time. If your key is "differences," then your organizational structure is contrast. If your key is "aspects," then your organizational structure is topical. Each of these structures gives you a different speech focus.

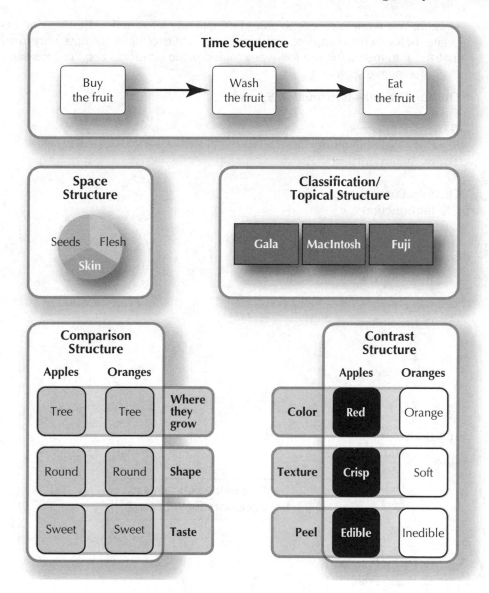

STEP 10: OUTLINING

Many students grimace when they are asked to submit an outline. Their attitude could change if they understand why outlines are useful. Think of an outline as a planning phase. When building a new condominium, the contractor doesn't just start building. First she must decide on the structure. How many stories? What kind of building materials will go in the frame? How will the electrical and plumbing elements be roughed in so they coexist? These are all questions that need to be answered before the building process begins. The contractor can look at the design and figure out if the pieces will work together. If there is a problem, there is time to reorganize before construction begins.

The same is true with your outline. When you organize your main points and subpoints in an outline format, you are building the structure of your speech. You want to reorganize or eliminate any information that isn't appropriate before you complete your project. While outline formats vary from instructor to instructor, the following includes the elements required for effective informative speaking.

Outline Format—Informative Speech
Title:
General Purpose:
Specific Goal Statement:
Thesis Statement:
Key:
Organizational Pattern:
  I. Introduction
      A. Attention-Getting Device
          1.
          2.
      B. Connection
          1.
          2.
      C. Credibility
          1.
          2.
      D. Preview
          1.
          2.
          3.
  II. Body
      A. (Main Point #1)
          1.
              a.
              b.
          2.
              a.
              b.
      B. (Main Point #2)
      C. (Main Point #3)
  III. Conclusion
      A. Review
          1.
          2.
          3.
      B. Connection Restated
          1.
          2.
      C. Concluding Statement
          1.
          2.
Bibliography

> Fill out the subpoints as necessary for your topic.

The purpose of ***outlining*** is to make sure your thoughts are sequential and thoroughly developed. Never show up for a presentation and say, "Well, I thought I'd just answer whatever questions you have." The only message the audience receives from this statement is that you did not bother to prepare and that you're arrogant—and the audience is correct.

A *title* is used to capture attention since it is read by the emcee before you stand up to give your presentation. However, it should not give away your topic, nor should it be the topic. How does the title "A Vitamin a Day" grab you? Boring? You already know what the speech is about and who cares? Be creative with your title. Some good titles we have heard are:

Digging Up Your Dead Relatives (speech about genealogy)
I Melt for No One (speech about M&M's candy)
On the Rocks (mountain climbing)
How to Play with a Bear (trading stocks)
What a Relief (drawing techniques to reduce stress)
Could I Get Some Bacteria with That? (stop eating hotdogs because of Listeria)

— Professional Perspective —

In the student loan business, communication is critical. It is of utmost importance that potential borrowers at the Arkansas Student Loan Authority first understand that the loan is an investment to better their future and it must be repaid. Herein lies the importance of public speaking.

How do I convey such pertinent information? Capture the moment, of course!! The opening introduction can seal the deal or break the bank. Be knowledgeable, humbly secure in your purpose, and speak to the beat of the drummer you hear. Explain why that particular someone should be listening to you at that very real moment in time; reveal up front the need for your important communication. Feel it. Believe it. Conceive it. Communicate it. Achieve it. Simply plan your work then work your plan and above all else envision your success!

—Corey D. Welch
Operations Supervisor
Arkansas Student Loan Authority

Note that our sample outline includes the elements of the speech design process. These are not comments you will make during the speech, but they are part of the outline to keep the speech focused. Be sure to include your general purpose, your specific purpose, your thesis statement, your key, and your organizational pattern. When you start to create an outline, you usually work on the body of the speech prior to writing the introduction. It is illogical to design an introduction for a presentation that is not yet created. Our discussion, however, will follow the order of delivery.

Introduction

The *introduction* of any informative speech has four parts: gaining attention, making a connection, stating credibility, and stating the preview. Although the total speaking time for an introduction is roughly 10 percent of your total speaking time, it is a key element of the presentation.

Gaining Attention

The *attention-getter* is the first statement you make. It should not be, "Hi, my name is . . ." or "My topic today is . . ." or "How are you today?" You need to prepare an effective way to grab the audience's attention that relates to the topic. There are a number of attention-gaining devices:

- *Painting a picture.* When you paint an image with words, you engage the audience. You might begin with, "It was a beautiful misty morning. From the window she could see dense clouds embracing the valley as though someone had poured milk from a stone pitcher. A fine mist fell on her upturned face." Speakers can use any description of a scene that encourages audience members to see a picture in their minds.

- *Quotations.* You can use literary quotations, historical quotations, or contemporary quotations. "Ben Franklin was quoted as saying, 'Many people die at 25 and aren't buried until they are 75'" (Voorhees, 2002). This quote could be a wonderful beginning to a speech about making the most out of every day.

- *Rhetorical questions.* This is a question where you are not expecting any response from the audience. Rhetorical questions are often used to set the tone of the speech. For instance, if you want to talk about a very serious topic like teenage suicide, you might ask the audience, "How many of you have been hurt, upset, and depressed to the point of thinking about taking your own life?" You aren't expecting audience members to raise their hands. While this may set the tone for a serious speech, it could also backfire. Imagine a smart aleck in your audience saying, "ME!" The audience giggles, and the mood evaporates. Sometimes people legitimately don't know whether you are using a rhetorical question. They may innocently raise a hand resulting in an awkward situation for you. You can set up a rhetorical question by saying, "Just think about this for a moment . . ." and then proceed with your question.

- *Actual questions.* You can also ask an actual question to get your audience's attention. You may need to set this up by saying, "Raise your hands if. . . ." But, make certain you know what the response will be. We have seen more than one speech introduction fail with the use of an actual question because the audience's response didn't match the speaker's expectations. It would be extremely rare for an audience member to have never eaten in a fast-food restaurant. So, you could use the question, "Is there anyone here who has never eaten in a fast-food restaurant?" It would be evident that everyone has done this because no hands would go up.

- *Startling or striking statements.* This needs to be done responsibly. Would it get your attention to hear the statement, "Americans are lazy and uncompetitive"? This might be a great attention-getter for a speech that compares the work schedule of Americans and Europeans. Another example is to begin your speech in a foreign language. You could begin a speech on Madrid with a quote in Spanish. Recently, a student who wanted us to reduce our consumption of meat began by saying, "Did you know the average American eats over 20 animals a year?"

- *Personal references.* If you have a unique or strong connection with your topic, a personal reference can be useful as an attention-getter, especially if your audience knows or likes you. One of the best personal references I (KSY) have heard came from a student who had leukemia. She began, "Some people live without arms, and some live without legs, but I live without hair," and she pulled off her wig. No one in the class knew she wore a wig, and she had our immediate and full attention throughout her speech on leukemia.

- *An audio or visual aid.* Sometimes an audio or visual aid can be useful as an attention-getter. One student who was going to give a speech on a Spanish festival played 10 seconds of festival music to gain the audience's attention. If you choose a topic of childhood obesity, you might begin with a visual of the number of obese children in 1980 vs. the number of obese children today.

- *Humor.* We urge caution with the use of humor. You should only use it if it is relevant to the topic. Sometimes, speakers tell a joke and then proceed with a presentation on a totally different topic. This is confusing to the audience. Humor must be appropriate for the topic and the audience. Any joke that is offensive whatsoever (and that really limits your choices) will lose the audience's attention instead of gaining it. Finally, the material must be genuinely funny. If a speaker delivers a joke and is the only one who laughs, that is an extremely awkward beginning. Given the diversity of audiences, we advise using humor with extreme caution.

⇒ **Try It!** ⇐

Write an attention-getting device for your speech on music.

_____

_____

Remember, an attention-getter will not affect everyone the same way. Some of the examples above will appear more effective to you than others. Most importantly, the attention-getter must be related to the topic in some way, must be appropriate for the speaker and the audience, and must actually attract the audience's attention.

Connection Step

Have you ever found yourself listening to a speaker and saying to yourself, "So what? What does this have to do with me?" That speaker forgot the second part of the introduction, which is the **connection step**. In this section of the speech, you must connect with the audience to let them know why the topic is important to them. This is also referred to as relevance. Audiences are egocentric—they care about what relates directly to them. You can make the connection with what the audience cares about in numerous ways. Looking at some of our attention-gaining examples, try to develop some connection steps. Why would an audience of college students need to know about Madrid or leukemia or childhood obesity? The need to know about these topics is a little less obvious than it is about some topics, such as time management, money management, or study skills, where you can immediately see the relationship to the college audience.

For example, you might state in the connection step for a speech on Madrid that learning about other cultures is valuable and that its architectural distinctions could be the subject of a future conversation, perhaps with a potential employer. You might address the connection step in a speech on leukemia by stating the percentage of children who get the disease, or the chance of having a child with it, or the likelihood of knowing someone who has it. You can then state what percentage of the audience is likely to come into contact with someone who has leukemia. Childhood obesity may not seem relevant to a college-age audience. Linking it with younger brothers, sisters, nieces, nephews, friends, or one's future children helps audiences see the problem as a national issue. If you don't make these connections, the audience will tune out because they cannot see how the information applies to them.

⇒   Try It!   ⇐

Write a connection step for your speech on music.

_____

_____

_____

Credibility

Once you have the audience's attention, and you've convinced them the information is important to them, you begin to present information that allows the audience to assess your credibility. *Credibility* is the believability factor of a speaker. A critical consumer of communication should always ask, "Why should I listen to you?" Effective speakers present solid information in the introduction of the speech, encouraging the audience to believe they are credible. Speakers can mention their credentials (certifications, degrees), their research (articles, books), and their personal connection (experience with the topic).

Even though speakers present information concerning their credibility, credibility is actually determined by the listener. A speaker cannot say, "I am credible because. . . ." For instance, as authors of this textbook, we cannot say we are credible. Instead, we might tell you we both have PhDs in speech, we've given numerous public presentations, and we have over 50 years combined college teaching experience in communication. This would state our qualifications and experience. Does that make us credible? Not necessarily. If you saw us in a public performance and we made a grammatically incorrect statement, spoke with vocalized pauses, or spoke with a local dialect although using a local dialect would enhance your credibility with certain audiences, we could lose credibility instantly.

In the credibility statement, it is best to state your research and your experience with the topic. Then, the audience can assess your credibility initially and throughout the speech. Consider the following two examples. Robert is giving a speech on a software program for the home computer. He states he has done research in *Computer Journal* and has been writing software programs for three years. Bernhard is also giving a software speech, and he states he read an article in a weekly popular culture magazine. Who will have better credibility?

It is important to maintain credibility before, during, and after the speech. When Patrick goes to the front of the room, takes numerous deep breaths, and states how nervous he is, he loses credibility immediately. When Gwen does not attribute any of the statements she makes to reliable sources, she loses credibility. The person who stomps over to the trash can to dispose of note cards immediately after presenting the speech loses whatever credibility was established. Similarly, a person who gives a persuasive speech on picking up litter and is later seen tossing a gum wrapper on the ground also loses credibility.

As speech professionals, either of us could create a dynamic speech to convince you to become a vegetarian. We know the right sources, the right persuasive techniques, and the right emotional appeals. However, we are not vegetarians; therefore, it would be unethical for us to try to persuade others to practice something we do not. The same rule applies to informative speaking. You must know your information and have valid facts and research. Misrepresenting your credibility in any way is unethical.

⇨   **Try It!**   ⇦

Write a credibility statement for your speech on music.

_____

_____

_____

Preview

The final step of the introduction is the ***preview***. This is the navigational tool for the speech. When you read something, if you get lost or confused, you can go back and reread the paragraph. But in presentational speaking, the audience has only one chance to follow you. By providing a preview that states your three main points, the audience can mentally join your journey through the topic. Audiences should know what you are going to discuss and the precise order in which it will be discussed.

— Professional Perspective —

A key principle for a student to remember is that your audience gets only *one* time to hear, understand, and comprehend what you are trying to tell them (unlike a newspaper or this book where a reader can go back and review something they don't understand).

—Robert Buchanan
Producer
NBC News/*Dateline*

The preview relates directly to the key you selected. Audiences have short attention spans, are egocentric, and may have difficulty seeing connections among main points. Reinforcing the commonality of your points helps your audience follow your speech. Be sure to use your key in the preview of your speech. However, try to be somewhat subtle in your preview. Speakers should not say, "My three main points are . . .", but they can say, "Today I'd like to cover the three historical aspects [key] of Faneuil Hall Market Place, which are its founding, the designer, and its original name."

⇨   **Try It!**   ⇦

Write a preview statement for your speech on music.

_____

_____

_____

_____

— Professional Perspective —

Lay members of our church are asked to speak during our services. While we have some wonderful speakers, others are less prepared and harder to follow. When I hear speakers at church, school, or in business, I find myself asking three questions:

• What is it you are trying to tell me?

• Why on earth should I care about what you're saying?

• Who the heck are *you* to be telling me this?

If these questions aren't answered within the first couple minutes then I'm less likely to listen.

Speakers who make it easy for me to follow keep my attention. The best way to make it easy for me to follow you is for you to tell me in the beginning what you're going to say and then stick to your points throughout the body of the speech. It is hard for me to know where a speaker is going when the points addressed are different from how they were listed in the introduction. If the points come out of order, or if the speaker adds points not mentioned in an introduction, I get lost easily. My mind wanders a lot without any help from anyone else! Speakers who wander in their presentation make it even worse and all I get out of it is what I was thinking—not what the message was about. Your audience can be distracted easily enough on their own. Why help them be distracted?

One way to help keep my attention and prevent unnecessary distractions is to answer the questions I mentioned earlier. Don't answer them just in the introduction; also look for ways to weave them throughout the entire speech. Doing this reinforces for your audience what you're saying, why they should care, and why they should listen to you.

Speakers who go the extra mile in their preparation and answer these questions gain and keep my attention and interest.

—Raymond R. Ozley
Lecturer
University of Montevallo

Transitions

Transitions are bridging statements that tie the organizational elements of your speech together. You need transitions between the introduction and the body of the speech, between each main point, and between the body and the conclusion. A transition statement is another place where mentioning the key is imperative to helping the audience follow along.

In the speech on Faneuil Hall Market Place, our key was historical aspects. After previewing the topic and order as stated above, you might get from the introduction to the first main point by stating, "The first historical aspect is. . . ." You can get to the second point by a transition like, "Now that you know the founder, I'd like to tell you about the designer," or simply, "The second historical aspect is the designer." These are the standard types of transitions.

You may want to be even more creative with a transition, using something like: "The men and women who settled Massachusetts in 1630 needed to obtain goods and other commercial services for survival. A farmer's market where the community could gather socially and obtain food was developed by. . . ." This transition could be used after the preview and lead into the body of a speech about the founding of Faneuil Hall.

Body

In the body section of the outline, list your main points and all your supporting material. We recommend a keyword outline. A *keyword outline*—is a list of the words and phrases you need to remember to remain organized. For example, if you are going to give a speech to introduce yourself, you don't need to write out, "Hello, my name is Mark Henry. I am from Newark, New Jersey. . . ." Instead, you can just jot down the words "name," "hometown," etc., on a 3 × 5 card. You should use enough keywords and phrases in your outline so you don't forget what you want to talk about. But you should not have so much information that you are reading your speech. Keyword outlines allow you to practice extemporaneous speaking. Extemporaneous speaking simply means conversational speaking. (We will discuss extemporaneous speaking again in chapter 9.) The extemporaneous style is the best delivery style for a public speaker because you aren't reading to the audience—you are talking to them in a relaxed, vocal manner.

You should also include *source citations* in the main point section of the outline. In addition to your credibility statement, you build credibility throughout the speech by using proper citations. A citation includes the name of the research source. For a speech, you need to use either a title or author and the date for the source. "According to a March 2004 issue of *Time* magazine . . ." or "*Field and Stream* stated in an article published in February 2005 that. . . ." You do not need to include a full bibliography. The purpose of citations is to allow the audience to judge whether the information is current and from a legitimate source. The attribution is normally given prior to the quotation in public speaking. This helps the audience to understand that the words are not yours but those of an established source. Once you complete your main points, you are ready for the conclusion of your speech.

Conclusion

There are three parts to an effective **conclusion**: review, restatement of connection, and a concluding statement. The conclusion, like the introduction, is a short segment of your speech. You should not spend more than 5–10 percent of total speaking time on your conclusion.

The **review** is the same as the preview. This is your chance to remind the audience what your three main points were. It helps the audience to solidify the points in their minds. It also lets the audience know you are wrapping up the speech. We recommend you do not say something like, "In conclusion. . . ." This phrase is not necessary for short speeches. It also shows the audience you lack creativity in your transitions. The audience will know you are concluding when you review your main points.

The second step of the conclusion is to **restate the connection**. Remind the audience why this information is important or relevant to them. It reemphasizes why the audience just spent their time listening to you.

A *concluding statement* is the last part of an effective conclusion. Unfortunately, many speakers do not plan their concluding statement, so they end up saying something like "that's it." This does not leave the audience with a favorable impression. A weak concluding statement destroys your credibility.

To maintain credibility, you need to find a unique way of restating the content of the speech to make a connection with the minds or hearts of the listeners. The concluding statement is the opportunity to strike a resonant chord with the audience. You want to leave them with a reaction of awe, joy, thoughtfulness, laughter, fear, sadness, or action. One student gave a speech on rock climbing. She ended it with, "The next time you hear 'on the rocks,' you'll think of another way to have some fun!"

⇨   **Try It!**   ⇦

Write a conclusion for your speech on music.

_____

_____

_____

_____

_____

When you finish your conclusion, check to make sure the thesis, preview, main points, and review contain identical information.

Bibliography

At the end of your outline, you should always include a *bibliography*. We talked about keeping track of your sources in the section on research. There are different bibliographic styles, such as APA, MLA, and others. Your instructor will tell you which style to use. We encourage you to consult published manuals or Internet sources that explain how to use each form of citation. The rules change with every edition of these manuals, so you need to check the most current edition.

Choices and Consequences

You procrastinate working on your speech until the night before it is due. You don't have time to research and organize the material. What are the consequences of this choice?

_____

_____

_____

SUMMARY

Researching, organizing, and outlining information is a logical process. Each of these steps must be followed sequentially. Once you have your information organized, you can focus on an appropriate delivery style. You will be ready for the final step in the speech design process, choosing a delivery style and delivering the speech, the subject of the next chapter. Listen carefully to other speakers. Critique their speaking style by following the speech design process as an active listener. The more you analyze others, the easier it will be for you to improve your speaking style.

Key Words

analogies

bibliography

body

comparison structure

concluding statement

conclusion

connection step

contrast structure

credibility

definitions

examples

expert opinion

facts

gaining attention

introduction

keyword outline

main points

organizational pattern

outlining

preview

research

restate the connection

review

space structure

statistics

supporting material

title

time structure

topical/classification structure

transition

Crossword 8: Constructing the Speech

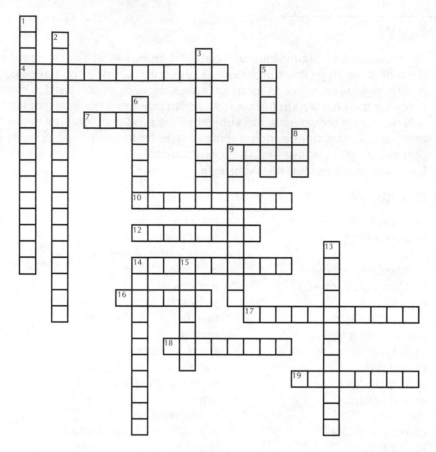

Across

4. Information from someone who has credentials to talk about the subject. This person is a type of supporting material.

7. If Tim talks about the chronology of a space shuttle blast-off, he is using a ____ organizational structure.

9. When Sybil talks about the three parts of the brain and how they work together, she is using a ____ organizational structure.

10. Henry needs to include a ____ of the term superconductor in his speech since so many students would be unfamiliar with the term.

12. This structure is used to show the differences between two objects or concepts.

14. _____ structure is used to show the similarities between two objects or concepts.

16. A summary of your three main points as you approach the conclusion.

17. Bridging statements used to tie information together.

18. An essential activity for you to perform even if you already know most of the information you will be talking about.

19. ____ can be real or hypothetical, but they paint a picture or tell a story.

Down

1. Painting a picture, quotations, and rhetorical questions are ____ devices.

2. The information you use to convey your point.

3. The part of an introduction that lets the audience know why a topic is important to them.

5. This structure is used whenever you want to talk about three characteristics of something.

6. An outline designed with simple words and phrases.

8. The concept that ties your main points together.

9. These are a descriptive use of numbers. They are a type of supporting material.

13. A list of all sources used to research a speech.

14. The believability factor of a speaker.

15. The navigational tool for a speech placed at the end of the introduction.

CHAPTER 9

Presenting the Speech

OBJECTIVES

After reading this chapter, you should be able to:

* List the four styles of delivery
* Understand articulation, pronunciation, and grammar
* Explain the importance of visual aids
* Recognize effective uses of visual aids
* Explain the importance of practice
* Understand communication apprehension

Your speech design planning and organization are about to pay off. The exciting final step of the design process is selecting the delivery style to highlight your detailed speech preparation. You have a mental picture of the entire speech as soon as you complete the outline. Now, it is time to lift the words from the page and articulate them as sincere personal thoughts for the audience. This mental transition from thoughts to verbal communication is occasionally an obstacle for some speakers. Many people know how to write and think on paper, but they don't have the vocal skills and confidence to translate their carefully prepared research into a form that will resonate with listeners. This final step may seem daunting, but it really isn't.

STEP 11: DELIVERY STYLE, VISUAL AIDS, AND PRACTICING

We want to remind you that this discussion sets general guidelines for delivery, presentational style, and the use of visual aids. Each professional discipline presents its own variations of these guidelines. Work closely with your academic mentors to find the presentational norms for your discipline. You must look and sound like a professional in your field when you speak to other professionals. Your credibility is on the line. Talk to your mentor.

Delivery

There are four *delivery styles:*

1. Impromptu: speaking with no preparation at all
2. Manuscript: reading from a written paper
3. Memorized: written out and committed to memory
4. Extemporaneous: using key words and phrases to promote a conversational style

Everyone must do ***impromptu*** speaking at one time or another. If a teacher calls on you in class, you do impromptu speaking. You also do impromptu speaking in an employment interview when you answer an unexpected question. However, this style is not appropriate for a formal speaking situation. Very few people are organized enough to pull off an effective impromptu speech.

Some professionals use ***manuscript*** speaking. The president of the United States, for example, must speak from a manuscript during national addresses to ensure every word that has been planned is delivered correctly. The speech is read from a teleprompter to make the president look more natural to the television audience. The audience may think the president is talking directly to them during an address, but in fact he is reading from a manuscript.

There are very few speech occasions where a manuscript speech is appropriate. Audiences get annoyed when speakers read to them. How do you feel on the first day of class when an instructor reads the entire syllabus to you? Most students feel offended. Students can read the syllabus themselves—and in more comfortable places than sitting in class. Manuscript delivery can remind you of your first-grade librarian who came into class and read a book. This is a condescending delivery style for an adult audience.

Memorized speeches also have problems. While memorized speeches sometimes sound very polished, they more frequently sound scripted, and the speaker usually lacks natural vocal variety. An actor works from memorized scripts because he or she is performing someone else's words, but a good speaker works from notes. Speakers need a relaxed conversational style. When we memorize, we concentrate on the fact that "this word" follows that "word," which goes after "this word." We do not think about the total concept and shape of the speech. Therefore, if we forget a word, it is much more difficult to recover mentally during the speech. We have seen numerous students who memorized speeches despite our warnings about potential problems. In almost all cases, either the speeches sounded unnatural, or the student forgot a word, panicked, and could not complete the assignment.

Extemporaneous speaking is conversational speaking. This is the preferred delivery style for most speaking situations. With extemporaneous speaking, speakers note key words and phrases on cards to help them remember the concepts they want to cover. They talk about those concepts, glancing at the written notes if they need to remind themselves about an example. If you want to call a company to lodge a complaint about a defective product, you might jot down some of the key points you want to remember. You don't write it out word for word or memorize it, but you refer to your list and make sure you cover all of the points on it. This delivery style helps listeners feel as though they are important because we are talking to them and not at them. The style also allows for adaptation on the part of the speaker. If you see that the audience doesn't understand a concept, you can add another example. If you see they are bored, you might add some humor or pick up the pace. One way to speak consistently in a conversational style is to imagine you are sitting at a kitchen table sipping a hot drink and communicating with a friend. An audience becomes your friend. This mental game keeps your voice warm and the delivery spontaneous.

Critical Thinking

Think about the last presentation you experienced. What style of delivery did the speaker use? How effective was it?

_____

_____

_____

_____

Articulation, Pronunciation, and Grammar

Articulation is the proper formation and release of the sounds that make up a spoken language. Using "proper" speech should be the goal of all speakers. Many local dialects don't use properly articulated English sounds, or they modify those sounds. For example, many people drop word endings. Going fishing becomes "goin' fishin'." In other regional dialects, people drop the "t," "k," and "p" sounds. So, gift becomes "gif." A word like "fact" should actually be articulated as "fa-k-t," but some people drop the "t" sound and simply say "fak."

If you have adopted the dialect of the region where you live, and you move to another location or into the business world, you may find that people will perceive you to be uneducated if you use this speech. For instance, some people from the town of Scranton, Pennsylvania, drop the "t" and say they are from "Scran-in." While that pronunciation is usually acceptable in their local area, people from that area who travel elsewhere lose credibility when they announce where they are from. Most people would wonder why they can't pronounce the name of their own hometown correctly. It is your job as a speaker to monitor your sounds and compensate for any errors in your local dialect.

You may think a discussion of articulation is mundane; however, proper articulation makes your message clearer to a diverse audience. People who articulate well stand out. In fact, proper articulation is so coveted that in South Korea some parents choose tongue surgery for their young children to enable them to articulate English sounds more clearly ("A Short Cut," n.d.).

Proper articulation relates to proper *pronunciation* as well. Pronunciation is the accepted sound of a word according to the dictionary. A word like "get" is often pronounced "git." People say "you are taking me for granite" instead of "for granted." "Ask" in urban speech is pronounced "aks" or "axe." There is also an interesting pronunciation rule for the word "the." There is a difference between "the" pronounced "thuh" and "the" pronounced "thee." You should use "thuh" before all words that begin with a consonant such as, "thuh choir."

But, you use "thee" before any words that begin with a vowel, such as "thee orchestra." This subtle difference can make you stand out to an audience.

Every time you read something out loud, focus on the rules of pronunciation and proper articulation. Remember your audience. The audience determines if you are credible as they listen to you. Your voice holds clues to your educational level and training. Do you want to be perceived as a professional? Then you'll need to practice pronouncing words correctly.

⇨   **Try It!**   ⇦

Read the following out loud.

The girl and the iguana walked through the forest. They were going exploring. The girl and the iguana saw the orange and the apple hanging in the tree. The sight of the enormous apple whet their appetite.

Did you articulate the "t" and "ing" endings? Did you catch all the "thuhs" and "thees"?

— Professional Perspective —

I was in the business 20 years before making it to the network level in New York. On day one, I was greeted by a coanchor who, after learning that I was from the South, replied, "Oh, diversity is good." But in fact I had gotten rid of my accent many years earlier.

When I started in commercial radio, I was 20 years old and going to college in Mississippi. My friends and family immediately noticed a difference in the way I spoke. Even though I was still surrounded by southern accents, my own accent hurt my ears when I would listen to daily "air checks." Eventually, I learned to correct the patterns that bothered me.

I also got some good advice in a college speaking class, including learning to pronounce the "e" in words like "get." I'd never noticed I pronounced it like an "i."

My editors still point out my accent on occasion. Especially the varying emphasis on words like umbrella, from "UM-brel-la" (southern) to "Um-BREL-la." I now say "in-SURE-ance," rather than "IN-sur-ance."

While I don't think a dialect necessarily hurts a person's radio career these days, I don't think one can work in radio worldwide without using universally recognized pronunciation. Throughout a long career, I've picked up dialects, vocabulary, and mannerisms from nearly every place I've traveled.

—Cami McCormick
Network Correspondent
CBS Network Radio News

Grammar refers to "a set of actual or presumed prescriptive notions about correct use of a language" (*The Oxford American College Dictionary*, 2002). Usually people think about grammar errors when they write, but grammar errors can also lead to credibility difficulties in presentational speaking. Review your speech patterns for the following potential errors:

- One of the biggest errors in spoken speech is the adverbial form. People drop the "ly" ending from adverbs. For example, many people say, "Please drive safe" instead of "safely," or they use an adjective instead of an adverb, saying, "He draws good" instead of "He draws well."

- Some people also misuse pronouns. Someone might say, "It is a conversation between my brother and I." Because the pronoun in this case is the object of the preposition, the objective form is correct: "between my brother and me."

- Verb forms may also be skewed, particularly in broadcast sports speech. "That team was beat last night" rather than "beaten." Listen carefully to electronic media sports personalities and announcers at a local game. What do you hear? Do you mimic their mistakes?

Choices and Consequences

You recognize you speak in a local dialect. What are your choices?

_____

_____

What are the consequences?

_____

_____

Following are other delivery qualities that will affect your speech:

- *Rate* refers to the speed at which you deliver a sequence of words. You do not want to speak too quickly or too slowly, because either one makes it difficult for the audience to pay attention.

- *Projection* is important so that everyone in the room can hear you comfortably. Audiences lose interest immediately if they cannot hear you. But remember, a booming delivery style can also be uncomfortable for an audience who may feel as though a speaker is yelling at them. Moderation is the key.

- *Vocalized pauses* are a repeated audible habit used by some speakers. They occur when you fill a natural pause with an "um," "uh," "like," or "you know" rather than a preferable, thoughtful silence. While one "um" in a speech is not distracting, if you do this on a regular basis, your audience will focus more on your vocalized pauses than on the content of your message.

- *Inflection* is important in vocal delivery. Inflection refers to your vocal pitch going higher or lower. Most people can do this naturally to some extent. The key to natural inflection is a relaxed, conversational style. Inflection eliminates a monotone performance.

Try to work to improve your voice, but don't get frustrated. It takes time to retrain old habits. Work on introducing new motor skills into your speech or alter the way you've learned to say certain words a little at a time.

— **Professional Perspective** —

To make a report easily understood, television writing needs to reflect the same language journalists hear "on the street" and from families, friends, and peers. There is a symbiotic relationship. "Audiences" influence our writing, and broadcasters influence the language of their audiences. But remember, don't let the rule of keeping it "simple" be an excuse to lose style and substance in your writing.

—Robert Buchanan
Producer
NBC News/*Dateline*

Visuals

Visuals are an important part of good presentational speaking. ***Visual aids*** (and to some degree, audio aids), including slides, videotapes, and overheads, can involve your audience in the speech and make your points easier to comprehend (Silk, 1994). When choosing a visual, think about which concepts in your speech may be hard for the audience to understand without seeing something. Visuals are used to clarify your message. There are many kinds of visuals you can use. A good general rule is to make sure your visuals do not take any more than 5 percent of your total speaking time.

Traditional Visuals

Poster boards or drawings on easels or chalkboards are quickly becoming outdated, perhaps because they appear far less professional than images prepared using computer technology. Another popular traditional visual is a transparency. You can put words, definitions, statistics, graphs, or pictures on transparencies. Learn how to do a computer-generated image so that your audience is not distracted by handwriting or hand-drawn images. The days of using transparencies are coming to an end, however.

Visuals also include objects. We have seen items such as sculptures, pictures from magazines (make sure the page is marked so you don't fumble through the magazine looking for it), horse gear, a newspaper, a hundred-dollar bill, clothing, craft items, or sports equipment. An object can bring a portion of your speech to life for an audience. But the object must fit the topic you are presenting and not be distracting.

You can also use video clips, cassettes, or CDs. These need to be extremely short. Generally, for a short speech, you need to limit video clips and audio clips to about 10–20 seconds depending on the length of the speech. Make sure the segment you need is cued to the exact spot. If you aren't cued, communication stops, and so does your credibility.

⇨   **Try It!**   ⇦

What traditional visual aid could you use for your speech on music?

Visual Technology

Visual technology refers to electronic equipment used to enhance a presentation, such as a PowerPoint presentation, laser pointers, and DVD players. Many speakers forget the purpose of a visual aid when they begin to use technology. Speakers may have a great time with the technology, but they generally forget to focus on the audience.

Most of you have listened to a presentation where the speaker dims the lights and puts a variety of words on a screen using PowerPoint software. PowerPoint is nothing more than an up-to-date filmstrip presentation or a cheap version of an arcade game if it is used as the entire focus of the speech. Some speakers use technology to entertain you. We have found that people who rely exclusively on PowerPoint usually are terrified of public speaking; they use PowerPoint to hide from the gaze of their audience. This is an abuse of technology, your time, and the speaking situation. When people use technology this way, they are eliminating the interactive and interpersonal dimensions of public speaking. Words on a screen are not a speech. Would you rather have someone hiding and showing you printed material on the screen that you could read at home, or do you want someone to talk directly to you in an exchange of information?

Of course, PowerPoint has its place in public speaking. When used correctly by selecting information that enhances the audience's understanding of a point, it can look professional and be extremely effective. But, the use of PowerPoint must follow the same time guideline as any other visual aid in public speaking.

To use PowerPoint effectively, make sure you check the color design combinations (yellow and some other light colors don't show up) and the font size (a 20–24-point font is necessary). You should have no more than five lines, no more than five words per line, and only one concept per slide (Weaver, 1999). The audience must be able to absorb the visual information easily without eyestrain. Some members of the audience may have color-deficient vision. The majority of these individuals see color images but with varying degrees of color intensity. You can be visually inclusive using color-designed aids such as PowerPoint if your presentation contains a great deal of color-intensity contrast (i.e., dark lettering on a light background or vise versa).

Rules for Visuals.   Simply having a visual to help the audience understand a concept does not ensure their understanding. The use of visual aids can enhance or detract from a presentation depending on how you use them. There are a number of things you can do to make sure that your use of a visual aid goes smoothly.

1. Make sure to practice with your visual. Visuals take time to set up and take down. You must also know how to run the equipment. You should never say, "Well, this worked before" or "How do you run the overhead?" This will instantly destroy your credibility.

2. Make sure the visuals are large enough to be seen and read by everyone. Most of you have heard a speaker say, "I know you can't see this, but. . . ." What is the point? The statement makes the speaker sound ridiculous. If an object can't be seen, then either figure out a way for the audience to see it or eliminate it. Sometimes a speaker can walk through the audience with a smaller object. Pictures can be scanned and the size increased so that the entire audience can view it.

3. Passing visuals through an audience is risky. It is distracting. Before the visual even gets past five people you will be on your next point. And, it never fails that the object will not make it through the entire audience before the end of your speech. If the purpose of the visual is to enhance understanding, then passing it is extremely ineffective. However, if you need your audience to refer to a paper during your presentation, you can explore the option of passing it out facedown ahead of time so they have it to look at when you tell them to do so. Or if it is something that they should take with them after the presentation, you can mention that you have a handout for them to pick up before they leave.

4. Only show the visual while you are talking about it. A visual should be shown in a place where all audience members can see it. You should reveal it at the point where it will complement your information, and then you should remove it. When you are displaying it, make sure you continue talking to your audience and not to the visual aid. Your back should never face the audience.

5. Do not bring anything illegal or harmful as a visual. Animals are generally not permitted in public buildings. Weapons of any kind (or even plastic guns, etc.) are inappropriate. Any kind of implement that could be used as a weapon is inappropriate as a visual (fishing knives, spears, etc.). Since alcohol is banned from college campuses, it should not be used as a visual.

6. Make sure to cite the visual source. If you got a visual from a Web site or a book, that citation should be at the bottom of your overhead or PowerPoint slide. If you borrowed the object from somewhere, you should be sure to credit your source.

7. Most importantly, have a back-up plan. Overhead projector bulbs blow out, transparencies smear, slides burn, tapes jam, and equipment fails. You need to be prepared for any of these situations. In some speaking situations, you may need to finish the speech without the planned visual aid. Don't panic. You have studied your topic thoroughly; use that knowledge to replace the visual information with a verbal description. Remain relaxed and in control.

Critical Thinking

Describe a time when you saw a speaker use a visual ineffectively. What was your reaction?

_____

_____

_____

Practice

It is essential that you *practice* out loud with a stopwatch. We do not recommend practicing in front of a mirror or with a tape recorder. The most important aspect of practice is to hear yourself say the words. One of our favorite student quotes is, "I didn't think I needed to practice. I sounded so eloquent in my mind." When you go through a speech in your mind, there are no vocalized pauses, no problems with transitions, no mispronounced words, no throat noises, and no delivery errors. But, there is no yellow brick road to a speaker's podium. You must practice out loud.

The first time you practice delivering your speech, it will probably sound pretty awful and will exceed the time limit. This is normal. The second time you say it out loud, it will get better and closer to the allotted time. By the fourth effort, you will start to sound like a polished speaker. You will change your wording during every practice session and even during the formal presentation using the extemporaneous style. Word changes are normal. Never panic. Concentrate. You will feel more comfortable with each practice session.

If your speech is consistently long on time, cut the material. Don't make the mistake of thinking you can shorten a 16-minute speech to fit a 6-minute time limit by speaking faster. If you are over the time limit, you need to hone the material to the essential points.

Ethical Considerations

Is it ethical to waste an audience's time if you have not properly practiced your speech?

Giving the Presentation

You should plan carefully for the day of your presentation. It is good to make a list of everything you need and get it ready and organized the night before a speech. Racing around before a speech or finding you have forgotten a crucial visual or required outline will only unnerve you. Try not to do this to yourself.

Know your own body chemistry. If you have an early presentation, but it takes you a couple of hours to wake up in the morning, you need to get up earlier the day of your speech to give yourself time to be mentally and vocally alert. Speakers should not take coffee with them to the platform. It's rude and distracting for an audience. Remember, your vocal chords take time to warm up. Your vocal chords are the key to good vocal technique. Articulation and pronunciation errors occur when your mind and vocal chords aren't working together.

If you are a little nervous before a speech, exercise can help you calm down. If that is not possible, you can try taking some deep, relaxing breaths. The best way to make sure you are breathing correctly is to make sure your chest remains stationary, but your abdomen moves when you breathe. Abdominal breathing increases the support for your voice and helps you to relax. Every speaker uses a different relaxation exercise to prepare mentally and physically for a speech. You can use an exercise that has worked for you in previous situations or you can search the Internet for hundreds of examples of relaxation exercises.

Communication Apprehension.   Throughout the last three chapters, we have given you advice about how to reduce ***communication apprehension.*** Fear of public speaking is perfectly normal. Most people, including ourselves,

---

— Professional Perspective —

First of all, when the occasion arises for you to speak, it is very important that you stick to the point and do not ramble; otherwise you will lose the audience, and they will stop listening to what you have to say. Second, it is equally important for you to be aware of your nonverbal behaviors. Maintain eye contact with the audience; this behavior reflects your interest in what you are doing. This is very important in U.S. culture. For example, when I first came to this country from India and started interviewing for jobs, I would not look the interviewer in the eye, thereby my credibility and honesty were questioned. I was unsuccessful in getting a job, and thankfully so, as that's what led me to study differences in communication styles between various cultures.

Pehali baat yeh hai ki jab bhaashan dene ka samay aye, to ye dhyaan me rakhana bahut jaroori hain ki aap mudde pe baat karein, nahin to sunnewale sunna band karenge. Doosari baat yeh hai ke, aapko apne haav bhaav ka bhi dhyaan rakhna chahiye, jaise ki sunnewalon ke saath aankh se aankh mila kar baat karna, is se yeh pata chalta hai ki aap is mudde per dilchaspi rakhtein hein. Is desh mein (U.S.) is baat ka bahut dhyaan diya jataa hai. Udaharan ke liye, hum jab pehali baar is desh main aaye aur naukari dhoondh rahe the, to naukri dhoondte samay, parichay ke samay main hum sawal poochne wale ke taraf aakh uthakar bhi nahi dekhte the. Iske vajah se, mujhe naukari nahin mili, lekin acchi baat yeh hui ki isi kaaran, hum is kshetra mein dilchaspi lene lage ki alag sanskriti ke logon ka bol-chaal aur haav-bhaav ka tareeka kaise fark hota hai.

—Dr. Aparna G. Hebbani, Lecturer
School of Journalism and Communication, University of Queensland,
Brisbane, Australia

---

get butterflies in the stomach or slight nausea or heart palpitations. Through careful planning and preparation, most of these symptoms will subside once you begin your presentation.

However, there is a small percentage of the population that suffers from extreme communication apprehension. These people may be so fearful of communication events that they cannot raise their hand in a class, call for a pizza, or engage in interpersonal communication. For many people, their fear may be localized to one of these situations. For others, they may experience extreme apprehension in all of them.

If you are not extremely apprehensive, then you can skip the rest of this section. But if you feel that you fit the description, there may be some tips to help you. I (KSY) taught a special section of oral communication at The Pennsylvania State University that was designed for students who had severe apprehension. The program was developed by Gerald M. Phillips, who published prolifically in the communication field for over 40 years. During the 1980s, Penn State had to offer three sections of the course every semester because of the number of students affected by severe communication apprehension.

The program encouraged students by having them first set a goal and then brainstorm scripts of communication encounters. For example, if Judy is afraid to call and order a pizza, she would set a goal ("I will call Joey's Pizzeria and order a pizza") and a date for when the event would take place. She would write what the person on the other end of the phone would most likely ask her and what her answer would be:

Judy: Hi, I'd like to order a pizza.
Pizza place: What size pizza would you like?

Judy:	Medium.
Pizza place:	Toppings?
Judy:	Yes, pepperoni please.
Pizza place:	Crust?
Judy:	Thin.
Pizza place:	Pick up or delivery?
Judy:	Pick up.
Pizza place:	Name?
Judy:	Judy.
Pizza place:	It'll be ready in 20 minutes.
Judy:	Thank you.

Once the script is brainstormed, Judy would practice reading the script out loud over the next couple of days, employing the help of friends if possible. Phillips believed that communication apprehension would be reduced by practicing the words that would be used over and over again. For someone who is not severely affected by communication apprehension, this may seem to be a simple and tedious process, but it is effective and necessary for those who suffer from this debilitating condition. There are other theories for reducing communication apprehension, including meditation or systematic desensitization. Finding the method that feels comfortable and repeated practice will make interactions seem possible rather than forbidding.

SUMMARY

Many people fear public speaking initially, but they learn that it can be mastered. You need to follow the speech design instructions given to you by a teacher or an executive, give yourself adequate time to prepare, know your information well, and practice out loud to sound natural for the audience. Your butterflies may never go away completely, but you can gradually learn to appear calm and to be confident in public speaking situations. Like anything else in life, it takes time to improve. Make sure you take the time to practice.

Key Words

articulation	practice
communication apprehension	projection
delivery style	pronunciation
extemporaneous style	rate
grammar	traditional visuals
impromptu style	visual aids
inflection	visual technology
manuscript style	vocalized pauses
memorization style	

Crossword 9: Presenting the Speech

Across

4. There are four _____ styles a communicator can use in public speaking.

7. A repeated audible habit used by some speakers when silence would be a better choice.

8. Speakers use _____ to make sure they can be heard easily.

11. A speech delivered without notes and committed to memory.

Down

1. The proper formation and execution of the sounds of a language.

2. The accepted sound of a word as indicated in the dictionary.

3. The accepted rules for the correct structure of a language.

5. A conversational speaking style prompted by notes with a few words or phrases.

6. A speech that is read to an audience.

9. The speed at which a communicator delivers a sequence of words.

10. A speech given without preparation.

CHAPTER 10

Understanding the Principles of Persuasion

OBJECTIVES

After reading this chapter, you should be able to:

- Define persuasion
- Explain the idea of perceived choice
- Explain the difference between informing and persuading
- Develop a reasonable goal
- List the three types of persuasive speeches
- Write purpose statements for three types of persuasive speeches
- Explain the importance of audience analysis for persuasion

Adam and Megan are newly married. They have lots of gadgets in their house: food dehydrators, a vacuum-sealing machine for food, and clothes storage bags. They own hundreds of pieces of jewelry and every tool in the world, all ordered from television shopping networks. They have name-brand cereal, sneakers, clothing, dishware, perfumes/colognes, and furniture. In addition, they rarely take overtime opportunities at their jobs because their friends constantly persuade them to go out partying. They are living the good life.

Adam and Megan are also in serious credit card debt. They can't resist persuasive messages. They pull out their credit cards rather than analyze the messages that influence their spending behavior. Although their lifestyle makes them look very successful, Adam and Megan are living on dream power rather than actual earning power. Persuasive messages in our culture are powerful. It's important to think critically about these messages before you take action. You are responsible for your own behavior.

Throughout this chapter we will discuss persuasion in the context of formal public speaking as well as in interpersonal and cultural situations.

DEFINING PERSUASION

Persuasion is a process that involves a communicator who tries to influence the attitudes, beliefs, values, or actions of another communicator through message design and delivery, both formally and informally. Basically, a persuader tries to change or influence someone's mind or personal actions with well-designed language and nonverbal stimuli. Persuasion happens in both public speaking (parts of school lectures, religious lectures, press conferences, electronic news, and corporate blogs and Web sites) and interpersonal communication (family gatherings, peers, and chat room) situations. For public speaking, each element of a persuasive message is crafted to influence others. If a message is designed well, it supports the audience's basic beliefs, values, and personal needs. Receivers often accept persuasive messages without thinking critically. On the interpersonal front, we use persuasion on a daily basis to influence the people around us to believe as we do, to do something with us, or possibly go somewhere. A simple comment like, "Let's go to the movies" is persuasive because you are targeting another individual and trying to get them to perform an action.

⇨ **Try It!** ⇦

List five examples of interpersonal persuasion you've seen or experienced in the past 24 hours.

_____

_____

_____

_____

_____

If you take a semester-long course in persuasion, you'll find there are many variations of the definition. For our purposes, we limit the discussion of persuasion to messages designed with persuasive intent. In other words, when someone is persuaded by information, we don't label that as a persuasive message. You can be persuaded by facts. Think back to your round of informative speeches. You may have heard a speech on rock climbing. If the speaker followed content guidelines properly, it was strictly an informative speech. However, by hearing the information about rock climbing, you may have been influenced to try this activity during your next vacation. The speaker gave an informative rather than a persuasive speech, yet you were persuaded by the information. Another example of pure information affecting behavior is when a student changes his or her major after taking a course in a particular academic discipline. The instructor is not actively looking for new majors and using the course to persuade. But when the instructor presents facts and the student finds the information interesting, the student could decide to change majors. While the end result was persuasion, we do not consider this situation to be an example of a persuasive message.

Ultimately, receivers decide the effectiveness of the persuasive message. Receivers are in control and must think critically about the persuasive messages they receive from friends, parents, bosses, advertising, news, and other media. You do not have to accept persuasive messages (such as your parents' political views) blindly. Some parents give their children a sense of family, set an example for personal standards and moral values, encourage them to study and succeed, and share their beliefs on many topics. As children mature, read, and reflect on various issues, they may find themselves at odds with some of the messages they have received from their parents. As adults, we are responsible for what we say and do—not our parents. Therefore, it is important to decide whether we are persuaded by a particular viewpoint, rather than accepting it without question because we have heard it so often. It is acceptable to change your views based on your own analysis of society and culture. "The ultimate power rests not with the source but the receiver, to attend or ignore, accept or reject, remember or forget, act or not act on the persuasive effort" (Benjamin, 1997, p. 12).

Persuasion Comes from Many Places

Some efforts to persuade are easy to recognize, such as when your roommate persuades you to turn out the lights because she needs sleep prior to a big test the next day. Or, you are out shopping with a peer, and they say you should buy something because you'd look good wearing it. You decline, but they continue telling you that you are worth the expense and haven't had anything new in a long time. When you went to the mall, you had no intention of buying anything. However, the persistent persuasion convinces you to purchase the item you don't need on your credit card without thinking. Do you regret the decision when the credit card bill arrives?

Or, an organization in which you are a member is raising money for some cause. The cause may be worthwhile, but you don't have a particular interest in it—yet you hand over your money to support it. These simple scenarios are reminders of how constant persuasive messages are in daily life. We often react to them without thinking about our actions. It may be time to think critically and actively support causes and values in which we truly believe.

Critical Thinking

How often are you persuaded to do something that benefits someone else, but may harm you? Think about the example of a roommate asking you to turn out the lights. If you have a paper due the next day, how will you handle this? Do you cater to the needs of someone else while ignoring your own situation? Or do you find a solution that works for both of you, such as taking your laptop out of the room and going somewhere else to write so she can sleep?

_____

_____

_____

_____

_____

_____

The media projects numerous persuasive messages, whether through programming or advertising. Media messages are strategically aimed at all levels of culture. Did you ever look at the set and prop design background in your favorite program or ad? Does your family live in a home like the one your favorite characters inhabit? Do you have the same furniture and room decorations? Probably not, but they make a subtle impression on you to make decisions about your own color and style, which can lead you to purchase items simply because you now believe that they will make you happy and look more sophisticated. What about the wardrobes or hairstyles of your favorite media celebrities? Do you stop to think that media talent have designers working with them to create the best look for them as individuals, or do you assume you'll look equally good if you style your hair similarly or buy clothing to match? If you buy in to the message, your money supports the advertisers and retailers promoting their products. It's possible you aren't even aware that your buying habits are shaped by the media's overt and covert messages.

The media can shape our views as well. Gender communication theory looks at the pervasive persuasive messages designed to show us that women should look a certain way. The size of women that you see on TV is far smaller than the average-sized female in the general population. Typically women in sitcoms are a size 0–2, whereas the average American woman is somewhere between a 12–16. Women you see on the covers of magazines and in advertisements have been made-up and then airbrushed and image-manipulated by a computer. In some instances the images are computer generated altogether and there is no real person there. When we look at a person in an advertisement for cosmetics, the intended message is that we will look like that if we buy that product.

Our culture also generates a multitude of persuasive messages. Look at the messages that American culture promotes. We'll examine just one example: Bigger is better. This message dominates American culture—houses have expanded, cars are larger, etc. In England, the closets in homes are quite small because British culture encourages individuals to have a few things of very good quality rather than a lot of stuff. Americans, on the other hand, desire huge walk-in closets because bigger is better and the more you have, the more successful you are perceived to be.

⇨　**Try It!**　⇦

Take a quick look at how American culture has persuaded you to have more. Count up the number of items you have:

Pairs of shoes _____

Shirts _____

Electronic/digital gadgets _____

As you experience daily persuasive messages, you need to think critically about each message and whether you are willing to be influenced by it. But in order to think actively through your choices as the receiver of a persuasive message, you need to have a perceived choice.

Perceived Choice

There is a fundamental distinction between persuasion and coercion. Persuasion, as defined above, is influence with a ***perceived choice***, whereas ***coercion*** is perceived force. Many people argue that we have choices in every situation, and we agree. However, we may not always perceive that there is a choice.

For example, Kathleen turns in the first draft of a paper. She includes information and an analysis she believes is accurate. She draws a conclusion about the information and feels great conviction that her analysis of the subject is correct. However, the instructor returns her paper, questions her analysis, and does not agree with her conclusion even though it was supported by evidence she presented. The instructor tells her to rewrite the conclusion in a specific way. Kathleen does not agree with the teacher's decision, but she knows this instructor assigns failing grades to people who don't comply. She decides to change the conclusion of her paper according to the teacher's wishes.

In this case, Kathleen has not been persuaded that her analysis is incorrect; she has been coerced to change it. Coercion means there is no perceived choice in a situation. We label it a *perceived* choice because obviously Kathleen has a choice. She can disregard the instructor's comments and write what she believes to be the appropriate conclusion to her paper knowing her grade might be lowered. She can also discuss the decision with the teacher hoping to convince her that her analysis is correct. However, because she needs a good grade in the class, and the teacher has a reputation for being close-minded, Kathleen doesn't perceive she has a choice in this situation. Therefore, she is coerced to alter the conclusion.

Coercion can frequently occur in interpersonal relationships with siblings, friends, and intimate partners. It takes time to realize that you always seem to do a lot of things for other people, and they rarely make themselves available to you. Our siblings usually know nearly everything about us because we

---

— Professional Perspective —

Some people always seem to get what they want. Other people only get what others want them to have. We need to ask, "Why?" The answer is, "Persuasion." In sales, like all other walks of life, persuasion is the difference between success and failure. Because so much depends on "making the sale," some agents are tempted to do *anything* in order to close a deal. This is an unfortunate, unethical implication of persuasion. Sales agents can become so skilled that they coerce or force a person into buying something that may not be suitable for them. In the world of investments and financial planning, for instance, an effective communicator must construct a range of persuasive appeals and arguments that can ethically be adapted to a range of clientele with differing needs. The ethical communicator constructs messages that accurately describe the rationale, the advantages and disadvantages, and the short-term and long-term implications of investment vehicles, recognizing that the needs of every client are unique. Ethical communicators use their persuasive abilities to construct messages that are based in truth and accuracy, allow the listeners to decide for themselves what action is best, and effectively demonstrate the implications of any decision for their clients.

—Barry McCauliff
Account Executive
The Investment Center

Choices and Consequences

Your roommate says, "I want you to type my history paper for me tonight. If you don't, I'll tell your mother what you've been doing." What are your choices?

_____

_____

_____

What are the consequences?

_____

_____

_____

---

shared our lives with them at home. Some of you may have had pleasant sibling relationships, while others of you did not. Regardless of which category you fall into, did a sibling ever use coercion to get you to do a task for them with the threat that they would tell your parents what you did or said? This is a common communication challenge in childhood, and yet it is coercion at a time in life when you aren't prepared to analyze the request and you don't perceive that you have a choice.

Friends use coercion to control our behavior by reminding us of what they did for us the last time we asked them to do something, so now it's our chance to return the favor. There is occasionally a payback theme to coercion, but it isn't a valid reason to do something for someone else. The emotional bond in this type of interpersonal exchange is usually applied to get the appropriate results. Even intimate relationships can display coercive techniques at times. One example of this type of coercion is family holiday visits. Which set of parents do you visit on which holidays? This discussion is always interesting with newly married couples, and the "traditional" visits are normally set before children enter the picture. If one individual is uncomfortable with their actions in an interpersonal situation, the action itself is probably the result of coercive messages. However, that person may have perceived that they had no choice in the matter when, in fact, they could have collaborated to achieve a different result.

Effective persuasion occurs when two people explore the options, share their reasons, look at all the information, and come to an effective agreement. One person will have persuaded the other to see their point of view, but each person should recognize that they have a choice.

Informing versus Persuading

We talked about informative speaking earlier in the book. Informative and persuasive speaking have different basic goals. The goal of informative speaking is to get the audience to remember specific, factual information. With persuasive speaking, however, you add the personal element of drawing conclusions about the factual information you are sharing in order to get the audience to believe something or do something. As a receiver listening to an informative speech, you only need to assess the factual information. With persuasion, however, you must critically analyze the factual information as well as the reasoning to arrive at the conclusion. A persuasive speech attempts to get the audience to believe a specific point of view and sometimes to act on that point of view.

It is useful to know what's happening in the country and the world, and it is also important to remember your unique position in both of them. Media is a form of public speaking. It is your job to listen critically, analyze the information and then alter your beliefs or actions based on sound judgment. It is equally as important to realize that we don't get all of the facts about any story unless we go looking for them. A lot of cultural persuasion occurs when people are complacent about obtaining all of the information.

Reality ✔

Is the nightly news informative or persuasive? While we are taught to think that the news simply gives us the facts about what is going on in the world, we would be naive to think that it is unbiased information. Just as we filtered the information presented in this textbook and chose to focus on choices and consequences, a news producer is responsible for framing the information broadcast and the facts that were omitted.

Broadcast news spotlights a limited number of events. Let's say the news reports an anthrax incident or a shark attack. Do you immediately think, "What percentage of the population is involved in such incidents?" Why not? Just because a story is reported does not mean that it influences your life in any way, so why worry about it?

Unfortunately, we do tend to focus on what is in the news. Think about some recent stories. After 9/11 there were a number of reports of anthrax attacks. The number of people who died from those attacks numbered less than 20, yet many people were fearful and opened their mail with rubber gloves. At the same time, we rarely hear about intimate partner violence (IPV). These are assaults that occur between two people who are in an intimate relationship—not random, violent attacks. According to the CDC (Centers for Disease Control, 2007) Web site, "In the United States every year, about 1.5 million women and more than 800,000 men are raped or physically assaulted by an intimate partner." And yet how much time do we spend fearing that we'll end up in an intimate relationship where that kind of horrible violence would take place? Chances are, you never even thought about that, because it is rarely brought to our attention.

The next time you watch the news, think of it as a persuasive presentation. What is the news channel trying to persuade you to believe about the world in which you live?

⇨ Try It! ⇦

What kinds of stories on the news make you fearful? What are the chances that those events could happen to you?

_____

_____

_____

_____

_____

⇨ **Try It!** ⇦

Write an informative statement about food. _____

_____

Write a persuasive statement about food. _____

_____

The definition of persuasion includes an actively designed message (i.e., opinion and reasoning are included), a perceived choice on the part of the listeners, and a goal of influencing the audience's attitudes, beliefs, values, or actions. Our definition also includes the concept that persuasion is a receiver-oriented phenomenon. People decide for themselves which messages will influence them and what actions they will take.

What Does It Take to be Successful?

While we would hope every persuasive message we design ultimately leads to total audience/receiver change, that isn't a realistic goal. So how far must an audience shift in its attitudes, beliefs, values, or actions for you to be considered a good persuader? We will argue that if you get even one person in the audience to think about what you've said, you have been somewhat successful. Persuasion happens over time. Most people aren't persuaded to change their beliefs on major topics in a five- to ten-minute speech. For example, in the 1980s organ donation became a topic of public discussion, and college students used the topic for their persuasive speeches. The first time I (KSY) heard about this program, I thought, "Well, that is interesting. I ought to think about that." I didn't initially change my actions, however, but the thought was introduced. In subsequent semesters, I heard more speeches on the topic. As time passed, I finally decided to sign a card, but I made sure to list all kinds of exclusions, such as my corneas and other various body organs. After a few more semesters of hearing the message and processing the information, I became a full-fledged organ donor with no exclusions.

Critical Thinking

What have you tried to persuade your parents to think about or do that took a number of attempts before you were successful?

_____

Sometimes your persuasive goal does not come to fruition for many years. Some people are persuaded by repetitive messages over time. Others may not change their beliefs until there is a personal connection. No matter how well crafted the persuasive argument is, there are some people who will never be influenced.

REASONABLE GOALS

Your best approach to a persuasive message is to have ***reasonable goals.*** Think for a moment about things that you have a strong opinion about: abortion, euthanasia, gun control, or capital punishment. Could a 6-minute presentation get you to change your mind and/or perform an action on any of these topics? It's highly unlikely.

To keep your goals reasonable for a persuasive speaking assignment, follow these guidelines:

1. Choose a topic that is *not a national debate*. We already have strong views on topics like abortion, euthanasia, the death penalty, and the legalization of marijuana. These topics are incredibly complex, and unless you have three days to speak, it is unlikely you can even begin to develop the details of the subject in a meaningful way.

2. Choose a topic that is *not a national campaign*. Persuading people to stop speeding, wear a seat belt, exercise regularly, and eat right are national campaigns with multimillion dollar budgets and marketing plans. If these persuaders, a loved one, or the police can't get the audience to change, we doubt you'll be successful. Plus, we already know the recommended behaviors for these issues; so unless you can provide new information on these topics for an audience, select another topic.

3. Choose a topic to which *you have a personal connection*. Find something you are involved in or you feel strongly about. Unless you have a personal connection with a topic, you do not have the motivation necessary to project sincerity. We all know that we should donate blood. We all know where and when, but we don't do it. Why? A story about a little girl who needs blood isn't enough to persuade a college audience to donate. We have watched over 50 donating blood speeches. There was only one truly effective speech. A young college student with leukemia presented it. He had the personal experience of needing blood and sitting in a hospital waiting until they found it. Because the audience of college students could relate to him, the speech was effective. Also, don't ever attempt to persuade us to do something that you don't do. It is unethical and ruins your credibility.

4. Choose a topic that is *easy for the audience to comprehend and to do*. For instance, one semester a student tried to persuade us to volunteer to work with people with intellectual disabilities. But it wasn't until the question and answer period, when she stated we could do something as simple as send a card, that we felt helping was within our realm. She might have had more success if she had selected an easier and more tangible topic: "I want my audience to send a card to Alicia or Kevin at the facility where I work."

5. Choose a topic most people don't do because *they don't know about it*. We all know we should floss, but do we know to change our toothbrush every three months? That is a bit more unique and most of us don't think about it. However, it is important not to choose a topic people find to be trivial. Think about everyday things you do that you feel other people should do and go from there.

6. Choose a topic that can be *phrased as a positive*. You need to tell us something to do rather than something not to do. Rather than tell us not to use Q-tips to clean our ears, give us the alternative, "You should use a washcloth to clean your ears." The audience will react better if you suggest an action rather than a prohibition.

⇨   **Try It!**   ⇦

Which criteria are useful as you try to keep your goals reasonable when persuading friends, family, and significant others?

_____

_____

_____

_____

_____

TYPES OF PERSUASIVE MESSAGES

There are three types of persuasive messages. Whichever one you choose becomes your goal statement for the persuasive speech. You must decide whether you are trying to convince, to reinforce, or to actuate. A message to **convince** targets the audience's attitudes, beliefs, and values. With this message, your goal is change. In a speech to convince, your audience disagrees with you or is neutral about your topic.

A message to **reinforce** also targets the audience's attitudes, beliefs, values, and actions. What makes this speech different is that the audience already agrees with you or is performing the action. You are strengthening the audience's convictions on the topic or reinforcing their motivation to continue doing the action.

A message to **actuate** is for people who are not *doing* an action you want them to do. A speech to actuate is best for listeners who are not hostile to your topic. You are more likely to get the audience to perform the action if they are already convinced the topic has merit, or if they are neutral about the topic but simply lack the motivation to take action.

Let's look at the topic "Using a campus tutoring center." Think about realistic goals for a speech to an audience consisting of typical first-year college students. If the audience believed the tutoring service offered no benefits for them, you could *convince* this audience they should use the tutoring center. The end goal would be to change their belief that the tutoring center is not useful. If you found that most of your audience is already using the tutoring center, then you might design a speech to *reinforce*. You want to strengthen their belief that the center is helpful and motivate them to keep going. If the audience felt they could benefit from the tutoring center, but didn't have the motivation or knowledge to use it, then you would design a speech to *actuate*. The end goal would be to get audience members to make appointments at the tutoring center. As you can see from this discussion, audience analysis is imperative in deciding on the type of persuasive speech to present.

⇨ **Try It!** ⇦

These three goals also apply to interpersonal persuasion. Come up with examples of persuasive messages you have received or have used on others in each of these categories:

Convince _____

Reinforce _____

Actuate _____

⇨ **Try It!** ⇦

For the remainder of this chapter and in chapter 11, we will use the following scenario for the Try It! boxes. Let's say you are a straight-A student who reads your textbooks each and every time they are assigned. You decide your goal will be to persuade your audience to do the same thing. Keeping this information in mind, what type of speech will you be designing?

_____

Purpose Statements

As you build a persuasive speech, you need to have a purpose statement. The purpose statements for three types of speeches are as follows:

Convince: I want my audience to believe that. . . .

Reinforce: I want my audience to believe more strongly that . . . **or**
I want my audience to keep doing X.

Actuate: I want my audience to. . . .

Convince: I want my audience to believe that the tutoring center could help them.

Reinforce: I want my audience to believe more strongly that the tutoring center is useful.

Reinforce: I want my audience to keep on using the tutoring center in their second year of school.

Actuate: I want my audience to schedule two appointments at the tutoring center.

Notice that depending on which type of speech you choose, the focus is totally different. Once again, your first decision involves the audience. What reaction do you want from your audience? Do you want the audience to believe something, believe something more strongly, or do something? If you want them to do something, then you don't design a speech to convince.

⇨ **Try It!** ⇦

Think about your speech to actuate students to read their textbooks. What is the purpose statement you should design?

AUDIENCE ANALYSIS

What should you know about the audience? In persuasive speaking, there are three main things you need to know. For a speech to convince, it is imperative to find out whether the audience agrees with you, is neutral, or disagrees with you (sometimes called a hostile audience). Obviously, if the audience already agrees with you, you do not need to convince them. If you are constructing a speech to actuate, you need to know whether the audience is always doing the action, doing it sometimes, or not doing it at all. In addition, you must know how much the audience knows about the topic. We are neutral about some topics. Sometimes we don't perform an action because we simply don't know the information. Some college students don't wash their sheets as frequently as once a week, nor do they think that it is important. The subject of clean sheets can become a good topic for a speech to actuate. Once students hear about the millions of dust mites that grow in sheets and crawl on their bodies at night, most of them will be quick to agree washing sheets is important, and many may wash their sheets immediately. This is a good example of how to examine the environment around you to find a clever way to actuate an audience.

The following continuums will help you with audience analysis.

We recommend the 50 percent rule of audience analysis for a persuasive speech: at least 50 percent or more of your audience should oppose your position on a topic to make the speech worthwhile. Look once again at the reasonable goals section before the discussion below. The discussion would not be a reasonable goal, but many college students persist in trying.

Tracy's best friend was killed by a drunk driver. She wants to give her speech on drinking and driving. So, she designs a speech to convince her audience drunk driving is wrong. Tracy makes a crucial mistake. Think about the audience for a minute. What do you suppose the audience's current belief is about drinking and driving? Do you imagine the audience believes drunk driving is right? Not a chance. Tracy argues with her instructor, "But people still do it!" OK, that is true, but that isn't a speech to convince. So, Tracy decides to actuate her audience to stop drinking and driving. Well, once again, while this is a morally wonderful goal, it doesn't fit the audience. Unless you live in an extremely reckless area, 50 percent or more of your audience doesn't drive drunk. With strong evidence of tragic consequences and stiff penalties for violating the law, most people don't drink and drive. Most people use designated drivers.

If Tracy persists in using this topic, she needs to find a new angle. At one time, a speech to actuate the audience to take keys away from others worked. But even that topic rarely meets the 50 percent rule anymore, since most college students already perform this action. Another possibility for an approach might be to persuade people in the audience to never get in a car with someone who has had even one drink. You'd have to do an audience analysis to see whether this meets the 50 percent rule, however. Many people don't have the personal strength to find another way home if their driver has had only one or two drinks. People still get in the car. This speech would focus on our personal responsibility to keep ourselves alive as more important than the possibility of offending a friend by refusing to accept a ride.

Remember, drunk driving is a national campaign. There are messages everywhere, and people who choose to drink and drive aren't going to stop based on a brief presentation. The only unique approach to this topic we have ever seen was a 23-year-old student who was widowed after her husband was celebrating a promotion at work and was then killed in a drunk-driving accident. The personal connection and the shock of her circumstances gave a compassionate edge to the speech that made it successful. So once again, unless you have a unique angle, you should stay away from topics such as this one.

Reality ✔

Here is your chance to have persuasive influence. Even one opinion can make a difference. Authors use the numerous persuasive messages they receive to evaluate their work. When we start working on the next edition we'd like to hear your ideas and feedback to improve this book and to meet students' needs. Please e-mail us at youngtravisbookreview@hotmail.com and persuade us.

⇨ Try It! ⇦

What audience analysis questions would be important to ask in order to design an effective speech on reading the textbooks? You should be able to generate at least eight good questions that will help design the focus for this speech.

_____

_____

_____

_____

_____

_____

_____

_____

PREPARING FOR PERSUASION

Before you begin a persuasive speech, it is a good idea to think about your personal feelings about the topic. You need personal conviction in order to be a successful persuasive speaker. If you haven't reflected on the issue and carefully evaluated why you believe what you do, then you won't be able to discover appropriate reasons and psychological motivations to persuade others. For example, if you automatically accepted your parents' opinion on an issue, you lack the necessary conviction. You need to carefully analyze your reasons for believing in a topic or doing a particular action as you design a persuasive speech. Careful analysis will help you discover what motivates you, the reasoning that convinced you to hold your position, and the language that will help you motivate others.

Critical Thinking
What topic do you really feel strongly about? If you could get the entire world to believe as you do, what would you argue for?

Another point of analysis is to discover why the audience disagrees with you or why the audience doesn't perform the action. Let's look at another national campaign issue. Let's say you want to persuade your audience to exercise five days a week. You can already see from the previous discussion, this is not a reasonable topic for a short persuasive speech. However, if you geared your speech to use time as your key argument, you could convince your audience that students really do have enough time to exercise at the university fitness center. Is time an appropriate key argument? Probably not. If you poll any college audience, as we have done numerous times, we find that only 20 percent of the audience does not exercise because of lack of time. Some do not exercise because they are admittedly lazy. Others do not exercise because they hate exercising. Many don't exercise because they don't think they need to or don't see the benefit. Many feel uncomfortable in the university fitness center because at some schools the climate is one of a sweaty singles' club. Still others don't do it because they are on a sports team and they exercise elsewhere. Many exercise at home. Some may be ashamed of their body type and feel uncomfortable exercising in public. Thus, there is no solid target for your speech; the audience is too fragmented in terms of these reasons for not acting. If you find out through audience analysis why at least 50 percent of the audience doesn't believe or do the action, then you have an appropriate approach to the topic.

As you select your topic and prepare your audience analysis, it is essential to consider the ethics of the persuasive situation. Your ultimate goal is to change beliefs, values, attitudes, or actions, which entails ethical responsibility. You must absolutely believe what you are trying to get your audience to believe. You must absolutely do the action you are trying to get the audience to do. We hope you don't ask why. But if you do, there are two reasons. First, you are believable only when you sincerely hold your opinion. An informed audience can hear the difference. Actors are trained to portray themselves as other people, but speakers don't usually possess such skills. Second, it is unethical to construct messages to influence your audience to do or believe something you yourself don't believe or practice. This is the equivalent of lying, and most people would agree that lying is wrong.

If an audience learns you lied to them, you lose credibility. For instance, Jerome constructs a wonderful persuasive speech about giving up red meat. He gives numerous statistics, emotional appeals, and well-reasoned arguments. Fred is really moved by his speech and thinks he might try to give up red meat so he can be healthier, as Jerome advised in the speech. Later in the week, after two days of meatless meals, Fred notices Jerome in the window of a fast-food restaurant wolfing down a triple burger. Fred now knows Jerome lied to him during the speech. He feels angry and betrayed because he believed Jerome was telling the truth. Fred now finds it difficult to believe anything Jerome says to him. Jerome's credibility is gone.

Ethical Considerations

What ethical considerations should you make about yourself and the audience when you proceed with your speech on reading all assigned textbooks?

_____

_____

_____

_____

_____

SUMMARY

Although understanding persuasive messages seems quite simple, we often fail to apply our reasoning skills to the constant persuasion around us. You need to listen critically to every message you hear. Without analyzing persuasive messages, you could find yourself in a financial situation like the example of Adam and Megan used to open this chapter. They were actuated to purchase items they did not need. You may think you can avoid their circumstances, but poor judgment for just a moment can place you in a similar situation.

Persuasive messages can be positive. For example, think of the emotional reinforcement you acquire from a weekly religious service or the thrill you get when you finally convince your parents you are right about something. On a daily basis, you need to find people to go with you to dinner, lend you some money, and take you places. Persuasion is the tool that accomplishes these daily goals.

Know your beliefs and values well so you can recognize whether persuasive messages match your needs before you take an action. Avoid reacting to messages unless you are thinking critically. Question everything and discover significant reasons why you should believe certain philosophies or hold certain values. This intrapersonal discussion makes you a stronger communicator and increases your ability to persuade others so you can help them. Persuade by example. Be ethical in all the roles in which you find yourself—within the family, the community, and your chosen profession. Responsibility for your behavior and actions is an indication you are becoming a good communicator.

Key Words

actuate
coercion
convince
entertain

perceived choice
persuasion
reasonable goals

Crossword 10: Understanding the Principles of Persuasion

Across

3. A speech strengthening audience conviction or strengthening their motivation to continue their current action.

5. Communicators must believe in their subject and perform the action they are suggesting for others to be considered ____.

6. A persuasive situation where the receiver does not perceive a choice in changing his or her thoughts or behaviors.

7. A persuasive argument is shaped once a communicator analyzes the ____.

8. A persuasive goal to make an audience change their attitudes, beliefs, or values.

9. A statement giving a persuasive speech its structural shape.

Down

1. A process in which one communicator tries to influence the attitudes, beliefs, and values of others.

2. A speech encouraging an audience to take the action you are presenting to them.

4. Realizing that people aren't persuaded quickly on big issues means that you must meet the criteria for a

_____.

CHAPTER 11

Constructing the Persuasive Presentation

OBJECTIVES

After reading this chapter, you should be able to:

- Explain credibility and logical and emotional appeals
- List the types of arguments/claims and write examples for each
- Identify other organizational patterns for persuasion
- List emotions that can be targeted
- Explain the five steps of Monroe's Motivated Sequence
- List and recognize the fallacies of reasoning

Think back to the newly married couple, Adam and Megan, discussed in chapter 10. They are typical of many people in U.S. culture who don't challenge the long-term effects of persuasive messages. Their dream was to have it all. The ease of using credit cards made the reality of the bottom line disappear. They had visible stuff, but their hidden weakness was their debt and an addiction to persuasive messages. Unfortunately, they reacted to persuasive messages without thinking critically.

It's easy to say, "That won't happen to me," but don't be so sure. You will use persuasion throughout your life to influence your children, your family and friends, gain employment, and live your dream. An understanding of persuasive reasoning makes you less susceptible to persuasive messages and, at the same time, helps you design effective messages.

Aristotle defined the three building blocks used in a persuasive message:credibility (ethos), logical appeals (logos), and emotional appeals (pathos). Credibility is constructed through the use of citations and testimony. Logical appeals are constructed from facts, figures, and reasoning. Emotional appeals are constructed with stories and examples.

BUILDING BLOCK #1: CREDIBILITY (ETHOS)

We talked about *credibility* in the informative speaking section. It always amazes us when students ask, "Do we really have to cite sources in a persuasive speech?" Our answer is, "Of course!" *Citations* are what make you appear to be knowledgeable. Without citations, your entire speech is nothing but opinion. If the audience is going to be influenced by your message, you must first convince them of your credibility. If you have not researched your topic and discovered experts who agree with your position, your ability to persuade an audience member approaches zero.

⇨   **Try It!**   ⇦

Find a citation for your speech about reading assigned textbooks.

_____

_____

_____

BUILDING BLOCK #2: LOGICAL APPEALS (LOGOS)

The term *logical appeals* refers to all of the structure and reasoning you build into a persuasive presentation. In the following sections, we discuss types of claims, persuasive organizational patterns, and types and fallacies of reasoning.

Types of Claims

In persuasive speaking there are three types of *claims:* fact, value, and policy. The type of claim you choose will influence the organizational pattern. Your claim will also relate to the persuasive goal you have chosen for your speech.

A *claim of fact* attempts to convince the audience (or reinforce existing beliefs) that a certain piece of factual information is true. For instance, you may claim that tuition at your school will rise by 6 percent in the next five years because of a new fitness center being built on campus. Since no one will know for sure what the actual percentage increase will be until the five-year interval ends, you need to provide evidence for your claim of 6 percent.

A *claim of value* attempts to convince an audience (or reinforce existing beliefs) that one thing is better than another. A speaker may try to convince an audience that the South Beach diet is better than the Atkins diet. Because of the word "better" (an opinion word), this is a speech of value. Sometimes speakers get confused here because they believe their opinions are factual. The statement, "The South Beach diet is the best" is a claim of value, not fact, no matter how much you believe it to be factual.

A *claim of policy* attempts to move someone to action. A speaker could try to get the audience to buy a product, sign a petition, go someplace, join a demonstration, or attend events on campus. Any time the goal is action, you have a claim of policy. Usually, a claim of policy statement includes the word "should," i.e., "You should. . . ."

So let's review:

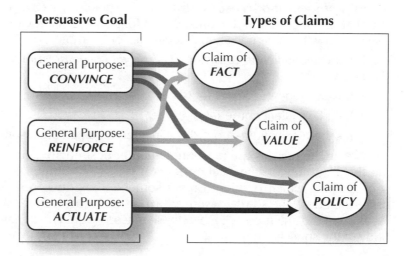

You must recognize that your goal is connected to your claim. In the next section, we'll talk about how your claim is related to your organizational pattern.

Persuasive Organization

Depending on your topic and your audience, you need to choose your organizational structure carefully. Statement-of-reasons and comparative-advantages structures are similar to one another and are best used for speeches to convince or reinforce. A problem-solution structure is used when you want to convince your audience of a policy claim where someone else should do the action. A Monroe's Motivated Sequence is used to compel the audience to perform an action themselves.

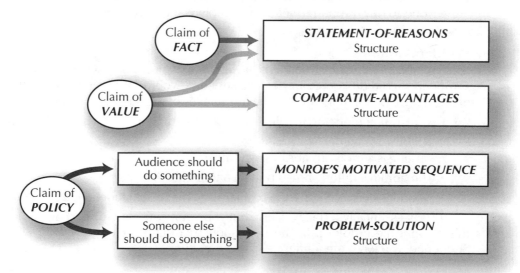

Statement-of-Reasons

In a **statement-of-reasons** structure, a speaker reveals the persuasive claim at the beginning of the speech and follows the claim with a number of reasons why the audience should accept it. For example,

I want my audience to believe *Everybody Loves Raymond* was the best sitcom ever.

- It was a top-rated show for CBS.
- It had excellent comedians.
- It's the most talked-about show in interpersonal conversations.

Notice the reasons are presented in order of strength. You can document the first reason with statistical evidence. You can document the second reason by citing expert opinion. Unless someone has done research, you can only document the third reason as a personal observation, making it the weakest of the arguments. Each of these reasons would be a main point in the body of the speech.

Comparative-Advantages

The **comparative-advantages** structure is similar to statement-of-reasons because the speaker states the persuasive goal first. The main points in this speech demonstrate the advantages this goal has over any other option. For example,

I want my audience to believe cotton underwear is preferable to silk underwear.

- Cotton material breathes better.
- Cotton material cuts down on urinary tract infections.
- Cotton material is cheaper.

In this speech, you would document each of these advantages, giving the audience reasons to agree with your proposition. Notice you aren't persuading anyone to buy the underwear. You simply want them to agree that cotton is superior to other fabrics.

Problem-Solution

A **problem-solution** structure is useful if you want to convince an audience someone should do something. In this structure, your main points are (1) the problem, (2) the solution, and (3) the advantages of the solution. For example,

I want my audience to believe that Anytown University should build a parking deck.

- Parking is a problem at Anytown University.
- The administration should build a parking deck.
- A parking deck will solve the problem and make the student body content.

This is essentially a policy claim, but you want someone else to do something about the problem. In the next speech structure, Monroe's Motivated Sequence, you want the audience to do something.

Monroe's Motivated Sequence

If you are choosing a speech to actuate, then you will probably go with **Monroe's Motivated Sequence (MMS)**. This is a five-part organizational pattern that is appropriate if the audience is not opposed to your topic—they just lack the motivation to perform an action. This structure is more complex than the previous ones because you are attempting to get the audience to take action rather than simply agree with you. You need to ignore the statement-of-reasons structure to be successful with MMS. You are no longer stating a claim and giving reasons why someone should do something. With MMS you must describe a problem for the audience so they will be motivated to take action.

MMS moves an audience through five steps (German, Gronbeck, Ehninger, and Monroe, 2004, pp. 266–270). All five steps are important, and we will cover each step in detail.

Attention Step: You first need to get your audience's attention. The attention step in MMS is similar to the attention-getter in an informative speech. After hearing this step, the audience should say, "I want to listen!"

Showing the Need: In this step you must convince the audience there is a problem that affects them. The first thing you do is state the problem; be clear and specific. To prove to your audience that this is indeed a problem, you will need to include lots of evidence in the form of supporting material. It is not enough just to say a problem exists—you must prove it. Obviously, some problems require more evidence than others. If you want to prove your audience is stressed, it will not take much convincing. However, if you want them to believe there are pollutants in their air, you may need a lot more factual evidence and emotional appeals to accomplish your goal.

Be careful not to reveal your claim in this step. The idea is to convince your audience that they face an urgent problem (air pollution). You will show them what to do about it in the next step (buy houseplants). Note the problem is air pollution. If you say the problem is that the audience doesn't have houseplants, you are building a circular argument.

Don't forget to link the problem with your audience; they must believe it is *their* problem. Think of the commercials for starving third-world children. You know it is a problem, but how many of you send money to help? If you don't, chances are the reason is you don't feel connected to the problem. It is something that happens "over there" and doesn't affect you personally other than the fleeting emotion you may feel when you see the commercial.

Satisfying the Need: You reveal your claim in this step. You tell the audience what it is you want them to do. There are five parts to this step. You must first reveal the action you want them to perform in a clear and concise manner. Second, you explain the details of what you want them to do. In some speeches, you will need a lot of explanation. In others, you will not. If I want my audience to buy houseplants to clean the air, I don't really need to explain what houseplants are in more detail other than to say, "By houseplants, I mean indoor plants like snake plants and spider plants." In your textbook example, however, you will need to explain precisely what you mean by reading the textbook. (Many of you may think reading simply means to drag your eyes across the lines of text. However, when I say read the textbook, I mean you must examine all of the chapter headings and see how they fit together, read and comprehend each paragraph well enough to write a small summary note in the margin. . . .)

The third part is to explain how the action you want them to do solves the problem you outlined in the need step. You must use strong reasoning and factual support here. In the houseplant example, provide evidence that snake plants and spider plants remove 87 percent of air pollutants in the first 24 hours they are in the room. The fourth part contains evidence that the solution has actually worked in real life. You might use personal testimony, research studies, and citations by expert authorities to prove this point.

Finally, the fifth part is designed to meet imagined objections. Keep in mind you can't persuade people if they are arguing with your claim in their minds. In this part of the satisfaction step you need to refute any potential arguments the audience could be composing. Here is where a thorough audience analysis comes in handy. You need to know why they aren't currently doing the action. If you chose stress in the need step and then propose a $2,000 cruise to Bermuda over spring break as the action, a discussion about how safe Bermuda is as a place to vacation and assurances that the audience won't be sucked into the Bermuda Triangle would totally miss the mark as to why the action solves the problem. Safety is irrelevant; students would be thinking, "Oh sure, like I have $2,000!" By the time you complete the satisfaction step, your audience should realize that executing your claim will solve their problem and that there are no barriers to prevent them from doing so.

Visualization: In this step, you want to show the audience how their world will be a better place if they perform your action. You can do this by describing how things will be better if they do the action, how things will be worse if they don't perform the action, or you can include elements of each.

Requesting Action: In this step, you convince the audience to begin the action. You need to give them every detail they need in order to do so. In our houseplant example, you would need to explain where to get them, how much they cost, and how to choose the right one. It is often extremely effective to give something out during this step. You might give them a handout with the info they need. You might give them a sample of the thing you want them to try. We find audiences are much more receptive to an action when they get a free product. Be careful, however, of the method you choose to distribute your aid. In many cases you can give your handout or product at the conclusion of the speech, but it is acceptable to alert the audience in the action step that they will get something. Think creatively here.

We have outlined the MMS sequence below (German et al., pp. 266–270).

I. Attention Step
   (Use an effective attention-getting device here)
II. Need Statement
   A. Make a definite, concise statement about the problem (avoid a circular argument!).
   B. Use one or more examples explaining and clarifying the problem. Be sure to include additional examples, statistical data, testimony, and other forms of support.
   C. Show the extent and seriousness of the problem.
   D. Make it clear that the problem affects the audience.
III. Satisfy the Need
   A. State the action you want the audience to begin (or stop).
   B. Explain your proposal thoroughly.
   C. Demonstrate with reasoning how your proposed solution meets the need.
   D. Refer to practical experience by supplying examples to prove the proposal has worked effectively where it has been tried.
   E. Forestall opposition by anticipating and answering any objections that might be raised against this proposal.
IV. Visualize
   A. Describe conditions as they will be in the future if the solution you propose is carried out; or

B. Describe conditions as they will be in the future if your proposal is not carried out; or

C. Use both the negative and positive potential results.

V. Request Action

(Tell the audience every detail they need to know in order to perform the action.)

Recently, a student gave a speech to actuate. She wanted the audience to use ginger for nausea. Following MMS, she did not mention her topic until the satisfaction (third) step. She built the problem that her prescribed action would solve by demonstrating that popular over-the-counter antinausea medications are potentially dangerous drugs.

In the need step, she built the problem that most of us take these products when we are nauseated. She cited a source that states using a particular over-the-counter product can result in ringing in the ears and a black tongue. She also stated that according to J. Jamison Starbuck (2000), "drugs like Dramamine work on the Central Nervous System, depressing the body's reaction to movement stimuli." By the time she was done with the need step, we were all appalled at the side effects or potential dangers of both of these products. We were left wondering, "What can we do?"

⇨ Try It! ⇦

Now it's your turn. Using your speech to actuate students to read a textbook each and every time it is assigned, fill in a brief keyword outline of what you would do in each step of the sequence. REMEMBER: You cannot talk about reading textbooks until the satisfaction step. You must build a problem in the need step that reading assigned textbooks will solve.

Attention

_____

_____

Need

_____

_____

Satisfaction

_____

_____

Visualization

_____

_____

Action

_____

_____

As she approached the satisfaction step, she told us ginger was an alternative approach for the condition of nausea. She cited evidence that there was no danger to humans from this natural root and cited studies that proved its effectiveness. She talked about the personal success she had with the product. She also met potential objections of expense and dislike of the taste.

In the visualization step, she created a hypothetical story about driving on vacation and missing everything because of sleeping due to the side effects of the drugs the audience would normally take for nausea.

In the action step, she showed the alternative products you could use, including ginger tea, ginger candy, ginger drops, and crystallized ginger. She told us where in town we could get it. And she handed out ginger drops to all audience members to try the next time they experienced nausea.

Reasoned Argument

Once you've decided on your goal, your claim, and your organizational structure, then it is time to support your claims with reasoning. *Reasoning* refers to taking facts, analyzing them, and drawing conclusions from them. If you take a logic class, you will learn various logical appeals. For the purposes of introductory speech building and for critical consuming of the persuasive messages you receive, the following three types of reasoning are generally sufficient: inductive reasoning, reasoning from analogy, and causal arguments.

Inductive Reasoning

When you use *inductive reasoning,* you take some facts and draw a conclusion based on them. For example, it is a fact Ben failed geometry. It is a fact that he failed trigonometry. Ben also failed calculus. What general conclusion could you draw about Ben and math? Probably it would be a safe bet to say that Ben is mathematically challenged. Let's look at another example. Jana ate kung pao chicken and got sick. On another day, Jana ate chicken and snow peas and got sick. Recently, Jana ate chicken and cashews and got sick. With these three facts, what conclusion can you draw? Well, you can quickly see that there are a number of conclusions you can draw from these facts. Jana may be allergic to MSG—a common ingredient in Chinese food. Jana may have developed an allergy to chicken. Jana may be visiting a restaurant that is not following FDA requirements for food safety and preparation.

When you hear an inductive argument, you should always ask yourself whether enough specific facts were documented to support the conclusion. Another question to ask is whether the examples presented were typical of the situation or simply an exception. Let's look at an example. Anytown, USA declares a medical emergency. Three people die from an unknown virus. It is reported in the national news, and people in your community become concerned they could be susceptible to the same virus. However, your community is on the opposite side of the country from the original incident. Your local mayor makes a statement that all residents should follow five precautions. He is using inductive reasoning. He thinks because three people died, the general population in his community is at risk. How logical is his argument? Do three deaths in a distant community warrant a conclusion that you are at risk? Thinking about the question of typical instances, you may want to research information about the victims. If the three people who died were elderly people who had compromised immune systems, then they are not representative of the general population. As a receiver of this message, you would ask for more information.

Reasoning from Analogy

When you compare two concepts saying that what is true of one will be true of another, you are *reasoning from analogy*. Let's say someone uses the argument, "If you liked Boston, you'll love Washington, DC." What they are saying is that these two concepts are so similar they can make this comparison. Now the question you should ask yourself when you design or hear an argument from analogy is whether the two cases are similar enough to be compared. Are Boston and Washington, DC similar enough that we can make this case? It depends. If you are enthralled by a variety of restaurants, then yes, those two cities are very similar. However, if you like Boston because of its colonial history, then your analogy fails because Washington, DC doesn't have that history.

Have you ever heard the expression "comparing apples to oranges?" This expression is talking about poor arguments based on analogy. If someone says that to you, he is saying the two things you are comparing are dissimilar. So whenever someone presents reasoning from analogy, think carefully about what is being compared and the facts presented.

Causal Arguments

Reasoning from analogy compares two concepts, but a *causal argument* puts two concepts together stating one concept is the cause of the other. For example, "A college education leads to success" is a causal argument. In other words, if you get a college education, you will be successful. We know there are some flaws with this argument. When you hear a causal argument, you should ask yourself whether another cause might produce this conclusion. It may not be the college education that produces individual success; it may be the professional connections you make during your college experience. It may be that your work ethic makes you successful. It could also be your maturity after four additional years of growing up that helped you to focus and become successful. A roommate's parent or someone you met on the college campus could offer you a job. Or it could be the college education itself. But you get the idea. There are many variables. Causal arguments are very hard to prove because there are so many potential causes for various phenomena.

Fallacies of Reasoning

A *fallacy* is an error in reasoning. Any time you do not logically design your argument, you have an error. The questions we told you to ask help you to determine whether a fallacy exists in your reasoning. If you take a logic course, you will study this concept in much more depth and with different parameters. In basic communication, be aware of the following fallacies: ad hominem, hasty generalization, false cause, bandwagon, circular argument, appeal to authority, and irrational reasons. All of these fallacy names are derived from Latin. However, only ad hominem is still commonly known by its Latin name.

Ad Hominem: This fallacy happens whenever there is an attack against a person rather than against a concept. Alexander says to Rita, "Don't choose Professor X for this class. She dresses like a hippie. She is horrible." This is a personal attack. The argument rests on the clothing choices of the professor and has nothing to do with the quality of her teaching, her teaching style, or her knowledge of the discipline. Therefore, it is a personal, irrelevant attack. As a critical consumer of communication, Rita should recognize this fallacy and ask some follow-up questions, such as, "Why does the professor's appearance matter?" or "How knowledgeable is she in the discipline?" "What

---

⇒   **Try It!**   ⇐

Now that you are familiar with three types of arguments, try to write one of each for your speech on reading textbooks.

Inductive:

_____

_____

Analogy:

_____

_____

Causal:

_____

_____

— Professional Perspective —

Recently I had an experience that illustrated for me the need to be very careful when making causal arguments. I listened to a presentation by a health-campaign administrator. He was trying to persuade the public that a stop smoking campaign that targets children in a nearby community should receive funding from tax dollars. His argument hinged on one comment: "Spending money leads to change in behaviors."

The reality is that no amount of money thrown into a program that doesn't work will help make changes. What leads to successful changes is, in part, the nature of the program not the money thrown at the problem. This speaker's focus on money as a solution opened doors for criticism and debate that was irrelevant to preventing smoking among children. A more effective presentation could minimize irrelevant debate by focusing on needs and solutions.

A better fund-raiser speech would be to identify (1) the need for a program, (2) talk about the successes of a specific program, then (3) explain that the program needs funding. I would be more likely to support the campaign if approached in this way. However, the presentation I heard was a sloppy causal argument that left me wondering, "How stupid does he think I am?"

—Raymond R. Ozley
Lecturer
University of Montevallo

---

teaching style does she use?" "Does she relate to her students?" These are excellent critical-thinking questions.

**Hasty Generalization:** Hasty generalizations happen when communicators draw conclusions from insufficient facts. Think about the arguments we talked about above. In which type of argument would hasty generalizations happen?

Sue says to Bia, "I swear, men cannot fold laundry. My husband has a PhD in engineering, but the man cannot fold a T-shirt without wrinkles." At another table in the cafeteria, Raule says to Christopher, "I swear, women can't drive. I came to school today and a woman was swerving all over the road." In both of these cases, Sue and Raule are guilty of hasty generalizations. Just because one man can't fold laundry and one woman can't drive straight does not mean they can generalize about the entire population of men and women. Think how often you hear hasty generalizations in daily conversation. Again, it is your responsibility to ask questions. "Do you have other specific instances of this event?" "How often does it occur?" "Are studies available that support your conclusion?" would be some initial questions to ask to determine if someone is making a premature generalization. Think how offended you might be if a teacher made a hasty generalization that all students are cheaters because one student was caught cheating on the last exam.

False Cause: False cause occurs in causal arguments when a different cause could have produced the phenomena. Let's say Shirley did very poorly on the test because she was out all night partying and didn't sleep properly. This statement could be false because it is possible she didn't read any of the chapters during the semester, didn't understand any of the material, or didn't go to class. All of these things could have caused her failure on the exam, or she might have failed because she was out late one night. Think how often you hear a friend say he failed an assignment because the teacher didn't explain it properly. Is it really the teacher's fault? What if everyone else in the class completed the assignment properly? Be careful of drawing false cause arguments in the workplace or in interpersonal relationships. These types of arguments are rarely accepted, and when bosses or friends hear them, it's the type of fallacy that breeds bad feelings. In our society, placing blame on false causes is becoming more and more prevalent. If you are the type of person who builds these arguments into your everyday speech, you may want to assess whether it is a behavior you need to change. Listen carefully for these arguments as well, so you aren't drawn into false argument.

Bandwagon: This fallacy is reasoning that you should be allowed to do something because everyone else is doing it. Think about the times in your teenage years when you said, "But Mom! *Everyone* is going to the party," and Mom replied, "If everyone were jumping off a bridge would you do that too?" What Mom knew, and you didn't, was that your argument was an error in reasoning. She knew that just because other people are doing something does not mean that the action is good. Think of the advertisers who use the bandwagon approach. Everyone who is anyone has product X. You are targeted with messages saying in order to be liked you must have the latest clothes, electronic products, or body adornments. Is this a valid argument? Of course not. Be alert to the bandwagon fallacy so you do not get persuaded to do something that is not good for you.

Circular Argument: You are guilty of a circular argument when your conclusion is the same as your statement. Think about a child who comes down to dinner, and the parent says, "Wash your hands." The child says, "Why?" The parent replies, "Because you haven't, and I said so." The parent is arguing in a circle, saying that the reason something should be done is because it isn't being done. No reason is given in this argument, making it a fallacy. As a child, you simply do what you are told, but when you are older, you need to ask questions. You will also be expected to give solid reasons for your assertions in the workplace or at school. When a teacher asks for your opinion on a speaker, you may find yourself saying, "I just didn't like that." When the teacher asks "Why?" and you reply, "Because it wasn't any good," you are using a circular argument. The teacher may press you for additional details about what you specifically didn't like. Some students cannot articulate what they didn't like and reply, "I don't know; I just didn't like it." This is a serious flaw for a competent communicator. If you suffer from this problem, start the process of change now. Think about why you are making the statements you make.

Appeal to Authority: This fallacy is not a common one for beginning speakers, but we include it because it is used in advertising. It is important for critical consumers of communication to realize that messages relying on a celebrity endorsement are actually fallacies in reasoning. Anytime you see a celebrity doing a commercial or supporting a cause, it is important not to buy into that product or cause simply because the celebrity endorses it. Can you find out whether the celebrity actually uses the product? Does he or she really support the cause? Or is the celebrity there to make a quick dollar? Realistically, you probably won't take the time to research the background of the celebrity, but as a practicing critical consumer of communication, the red flag should go up, and you should question the validity of the argument when you see your favorite celebrity endorsing a product or cause. There are advertising laws to protect the public, but when a gorgeous performer says, "I'm not a doctor, but I play one on TV, take product X . . ." there is a tendency to ignore the disclaimer and to identify with the celebrity. You should analyze your reaction to the performer carefully before you race out to get the product.

Irrational Reasons: This fallacy occurs when we use unrelated or irrelevant reasons to support our conclusions. It takes a little practice to recognize this fallacy. Tom comes in to see his instructor. He waits until his last semester to take his oral communication course. He just failed his first speech and is terrified he won't pass the course. He tells the instructor, "But there is no way I could fail this speech. I practiced eight times." The instructor refers him to her comments on the grade sheet that indicate the problems with the speech, including items such as a missing bibliography, missing citations, no attention-getting device, information that is not targeted to the audience, inability to conform to the time limit, lack of transitions, inappropriate organizational pattern, reliance on a manuscript for an extemporaneous assignment, and no eye contact with the audience. The student continues to repeat, "But I worked

⇨ **Try It!** ⇦

While you should never use fallacies, we think it is a great learning experience to design some intentionally so you will be more familiar with such arguments and, therefore, more able to identify them in a message. Using your speech to persuade your audience to read their textbooks each and every time they are assigned, write a statement for each type of fallacy.

Ad Hominem _____

Hasty Generalization _____

False Cause _____

Bandwagon _____

Circular Argument _____

Appeal to Authority _____

Irrational Reasons _____

really hard on this and practiced a lot." You should be able to see how his reasons do not support his conclusion that he should not have failed the speech.

Once you have determined your claim, type of persuasive speech, organizational pattern, and reasoning, your speech should come together successfully. You need to use supporting materials effectively and include citations as well. You may think you are done now, but you aren't. For the greatest persuasive effect, it is time to add emotional appeal.

Ethical Considerations

What are the ethical implications when you design a biased argument?

_____

_____

_____

_____

BUILDING BLOCK #3: EMOTIONAL APPEAL (PATHOS)

To make credibility and logical appeals work, you need to add an *emotional appeal* that allows you to connect emotionally with the audience. We know most audiences are not persuaded by facts alone. If that were true, why would so many people smoke? Everyone knows smoking is a dangerous action. Smokers know how many people die annually from related health problems. Those facts are not enough to get people to stop smoking. If you were going to try to persuade someone, you would need to connect on an emotional level.

I (KSY) often tell my students a true story of a young 23-year-old woman named Teri who was my neighbor when I was first married in the late 1980s. She had her own townhouse and a beautiful new Iroc-Z (a very popular sports car at the time). She was beautiful and had the world at her fingertips. She found out in December she had lung cancer. She was a smoker. By June, she had lost all of her hair and was unable to move about her house without assistance from a nurse. A few weeks later, she died. You may find this true story to be more touching than a statistic about how many people die, even if you don't know me or the person in the story. It's real. The story is emotionally powerful.

Types of Emotions

There are many types of emotions to which we can appeal. Think about speakers who make us fearful of something. In regions where tornados occur on a regular basis, students can design an element of *fear* into speeches to actuate the audience to keep a 24-hour emergency kit in their house. The government currently uses fear appeals in public service announcements in our rural areas to encourage families to have an emergency plan in case a terrorist event occurs. Emotional connections help motivate an audience to do something or believe something.

Another emotion is *anger*. If we can get an audience angry about something, then we can often get them to do or believe something. You may get an audience to buy used textbooks online by appealing to the emotion of anger. Tell your audience the profit their campus bookstore makes on the used textbooks they sell. You will have everyone's attention.

Speakers can appeal to happy emotions, too, such as *pride*. Think of a patriotic speech that builds on the pride we have in our country. Freedom is a powerful word, and the emotions it can release when used appropriately will surprise you. Maybe a speaker can also appeal to your personal pride in doing a job well. Most people enjoy doing a job well, and they like to be reminded that a work ethic is important.

Think of a speaker trying to get you to donate five dollars to Habitat for Humanity. He may try to make you feel *ashamed* that you willingly spend five dollars for a latte when there are people without homes.

These are just a few of the emotions that you can target effectively in a persuasive argument. It is important to remember that not all emotional appeals work on every audience member the same way. Some people are persuaded by fact, others by emotion. Some people will be touched by an appeal to shame, others will say, "Oh, for crying out loud—big deal—it's not my problem." Therefore, your best choice is to design a speech with a variety of appeals so you have the best chance of reaching the majority of your audience.

Let's take a quick look at the difference between a strictly factual account of an event and one that uses a carefully designed emotional appeal. Look at the difference between the two passages for persuasive speaking in the box on page 193. Which technique would reach the majority of the audience?

Emotional appeals are powerful in persuasive speaking. Without these appeals, it is difficult to persuade. You must, however, be ethical. Using emotional appeals to deceptively manipulate or take advantage of an audience is no different from coercion. Think of the various companies who used fear appeals after the September 11, 2001, tragedy to sell gas masks and other equipment to protect people from terrorism. These gadgets were overpriced and unnecessary. The companies incorporated fear appeals in their advertising by suggesting the possibility of another attack. They took advantage of a fearful public during a time of national tragedy. As the receiver of emotional appeals, think critically before you act. The act of communicating with others carries tremendous responsibility.

Choices and Consequences

Now that you understand the various persuasive techniques, what choices will you make in your daily life relating to your own use of persuasion as well as to analyzing the persuasion of others?

_____

_____

_____

_____

_____

Reality ✔

Factual Account:

Every night in the United States, over 600,000 people are homeless according to Tommy G. Thompson, Secretary of Health and Human Services, in a March 2003 report called *Ending Chronic Homelessness: Strategies for Action*. One of these people could be you. We all need to help the homeless.

Account with Emotional Appeal:

My family celebrates Thanksgiving as its major holiday every year. All of my siblings and their families come home to mom and dad's house where we were raised. The sight of everyone, the assortment of food, and the stories about growing up make this day very special for all of us. We look forward to it each year. As far as I'm concerned, this is the only way to celebrate the Thanksgiving holiday.

But not everyone celebrates the holiday this way. [pause] My brother didn't come home this year. I was very upset when I didn't see him at the table. Mom and Dad said he called to say he had to work and couldn't make it. The normal glow of the Thanksgiving festivities dimmed because my brother wasn't there. Yes, we all talked, ate, laughed, and enjoyed ourselves, but we wanted to know why he didn't make it for the holiday we all held sacred.

I called him to say happy Thanksgiving from the family. All of us were ready to yell and sing when he answered the phone. But, all that greeted me was his answering machine. The look on my face silenced the excitement in the room. My voice stood alone as I said, "Hi, Jim." The happy Thanksgiving part of my message evaporated and out came, "Are you OK? Where are you? Please call when you can. [pause] I love you."

My phone rang at 2 AM. It was Jim. Before I could say a word, the excitement in his voice caught my attention. He told me his closest colleague at work, a 32-year-old man named Ed, had been fired the previous week. Ed had not managed money well and was being evicted from his apartment because he couldn't pay his rent. He and his wife and three young daughters, Laura, Samantha, and Claire, had no place to go, and he was embarrassed and depressed because they would be on the street for Thanksgiving. My brother invited Ed and his family to move in with him temporarily.

Rather than drive home to be with his family, my brother spent the entire day racing around trying to throw together a Thanksgiving dinner for Ed's family and make them feel at home. He apologized to me and asked me to explain the situation to everyone at breakfast. [long pause] I don't think I have ever been more proud of my brother. He never struck me as a generous person, but like a bolt of lightning, he had done the most unselfish act I had ever known. I had always written checks to help the homeless. But my brother took action. His spirit made me see Thanksgiving properly for the first time.

[Note: Keep in mind that an emotional appeal does not have to be this long, but we have included an extended example to demonstrate the variety of emotional appeals you can use.]

Critical Thinking

From the Thanksgiving story in the Reality Check box on page 193, try to identify the following persuasive techniques and how they are used:

Paralanguage:

_____

_____

Language:

_____

_____

Personal Connection:

_____

_____

Emotional Appeal:

_____

_____

Ethical Considerations

When does using an emotional appeal cross the line from effective persuasion to manipulation or coercion?

_____

_____

_____

_____

SUMMARY

One of the most valuable skills a communicator can learn is to recognize the persuasive techniques others use. All advertising is based on the persuasive techniques we have presented here. Listen to any commercial or infomercial to pick out the parts of Monroe's Motivated Sequence. Does it use emotional appeal to help convince or actuate you? As people construct persuasive messages through credibility, logic, and emotional appeal, they are banking on the hope that you aren't thinking critically as you react to the message. If Adam and Megan had thought more critically and analyzed their resources, they would not have faced the possibility of bankruptcy.

In addition to analyzing persuasive messages critically, you can use your improved skills in a positive and ethical manner to make changes in your environment. For example, you may be able to convince someone at your school there should be a rape-awareness day. You may actuate the PTA at your child's school to implement an antibullying program. You may actuate students on your campus to create a fundraising event for a local charity. Too often, students think their opinions don't matter, or they believe they can't make a difference. This is not true. All it takes is one determined person with knowledge of persuasive principles to get the ball rolling.

Key Words

ad hominem
appeal to authority
attention step
bandwagon
casual arguments
circular argument
citations
claim of fact
claim of policy
claim of value
comparative-advantages
credibility
emotional appeal
fallacy
false cause
hasty generalization
inductive reasoning
irrational reasons
logical appeals
Monroe's Motivated Sequence (MMS)
problem-solution
reasoned argument
reasoning from analogy
requesting action
satisfying the need
showing the need
statement-of-reasons
visualization

Crossword 11: Constructing the Persuasive Presentation

Across

3. An error in reasoning.

6. A claim that attempts to convince an audience of whether something is true.

9. Reasons created when unrelated information is used to support a conclusion.

16. Influence created by a celebrity endorsing a product or cause.

17. A persuasive structure revealing the reasons why the goal of a speech will work.

18. A five-part organizational pattern to actuate an audience was developed by _____.

19. A fallacy resulting when another cause could have produced the same phenomenon.

20. A persuasive structure where a communicator tries to convince someone to take action.

21. An argument where the conclusion is the same as the opening statement.

22. Trying to connect with the audience's sense of fear, anger, happiness, or compassion to create an effective persuasive message.

Down

1. An argument developed when a communicator states one concept was created by another concept.

2. A claim that attempts to move a receiver to action.

4. Where concepts are compared with the conclusion that what is true about one concept is also true of the other concept.

5. The reasoning you build into a persuasive speech.

7. A process where facts are selected, analyzed, and then conclusions drawn for an audience.

8. A value judgment audience members make about a communicator.

10. A conclusion drawn from insufficient facts.

11. A fallacy created when a person is attacked rather than the concept.

12. Based on taking specific instances and drawing general conclusions from them.

13. A claim trying to convince an audience that one thing is better than another.

14. A fallacy created when you are asked to do something because everyone else is doing it.

15. A persuasive structure where the speaker tries to convince the audience that one action is better than another.

Crossword 11: Constructing the Persuasive Presentation

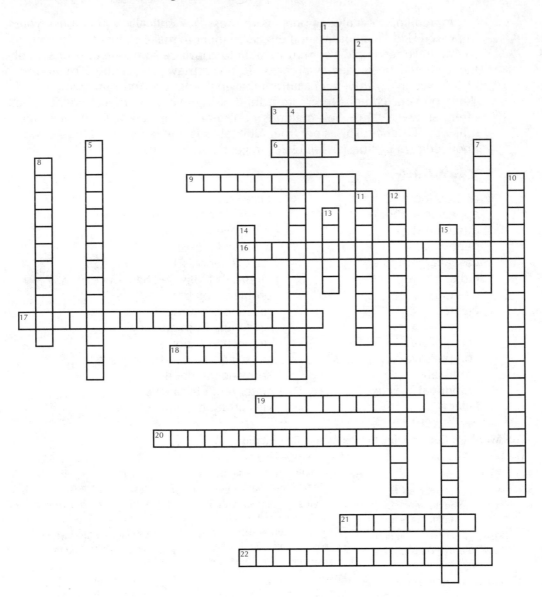

CHAPTER 12

Interviewing

OBJECTIVES

After reading this chapter, you should be able to:
- Identify the elements of an effective resumé
- Explain the importance of personal artifacts in the interview
- Explain the concept of behavioral interviewing
- Answer questions using behavioral interviewing techniques
- Identify unique aspects of phone interviewing
- Describe the elements of a stress interview

Interviewing is a process where a person demonstrates effective communication skills to obtain employment or promotion. Why do we cover interviewing in an oral communication textbook? The answer is quite simple. Interviewing (both the oral process and the written resumé) is the most important piece of persuasion in which you will engage when you complete school. Without a persuasive resumé, you will not get to the interview. And many job applicants who look terrific on paper don't make a good first impression during the interview. Your oral and written skills need to be outstanding.

There are no absolutes in the world of interviewing. The most up-to-date interviewing information changes constantly. Tips for effective resumé writing and interviewing vary from profession to profession. Therefore, in addition to the general tips we provide, we strongly recommend you do a thorough Internet search for interviewing tips in your field before you embark on the interview adventure. A knowledgeable faculty advisor is also a valuable resource.

— Professional Perspective —

An interview is a conversation to determine if a candidate's skills and experiences are a good match to the needs of the organization. You must prepare appropriately for the conversation. This includes, but is not limited to, ensuring your resumé is accurate (no typos please!), researching the company, and presenting yourself in a professional manner.

Quite frankly, your resumé is a reflection of you. It should be clear and concise, listing practical experience as well as academic success. How you format it is a personal choice, but it should be easy to read without filler. If it has a typo or is not professional I won't even look at it. A sloppy resumé speaks volumes about an individual.

All too often, I have interviewed recent college grads who responded to my inquiry about their knowledge of the company I represented with an uninspiring answer along the lines of, "I looked at your Web site when I applied for the job." Simply put, "and . . . ?" Looking at a Web site career page does not constitute research. To prepare for an interview, learn everything you can about the company—including what they do (products, services, etc.), where they're located (local, regional, national, global), how long they've been around, and if possible, how they're doing.

Once you get to the actual interview, don't blow it by not dressing or acting professionally. Dressing for business is the key, regardless if the company allows a casual business environment. There is a fine line between confidence and arrogance. You should be able to speak to the accomplishments and experience listed on your resumé.

Getting an interview is not easy, so don't blow it by not doing everything possible to prepare.

—Dean De Peri
Director, Human Resources
CIGNA HealthCare

Resumés

Most employers only spend about ten seconds glancing at your ***resumé,*** which is a written summary of your accomplishments and capabilities. Imagine trying to read a stack of 60, 150, or over 1,000 resumés to fill one opening in a company. The task is daunting. In order to whittle the pile of applicants down to a manageable size, employers look through the stack very quickly to see if they can eliminate any candidates immediately. Think of this as an altered corporate version of the cliché where "your life flashes before *their* eyes." Only in this case, your life is in print. A resumé immediately goes into the discard pile if it is not visually attractive or easy to read.

An effective resumé must:

- Be visually attractive
- Contain no typos
- Showcase your qualities, strengths, and experience
- Follow the format required by your professional area

To demonstrate the quality differences between an ineffective and an effective resumé, we provide two samples on the following pages. Each is a real resumé created by a student (her name has been changed to protect the innocent). Please don't look ahead to the effective sample, but take a look at the following ineffective sample and see if you can determine some of the problematic issues.

Reality

Wanda Fitzgerald
28 Fuller St., Detroit, Pa 16842
(000) 555-0000
WandaFitzgerald@notcoldmail.kom

Objective	To get a video-editing position
Education	***Mansfield University*** Graduated May 2002 B.S. in Mass Communication
	New York Institute of Photography Currently enrolled for professional certification Home corespondence course Expected graduation December 2002
Experience	***Country Ski and Sports***—**Sales / Bike and ski technician** April 1998–Present • Sales of outdoor products and services to customers. • Repair and assembly of bicycles. • Mounting and testing of ski equipment.
	WNQV 104.5 FM—**On-air announcer** February 2000–Present • On air announcing. • Live remotes and engineering. • Interviews and production of commercials and liners.
	Good Vibrations Entertainment—**Co-owner** May 1998–Present • Formed mobile disc jockey business with partner. • Promoting ourselves. • Building and maintaining our reputation. • Attracting new clients.
	Rossignol Ski Company—**Area Sales Ambassador** November 1998–Present • Attracting new customers to the Rossignol Company. • Promoting the company in the area. • Assisting the sales reps with product displays and demos.

References available upon request

Critical Thinking

Pretend that you are an employer. Write an assessment of Wanda Fitzgerald's resumé.

_____

_____

_____

_____

This resumé does follow the format for her chosen profession; however, it does not highlight her strengths. You'll notice the jobs this student has held have absolutely nothing to do with a video-editing position. This more traditional resumé format places jobs in a centrally-focused position. The format does not sell the student. You'll also notice the information is crammed together without bolding or highlighting to differentiate among its sections. As the employer scans the text, typos create an unfavorable impression (did you catch all three of them?). If there are any typos in a resumé, most applicants are disqualified instantly. Employers look at a resumé as your best piece of work. Nothing about this resumé encourages an employer to look at the candidate more closely.

Some resumé requirements that may vary from person to person or from field to field are:

- Whether to use an objective
- Whether to limit the resumé to one page

In reviewing interviewing research, we found that about 60 percent of sources recommend using an objective whereas 40 percent do not. In making your decision about whether to use one, you should consult with professionals in your field. If you do decide an objective is important, you must keep in mind that this statement is the very first item on the resumé and makes an immediate impression. An objective must be brilliantly written, or you will end up in the discard pile. Everyone knows your objective is to get a job. Don't state the obvious. You must highlight your abilities in the objective.

The best objective uses a format that highlights the applicant's strongest skills

Objective: An xxx position in an organization where yyy and zzz would be needed.

Xxx is the name of the position you seek. Yyy and zzz are the most compelling personal qualities, abilities, or achievements that will communicate your potential value to the organization and will make you stand out from the other of applicants. The research you have previously done to find out what is most important to the employer will provide you with the information to fill in yyy and zzz.

For example:

Objective: A software sales position in an organization where an extraordinary record of generating new accounts, exceeding sales targets, and enthusiastic customer relations would be needed.

The objective is your attention-getting device; it immediately showcases your best skills. When written well, the objective captures the attention of the employer and invites further exploration of the resumé. Consider the difference between the two objectives below.

Ineffective: To get a video-editing position.
Effective: To obtain a video-editing position in a company where enthusiasm, technical skill, and self-motivation are desired.

The effective objective would be a great persuasive statement at the top of the resumé. If Wanda's work experience included a few video-editing jobs, the objective coupled with the job highlights and some effective changes in formatting could be enough to secure an interview. However, because none of her jobs relate to a video-editing career, that format is not to her advantage even with a strong objective. So, let's take a look at a more effective resumé format for Wanda.

Reality ✔

We advised this student to use a different format for her resumé. Analyze the differences.

Wanda Fitzgerald

28 Fuller St. • Detroit, PA 16842
000-555-0000 • WandaFitzgerald@notcoldmail.kom

Qualifications

- Experienced in linear and nonlinear editing procedures. Own Canon XL-1 mini-DV camera. Proficient with AVID and Adobe Premiere 6.0 video-editing software and Cool-Edit BSI, Goldwave, and Multiquence audio-editing software.
- Produced music videos for the bands Backstreet Law and Fourfourteen. Produced promotional videos for Nightwind Studios and Benchmark Audio. Produced various interviews, PSAs, newscasts, and miscellaneous video projects.
- Started own company, Good Vibrations Entertainment. Responsible for inception of idea with partner, self-promoting through marketing, and building the business.
- Experienced in sales, customer service, promoting business, attracting customers, keeping records, and working independently.

Education

Mansfield University, Mansfield, PA
Bachelor of Science—Mass Communication, Broadcasting   **May 2002**
Coursework in TV Production I and II, Writing for Broadcast Media, Television and Radio Announcing

New York Institute of Photography, NYC
Professional Certification   **expected December 2002**
Currently enrolled in home correspondence course

Work Experience

Good Vibrations Entertainment
Co-Owner   **5/98–present**
- Initiated mobile disc jockey business with partner—began with a $20 mixer hooked into a school PA system
- Reinvested to grow the business to approximately 90 jobs per year and own $30,000 of sound and lighting equipment
- Responsibilities include: booking clients, talking to a variety of customers, ensuring customer satisfaction, purchasing and maintaining equipment, handling finances, maintaining Web page, setting up, and performing

WNQV 104.5 FM
On-Air Announcer   **2/00–7/02**
- On-air announcing
- Conducted and engineered live remotes
- Produced commercials and promos, conducted interviews

Country Ski and Sports
Sales/Bike and Ski Technician   **4/98–present**
- Sales of outdoor products and services to customers
- Customer service on various levels from greeting customers to handling dissatisfaction and complaints

This rewrite of the resumé takes advantage of using a proper format to showcase Wanda's skills. It contains the same information, but in a format highlighting the applicant's strengths. The resumé is visually appealing, from the balance of white space to the use of italics and bold. It contains no typos that would immediately disqualify her. This format allows Wanda to put relevant qualifications at the top, selling her immediately. Instead of a huge focus on the jobs, the employer can see she has done some professional work in her field and owns her own equipment.

⇨   **Try It!**   ⇦

Wanda's resumé is still lacking in some important areas. She only shows her work history and qualifications. What other categories should she include on her resumé to help sell herself?

_____

_____

_____

_____

Page limitations are another area where you need to check resumé standards in your field. At one time, resumés were only one page in length. That is still true in some fields. One of our former students wanted to work on Capitol Hill. She sent out 100 copies of a two-page resumé. She was bewildered when she did not get a single inquiry. Then, she did some more research and found the norm on Capitol Hill was a one-page resumé; anything over one page went into the trash immediately. She retooled her resumé to one page and received a number of interviews. A two-page or greater resumé may be perfectly acceptable in certain fields. In these professions, you would not want to limit yourself to only one page if you had enough relevant information to include.

Remember, many large companies scan resumés. This means no human being looks at your resumé initially. Instead, a computer scans each incoming resumé for key words. Be sure to emphasize qualities valued by employers, such as "organized" or "innovative." Keep in mind that fancy formatting and marbled papers do not scan. Those choices would put you immediately into the discard pile. If the company requires electronic submission, in most cases, the text of your resumé must be left-justified, with no formatting. Most company Web sites explain their process and format requirements for resumé submissions.

Once you have perfected your resumé and sent it to a potential employer, you should prepare for the next step. If you have effectively persuaded the employer to contact you, you need to remember the material from chapter 5 on electronic channels. An immature or inappropriate e-mail address or message on your telephone answering machine can halt the interview process. The potential employer looks at the e-mail address on the resumé and may listen to your answering machine recording. Everything must be professional. If all goes well, you will get an invitation to continue the interview process.

— **Professional Perspective** —

As a recruiter who skims through several resumés a week, a potential candidate has about 30 seconds to capture my attention before I'll move on. Some of the more important areas are:

Presentation: Your resumé should look professional and does not need to include fancy fonts, graphics, or a lot of bells and whistles. Often, if you are sending via e-mail or replying via a Web site, they do not transfer in their original format.

- Use a standard one-inch margin.
- Single space between listings and double space between sections.
- Highlight items using a boldface rather than changing fonts. Items that you want to stand-out can be bolded, such as your name, the employer's name, or the name of the institution.
- Use bullets to highlight accomplishments. Keep bulleted items to one or two lines. Bullets make a resumé look clean, clear, and crisp.
- No spelling, grammar, punctuation, or typographical errors (a personal pet peeve . . . no interview from me).

Be Brief: More does not mean better. Do not include every detail of your work history; a resumé should highlight your experience and accomplishments. Your finished version ideally should be one or two pages.

Never Lie: Aside from the moral implications, if you are hired and your fabrications are discovered, you can be dismissed.

In the end, for the best results, be concise yet compelling.

Julie Allen
Sr. Human Resources Specialist
The Summit Federal Credit Union

Ethical Considerations

What are the ethical implications of making exaggerated statements on your resumé? Is it ethical to say that you volunteered for community service if your fraternity or sorority required that work of you? Is it ethical to imply you worked somewhere longer than you actually did or had more responsibilities than you actually had?

_____

_____

_____

_____

_____

INTERVIEWS

Once your resumé attracts an employer's attention and leads to an interview opportunity, you must diligently prepare for the interview. Some students think they can just talk and be themselves. This casual attitude is not what an employer desires. Employers prefer concise, logical answers to their questions.

To be effective in an interview, you must:
- Spend time preparing for the interview
- Make a great first impression
- Be able to answer questions effectively
- Be prepared for phone interviews
- Be prepared for stress interviews
- Communicate effectively after the interview

Spend Time Preparing

Once you get the interview confirmation, there are a number of things you can do to plan for success. Make sure you have a correct address and directions for exactly where you need to go. If it is a long distance, or in a complicated place, you can use one of the Internet mapping services such as MapQuest or GoogleMaps to plan your route and also take a street map in case you make a wrong turn. You should plan for where you are going to park your car as well. Remember to take the phone number along in case you have an unusual complication. Don't hesitate to ask questions of your contact person at the organization. You are in much better shape if you overplan than if you get lost.

Another question to ask the contact person is whether you will be interviewing with an individual or a group. Ask for the name(s) of the people with whom you will be interviewing. If possible, look the people up ahead of time on the company Web site. This will give you a familiarity with how they look and possibly some information about them. Keep in mind that names don't always give away the sex of a person. Don't assume that people are male or female just because they have a certain name. You don't want to look shocked when the person you thought was going to be a man is actually a woman.

Research the company so that you know all of the basic information about it. We once had a job applicant who arrived for an interview and asked how many students were enrolled at our institution. That immediately told us the person had not done any preparation for the interview.

If it has been a few days or weeks since the original appointment was scheduled, it is a good idea to phone your contact a day before the interview is scheduled just to confirm the details of your appointment. Also be prepared that there are sometimes corporate or personal emergencies that arise, and you might arrive for the interview and be asked to come back another day.

Be aware that anything can happen. A colleague told us about an unusual circumstance. Her friend arrived at a job interview, and the interviewer asked her to drive them to lunch. She was horrified because her car was littered with fast-food wrappers, coffee cups, and multiple personal items strewn on the floor and back seat. What would the perception of the interviewer be after that short ride?

Finally, remember that you are "on" the entire time. From the moment you step out of your car, people may be watching you from windows. The same goes with your departure. Until you are safely down the highway, you should be a model of a responsible employee.

Making a Great Impression

The *first impression* is extremely important. Think back to chapter 2 on perception. Most people decide in the first minute whether you are competent, whether they will like you, and whether you belong in their company. The way you look when the interviewer first sees you, the way you move as you enter the room, and how you shake an interviewer's hand can affect your chances of being successful.

— Professional Perspective —

An important lesson I learned in an organizational communication class was that your hand-shake is a great way to make a good first impression. My professor in college would not let us leave the classroom until we had successfully completed a professional handshake, which was classified as a firm grip while looking straight into the other person's eyes. It took a few tries to get it right, but I am still using this technique in my professional environment. My company had an open position where many candidates who were recent college graduates applied for an entry-level position. One candidate in particular had a handshake like a cold, dead fish. This was an instant turn off for me. I immediately considered him to be weak and untrustworthy. This impression carried through the interview, and I was uncertain whether he would be an asset to our team and company. He did not get the job. My first impression of him through his handshake was never proved wrong through his responses to questions. In a professional setting, a firm handshake is necessary for a good first impression; you cannot afford to make into a bad impression.

—Angela Dickson
Senior Coordinator of Communications
American Architectural Manufacturers Association

You must choose your personal artifacts carefully. For example, Maurice walks into an interview with an advertising agency in a crisply pressed, jet-black suit. He has a silver dress shirt and black silk tie. His shoes are shined to reflect the light. His belt is black leather with a silver tip. Maurice's appearance places him two steps ahead of his competition when he is introduced to the interviewer.

Anita is not aware of how important artifact choices are, however. While she can afford much more expensive clothing than Maurice, she has made some unwise choices. She chooses a flowery dress that is not pressed. Her shoes have open toes and heels because it is August. The tattoo around her ankle is visible through her nude-colored pantyhose.

Maurice communicates success and confidence. There is nothing in his appearance an interviewer could interpret as objectionable. He sticks to the basic principles of a corporate dress code for that company. He realizes, however, if he were interviewing in a more traditional corporation, he should wear a dark suit, a white shirt, and a conservative tie. Anita is clueless. A flowery dress is simply too casual. Her visible tattoo gives the employer personal information that could be interpreted in a negative manner. (It is quite possible that Maurice has a tattoo, but it is covered by his suit and not visible to the interviewer.) The best choice is to analyze the company and be as conservative as possible.

Attire and overall appearance are essential to your success in the interview. You may not be able to afford all natural fibers in clothing or gold and sterling silver jewelry, but you can choose colors and fabrics that make you look good. Employees in many companies have a specific look, and you must find out what it is. In some cases, the dress code is casual, and you may look out of place in a formal suit. Research the dress code for that specific company.

Get comfortable with dress clothing and begin building your professional look while you are still in school. If you and your family do not have a lot of money, ask for items such as shoes, jewelry, ties, scarves, and belts for holidays and birthdays.

⇨ Try It! ⇦

Do an inventory. List what pieces of interview attire you already own.

_____

_____

_____

List what you still need to acquire.

_____

_____

_____

Make a plan to acquire these items by your senior year in college.

_____

_____

_____

Clothes are a costume. You must look the part. While you may enjoy being an individual by wearing green hair and face hardware now, that look will not be accepted in most companies. You must also look like the people who have the job you desire. In most companies, the dress code is conservative. Your first impression will make or break you.

Choices and Consequences

You have choices as a college student. You need to think ahead to the consequences. A female who gets a tattoo around her ankle and then wants a corporate job will have a limited wardrobe choice since the tattoo will be seen unless she always wears slacks and opaque stockings. Men may believe tattoos will be covered, but think about going to the health club with other people in your company. As soon as you change in the locker room, your tattoos are visible to others. While tattoos may be widely accepted by your peers, the people who are hiring and promoting you are usually at least a generation ahead of you. Remember attribution theory? Interviewers may assign a negative meaning to people who get tattoos and body piercings, thinking they are easily influenced by fads and cultural trends. Therefore, the interviewers may draw the conclusion that the interviewee cannot think or act independently.

Remember to select clothes that complement your body type. Here are some of the fundamental rules for conservative interviewing.

Dos

- One earring per ear (no earrings for men)
- Either a necklace or a bracelet
- One ring per hand
- Shined shoes
- Plain, conservative tie (no cartoon characters!)

Don'ts

- No open-toed/open-heeled shoes
- No sleeveless outfits (women), no short-sleeved shirts (men)
- No gaudy or noticeable makeup
- No work boots/sneakers

⇨ Try It! ⇦

Do a quick Internet search to find three specific recommendations about clothing, jewelry, or appearance for an interview that have not been discussed here.

_____

_____

_____

Once the interviewer sees you, you have made your first impression. But it doesn't stop there. As mentioned earlier, your handshake will add or detract from the first impression. A firm handshake sends the nonverbal message of confidence—a quality desired by most interviewers. Wiping sweaty hands on your pants or fumbling with papers so you can extend your hand for a handshake sends a message of incompetence and lack of professional interpersonal experience.

The requirements of making a good first impression vary with culture. For instance, in U.S. culture, business cards are exchanged after a meeting is completed. In some cultures, however, business cards are exchanged as you meet someone for the first time. If you don't know the culture, you could ruin an interview in the first few moments. If you do any business travel or have the potential to meet someone from another culture in this country, you should research the culture carefully to determine what you need to do to make a good first impression.

Answering Questions Effectively

Once you have made the first impression, you need to be able to sound intelligent when you speak. You must be aware of nonverbals such as volume, rate, and inflection. Some people speak very loudly or very quickly when they are nervous, which can be annoying to others. You should also work on the coherency and uniqueness of your answers to questions.

— Professional Perspective —

In Japanese culture, the handling and presentation of business cards are paramount because they are an extension of one's self. When meeting a Japanese executive for the first time, the business card should be skillfully removed without fumbling and presented to the executive by holding the card in front of you with two hands. The executive will always take the card with his two hands, grabbing the card by the lower ends with two fingers. Accept a card from the Japanese executive using the same procedure.

Once you have accepted the card, you will talk to the executive by holding the card in front of you at chest level. Never look him in the eye. In Asian cultures, this is considered aggressive and threatening behavior.

The business card should be placed in a respectable place only—a cardholder or breast shirt pocket. Placing a card in a wallet or a money clip is considered very insulting. When working with any internationally based organization, it is a worthwhile activity to understand the culture of the home country.

—Robert. H. Christie
Senior Public Relations Manager
Dow Jones and Company

It is essential that your answers to questions demonstrate that you have a basic understanding of the company. Research is imperative. Let's say you are interviewing for a job at a famous ice-cream company and you ask, "So what kinds of ice cream do you manufacture?", or "How many employees are in your company?" The immediate impression is that you aren't prepared. The interviewer would obviously think, "If you can't take the time to look up simple facts, why should I consider you for this job?"

A common concept in interviewing is called behavioral interviewing. In a **behavioral interview,** employers expect interviewees to provide detailed stories that demonstrate competence in a particular area (Half, 1993). Recruiters value interviews as an employment tool because applicants showcase their oral communication skills, interpersonal skills, critical-thinking skills, leadership skills, and teamwork skills (Moody, Stewart, & Bolt-Lee, 2002). To be successful

Reality ✔

Behavioral interviewing is used to weed out "polished" people who interview well without saying anything. Companies use this technique to find the candidate who can offer specific examples of the skills they possess.

Behavioral interviewing requires candidates to respond with specific examples of past experiences rather than generalized or hypothetical responses. At the root of this interview style is the belief that past performance is the most accurate predictor of future performance. Typical behavior-based questions begin with, 'Tell me about a time when . . .' or 'Give me an example of . . .' and require candidates to provide a complete, three-part response in a format known as SAR: situation, action and result.

While behavior-based interviewing is not a panacea for complex recruitment and retention challenges, it is a time-tested methodology for improving hiring results. It has been studied, evaluated, and practiced for more than 30 years and is a central component of selection strategy at some of the world's best known companies. (Kursmark, 2007) at behavioral interviewing, a candidate must be prepared to use stories to demonstrate their competence for the job in a meaningful and memorable way.

You must tell a strong 1–2 minute personal story that has characters, a plot, a climax, and a resolution. If you answer the question, "What is your greatest strength?" with "I'm very calm under pressure; I can really get the job done; I don't sweat the small stuff," you haven't said anything. The interviewer will not remember these clichés. There is no way you can make an impression with that answer.

Instead, when Veronica is asked that question, she answers with a one-minute story. "Well, I'm very calm under pressure. For example, when I was working at the ice-cream shop, a customer received a cone that had a hole in it. It was a small hole in the bottom, but the ice cream began to drip through it, because it was a hot day. The woman was so irate that the ice cream had dripped on her suit, she came up to me and threw the ice cream in my face. I had to stand there in front of other customers and handle the situation without losing my cool. My first reaction was to get really angry and say something I would have regretted, but I bit my tongue, wiped off my face, and said very nicely, 'Is something wrong?' And with that, all of the other customers turned their heads and stared at her. Once the focus was on her rather than on her actions, she stormed out of the ice-cream shop. While I was disappointed I couldn't make her happy, at least the other customers complimented me on the way I handled the situation."

Note that this is a 1–2 minute answer. It meets all of the criteria of storytelling in that it has characters, a plot, a climax, and a resolution. It paints a visual picture the interviewer is not likely to forget. And it answers the question. This type of answer will make Veronica memorable to the interviewer and much more likely to get the job.

Some of the basic questions you should be prepared to answer are:

1. Why should we hire you?

2. What is your greatest strength?

3. What is your greatest weakness?

4. What accomplishment has given you the greatest satisfaction?

5. What motivates you to put forth your greatest effort?

6. Why do you want to work for our company?

However, as more and more interviewers are looking for behavioral interview answers, you may find that you are asked questions that lead you directly to a story such as:

7. Tell me how you handled your last conflict.

8. Tell me about a time when you had to work on a team.

9. Tell me about the last time you had to handle a really stressful situation.

As you create your answers to these questions, keep your interviewer in mind—just as you think about your audience in public speaking. If you answer, "Why do you want to work for our company?" with "Because I really need a job," or "Because I find this company to be prestigious," you are not thinking about your audience. Your answer is egocentric; you should respond with information that is useful for the company. Show how your greatest strength can benefit the company. A personal story about your dependability and how that quality will benefit the employer can work to your advantage.

As you get ready to create your stories, it will be helpful for you to prepare a list of your skills and personality traits. Skills are competencies you've learned, such as computer programs, problem solving, or speaking a foreign language. Personality traits are desirable qualities you possess, such as being dependable, energetic, and detail oriented. Once you have developed your list of skills and personality traits, you can then create your stories to highlight them. Good stories will make you stand out.

⇨ **Try It!** ⇦

Take one of the six interview questions and write an answer that includes a true story from your personal life. The story should have characters, a plot, a climax, and a resolution.

_____

_____

_____

_____

_____

_____

_____

Sometimes the interviewer is looking for your ability to think creatively. The interviewer may ask a **brainteaser**—an open-ended hypothetical question that tests the problem-solving ability of a potential employee and necessitates a factual, logical, descriptive answer. Brainteasers are common in interviews for creative jobs. "Why use logic puzzles, riddles, and impossible questions? The goal . . . is to assess a general problem-solving ability rather than a specific competency" (Poundstone, 2003, p. 20). Here's an example of a brainteaser: "How much does the ice in a hockey rink weigh?"

Brainteasers are also used in noncomputer-related industries such as those that deal with the public or the law. The goal of this type of interview question is to test your experience with problem solving as well as your ability to remain calm under pressure. Many brainteasers do not have a correct answer. Your verbal ability to piece together logical thoughts in an impromptu manner is important. The brainteaser is somewhat different from the storytelling answers. The details and sequential logic in your answer must impress the interviewer.

Telephone Interviews

Telephone interviews add an interesting dimension to the interview process. This is a good news/bad news situation. The good news is you don't have to worry about your attire or posture. You can use interview notes with answers to potential questions and lists of skills or qualities that you don't want to forget. The bad news is your vocal technique, vocabulary, and verbal style is all an interviewer hears. Therefore, you must concentrate on your grammar and the completeness of your thoughts. Stand up while you talk so you have the best breath support for energy and vocal quality. You can tape your notes and resumé on the wall. Also remember you will have no nonverbal feedback. You cannot tell whether the interviewer is smiling and nodding or looking disgusted. Think positive thoughts. A positive image of the interviewer will help you remain calm.

Stress Interviews

Another situation you should be prepared to handle is the stress interview. In a **_stress interview,_** the employer will test you to your limits. I (KSY) had an accounting major who went for an interview to be a financial planner. The interviewer looked at her and said, "OK, Heather, here is a stack of travel brochures. I'll be back in 20 minutes, and I expect you to have a persuasive presentation ready for me concerning where I should go on vacation." He exited the room. When he got back and heard her presentation (using Monroe's Motivated Sequence!), he immediately launched into the questions. She was not allowed to use any material twice for her answers to 16 questions. When he asked her what her greatest weakness was, she paused for a brief moment, and he badgered her with, "What's the matter Heather, do you think you are perfect?" In this situation, the employer is trying to see how she will hold up under stress. Although this may seem unfair, a job as a financial planner entails dealing with very unhappy customers when the stock market goes down, and the employer needs to know she can handle pressure.

One of my (HPT) students who had a degree in broadcasting interviewed for a video-editing position. When the student arrived at the studio, he was handed video clips from a breaking story aired earlier the same day. He was given 30 minutes to cut his own version of a news package for the station. He was given no training or explanation of the company's equipment in the editing suite. He finished creating his version of the story within the time limit. The supervisor thanked him for his time and said the senior producer would contact him upon screening the package. No further questions were asked. The interview was over.

A third example of a stressful interview situation is if you are interviewed with other applicants. There are times when all applicants are brought into the same room and asked to answer questions in front of one another. We know of two people who have reported being asked to answer the question, "Why should we hire you instead of the specific person on your left?"

Thinking about the three scenarios above, it is important to find out what the interview norm is in your field. Are you likely to run into stress interviews? Make sure you can do what you say you can do on your resumé, because you may be tested on the spot. Any hesitation on your part in performing a task or answering a question may give the interviewer a bad impression. Be prepared and remain as relaxed as possible to handle whatever the interviewer throws at you.

Reality ✔

Many companies now give spelling tests during the interview. If a job you are seeking requires a lot of writing, be prepared for a spelling test on words commonly used in your profession. Typing tests for speed and accuracy are also given. Employers may ask you, especially if you are applying for a teaching job, to hand write an essay so they can check your ability to spell and the clarity of your writing. You may experience writing tests on a computer in the corporate world.

Communicating after the Interview

It is essential that you use the utmost caution when writing to a prospective employer in *post-interview communication*. While hand-written thank-you notes should be sent, one misspelling in a thank-you note or e-mail will reveal additional information about your ability. Be especially sure to get the correct spelling of the interviewer's name and title. You can always type a thank-you note in a word processing program to check your spelling, and then hand copy it onto an appropriate note card. It is also wise to write your e-mail the same way.

— Professional Perspective —

A former intern contacted me regarding opportunities for future employment. The student was graduating from a prestigious East Coast university and had been reliable and hard working throughout the course of the summer.

The intern was extremely excited about two possible opportunities I could offer, so I contacted my associates. The positions were in competitive fields; without my assistance, it would have been difficult to obtain an inside contact. My associates asked for a resumé and letter of inquiry to be sent to their e-mail addresses.

I expected the intern's transmittals would be forthcoming, but my colleagues did not receive any e-mail from the intern for nearly two weeks. When I finally received an e-mail from the intern, the intern had decided to inquire about only one of the positions. I had expected the intern to contact both of these individuals regardless of the intern's preferences and as a professional courtesy to my colleagues and myself.

When the intern finally drafted a letter to my associate, I received a call from this colleague who was shocked at the typographical errors and lack of formality in the intern's e-mail. The intern also did not send a resumé. The opportunity was lost.

When attempting to make a virtual impression on a potential employer, carefully draft and proof your letter of inquiry, resumé, and any follow-up e-mail, always address your potential employer with a professional tone and formality, and promptly respond to any messages regarding the opportunity.

—Anonymous
A member of the Professional Staff at a Large Museum

As a student, you may not think about the personal implications that are present when someone agrees to give you a reference or to help you make a professional connection. Rather than just providing a critical assessment of your skills, the person is putting his or her reputation on the line. Inappropriate or unprofessional behavior on your part reflects on the person recommending you. Many professors and professionals are extremely cautious about giving recommendations because they have been burned by students and other colleagues. A recommendation is a transaction involving mutual respect. If Professor Smith gives Dominick a contact person, Dominick is obligated to contact that person and to let Professor Smith know he has followed through. Additionally, it is respectful to keep Professor Smith informed of the process, since she put her reputation on the line to help Dominick. A thank-you note to Professor Smith would also be in order. All of this reflects on Dominick's credibility.

SUMMARY

Remember interviewing communication is a package deal. Your written material allows you to be selected for a job interview. But once you walk into a corporate environment, the employment pendulum swings away from your writing to your appearance and verbal communication skills and style. You must concentrate on verbal and nonverbal messages throughout your exposure to a potential employer. Everything you do and say is remembered. Practice and improve your written and oral skills while you are still in school. Remember to concentrate on your vocal technique during telephone interviews. Electronic interviews focus on only part of the communication package. Vocal technique and use of paralanguage become your selling points. It is important to develop your communication skills early. Sell your ability during an interview in a warm and friendly way. Your future depends on consistent communication skills and style.

Key Words

behavioral interview

brainteaser

first impression

interviewing

post-interview communication

resumé

stress interview

telephone interview

Crossword 12: Interviewing

Across

3. A written document detailing your employment history, skills, and strengths.
8. These answers must include characters, plot, climax, and resolution.
9. An interview that focuses on your vocal style, grammar, and completeness of thought.

Down

1. These should be sent immediately after the interview. They should be hand written.

2. A type of interviewing where applicants must be prepared to tell stories to demonstrate their competence, strengths, and skills.
4. Since most people make a strong first impression in the first 30 seconds, your _____ must be impeccable.

5. An interview question that assesses your ability to generate facts and logical sequencing while remaining calm.
6. A process where a person demonstrates competence through communication skills with the specific goal of gaining employment.
7. An interview where your interview skills are tested under a deadline.

CHAPTER 13

Working in Teams

OBJECTIVES

After reading this chapter, you should be able to:

- Explain the organizational elements of an initial team meeting
- Describe the importance of discovering the needs of team members
- Describe the importance of a team contract
- Describe the three styles of team leadership
- Explain how to select a leader
- Define task versus social elements of teamwork
- Explain how to keep proper records
- Identify ways to motivate team members
- Identify elements of effective planning for meetings
- List the six steps of The Standard Agenda
- Explain why The Standard Agenda is effective for problem solving
- List three types of team presentations

Groups are integral to modern life. Everyone congregates in groups during family functions, at school, during community or religious events, as well as in corporate life. At other times, we are assigned to work in groups. Groups help people to accomplish social and professional tasks that benefit their family, community, religious establishment, and business organization.

Groups are composed of individuals with similar ideas or goals coming together to complete a task or to solve a problem for a common good. *Teams* do exactly the same thing, but they go one step further. What makes a team different from a standard work group is the sense of cohesiveness they experience while working together for a brief period of time. An ideal team becomes cohesive as team members work to accomplish their task. This cohesiveness can be seen and felt by other people who aren't even part of the team. There are many facets to good team problem solving because you must work on a task and deal with the intricacies of interpersonal differences at the same time. Only when you combine effective task work with effective interpersonal skills do you have a true working team. Some groups never achieve team status.

There are many task groups in the workplace, but many are comprised of people who don't feel a sense of belonging, don't support a common goal, and don't worry about their interactions with each other. This is not a team. Some corporations use the team concept in the workplace successfully. By using the word "teams," corporations encourage a spirit of family, cohesiveness, and productivity. However, some corporations promoting the team philosophy still do not achieve their goal. Many employees never actively contribute to this spirit even though they do their work. These members hold the group back from becoming a team. Everyone must fully cooperate with other members throughout the duration of a task to achieve the team label. Forming a team is an ideal goal for any small group working on a task.

AN EFFECTIVE BEGINNING

So how do you become a team? The first few minutes of interacting with a new group of people present the same challenges as a first impression in an interpersonal relationship. Members may like or dislike each other based on their appearance or their nonverbals or preconceived notions about each other. The group must become cohesive quickly and forget their differences in order to be effective and complete the task.

For example, you walk into your oral communication class on the day the teacher is starting to talk about communicating in groups. Then, the teacher announces you will be doing a group project and assigns students to specific groups. You immediately think this isn't fair, but the teacher is actually preparing you for a potential team experience. You soon discover you are working with Tony, Nancy, Juan, George, and DeShara. Your disappointment mounts quickly because Tony is in your group. He hasn't come to most class sessions all term. When Tony is there, he is obstinate and argumentative. You are not looking forward to dealing with him. You are somewhat thankful, however, that DeShara is in your group, since she expresses her opinions in a positive way.

You meet with your group for the first time. If you don't know the people in your group, it makes it more difficult to talk to them effectively. Spend some time getting to know one another. The next task is to assess everyone's skills, goals, and needs. Groups often fail to talk about the skills each member brings to the task; this is an error that may prevent a team from ever forming. An initial skills assessment is necessary to determine who is good at research, writing, editing, proofreading, and visual and oral presentation. Once you know who can do what, members can be assigned to the right tasks. It is obviously self-defeating to assign the final draft randomly to someone who can't write. Assess member skills immediately.

As your team members talk about their skills, you discover the following:

- Tony says he is good at computer layout and graphics. He likes to make information look good on paper.
- Nancy says she is an excellent writer and editor. She pays a lot of attention to detail.

— **Professional Perspective** —

The most useful function of any member of a team is based on the old saying, "A chain is no stronger than its weakest link." Everyone on a team has to realize the team's strengths and weaknesses and adjust their plan based on those attributes.

In the news business, it takes a well-oiled team to get stories on the air. Reporters, producers, camera people, and audio techs work in the field and coordinate their actions with assignment editors and producers back at home base. When there is a breakdown in teamwork, bad things can happen like missed deadlines. While working for a major news network during a presidential campaign, a new producer didn't realize the reporter he was working with was strong on reporting and doing live shots but weak on writing. He left the reporter alone to write his script. The result was a blank computer screen with less than 30 minutes to go before air.

You need to know how good your teammates really are and play to their strengths in order to get the best possible job done.

—Tom Donahue
Assignment Manager
Court TV

Ethical Considerations

What are the ethical considerations of telling the group that you are strong at something when you really are weak?

_____

_____

_____

_____

- Juan says he is creative. He likes to do original research, think of new approaches to material, and come up with unique ideas. He also enjoys talking to people.
- George says he is very task oriented. He likes to lead a group and make sure they are progressing through the task. He likes to preplan and is interested in being the group leader if no one objects.
- DeShara says she is a good critical thinker. She likes to analyze ideas and find flaws and positive qualities in arguments.
- You are a little shy. You want to be involved, but you can't see yourself confronting Tony and DeShara. You like to take notes, and so you offer to record all of the ideas and minutes for the group. You also enjoy research, so you can work on your own. But if anyone needs a hand, you offer to help.

All group members should reach a common understanding of the goals of each member. What does each person want out of the experience? If some of the members are willing to work hard to achieve an A on a project but others want to do minimal work for a C or D, you already have conflicting goals. An initial conversation about goals can save a lot of misunderstandings and hard feelings later. In the workplace as well, we end up on committees where we have a really exciting project to do, and everyone is committed to doing their best. On other committees, the task may be "busywork" where everyone knows no one will ever look at their work and evaluate it. In that case, we may decide just to get the task done and not put a lot of effort into it. The clearer the members are about their goals, the more cohesive the group will be and the closer they will be to ideal team status.

Critical Thinking

Typically, what are your goals for a group project?

_____

_____

_____

Everyone says they will do whatever it takes to get an A on the project. You are skeptical, however, because you know Tony and Nancy have not done stellar work in the class so far. When you hear them say that, DeShara says, "Tony, you are never in class—are you sure we can count on you to do quality work?" Tony says, "Yeah, I just don't like going to class, but my computer work is spectacular. I'll bring in a copy of a report I did in high school, and you tell me if you've ever turned in anything that looked that good." DeShara says, "You're on! Make sure you bring it to the next meeting."

— Professional Perspective —

International differences might make the meeting challenging until you understand how everybody communicates.

In the United States, people change their reactions to others based on age, but only slightly. In Korea, if you are around anyone who is older, there is not much contact with them. If the older person speaks, you don't look at them. There are specific verbs and nouns used to signify that you have respect for them. You will never go against what an older person has to say. You can't express disagreement with their opinion unless you know them extremely well.

It would be easy to see how an American entering a Korean group would be seen as rude and/or arrogant when h/she offered a conflicting viewpoint. At the same time, a Korean who enters an American workgroup might not be willing to share a point of view and be seen as incompetent for not having an opinion. By doing what each has been trained to do through social communication, they will actually be giving a poor impression to group members even though they believe themselves to be acting in an effective manner.

Hyun Mook Kim
Former International Student
Mansfield University

In your first meeting, everyone begins with the premise that the group would like to do well as a team. Whether it will actually happen is up to the long-term efforts of each member. Doing an inventory of members' skills does not guarantee success. If a member fails to follow through with a commitment, simply knowing what he or she is good at doing doesn't do the group much good. However, an honest assessment during the members' skills inventory can be an effective beginning to bringing the group together as a team.

MEMBERS' NEEDS

To facilitate your group becoming a team, it is a good idea to talk about and analyze each ***member's needs***. It's easier to work interpersonally if you understand one another. Some people need a lot of encouragement; they need to hear people say they are doing a good job. Other people are self-satisfied and find comments like "good idea!" to be condescending. Some people need to be in charge. Others have a high need for organization. And others just want to goof off. The more you know about people's needs, the better you can interact with them. If all members choose to interact effectively on an interpersonal level, your group will be well on the way toward a team feeling.

George suggests everyone should make a statement about his or her personal needs, but his nonverbals suggest he isn't sincere. Nancy looks at George and says, "You think this is stupid, don't you?" George replies, "Well, sort of. I've never had to do this with other people before. It is weird to talk about my needs. But as I think about projects I've done before, I've been disappointed in the lack of feedback by group members regarding the research I've collected. I'd like to know what they think is good or bad." Tony says, "I know what you mean George. Every time I get a paper back, the teacher says, 'The ideas are not written well, but the layout is great.' I sure wish they'd explain why it isn't written well." DeShara says, "It is important to me that you listen when I talk. I get really irate when people don't look at me and pay attention to my ideas. A simple 'good idea' once in a while would be nice too." You know it is important for you to feel valued and included in the team. But because you are shy, you don't feel that you can say this to everyone. So, you don't share your feelings. This decision is not a wise one because the other members of the group don't know how to support you properly during the task.

Critical Thinking
List two personal needs you have that will be important for you to share with your group:

Tony, George, and DeShara have provided valuable information to other team members. DeShara's simple statement lets every team member know it is important to make eye contact and to pay attention to her when she is talking. Think about the hard feelings this team avoids later by simply having this small piece of information about DeShara.

Choices and Consequences

Describe the most difficult person you've had to work with.

_____

_____

_____

What choices did you make?

_____

_____

What were the consequences?

_____

_____

What would you do differently now?

_____

_____

TEAM CONTRACT

You may want to think about a written *team contract*. While this may not happen in the business world, we find it is extremely useful for students. The purpose of a contract is to outline what the working expectations are for each team member. You might also talk about penalties for not meeting individual obligations. In this way, there should be less misunderstanding on an interpersonal level as the task stages develop.

One example of a team contract has six sections:

1. A team goal
2. A list of what each member will do
3. A list of what the members will not do
4. A list of penalty points for each of the items in numbers 2 and 3: For example, "For each missed meeting, a member will lose five points for an excused absence (defined as . . .) and 10 points for an unexcused absence (defined as . . .). Think ahead for potential problems.

5. A list of the roles of team members (include the leader, secretary, and others)

6. A list of the strengths of each participating member

The contract is particularly important if you have a peer-grading element for the project. You may actually critique group members at the conclusion of the project, and it will be easier to assign points later with a solid contract. It is important to have a peer critique after any team project. Even if you don't have the opportunity to grade one another, you can still do a contract and share your reviews verbally or in writing once the project is completed.

STYLES OF LEADERSHIP

Before you discuss who will be the leader, everyone should decide what style of leadership works best for him or her. There are three types of leadership: authoritarian, laissez-faire, and democratic. ***Authoritarian leaders*** tell people what to do. They don't ask a lot of questions, don't get input, they make all the decisions and expect people to follow their orders. ***Laissez-faire leaders*** are laid back. They are "hands off," letting the group do as it pleases. They are not involved in much decision making and don't synthesize needs and ideas. ***Democratic leaders*** are characterized by their ability to solicit and synthesize ideas, attend to people's needs, keep the group on task, and reach decisions that consolidate the concerns of each member of the group.

⇨   **Try It!**   ⇦

Based on the descriptions in the text, which group member in our example would be the best . . .

Authoritarian leader _____

Laissez-faire leader _____

Democratic leader _____

The best leader for most discussion/task groups is going to be the one who can be flexible with all of these styles. There are times when the leader needs to back off and let the team run with an idea. At other times, the team may be unmotivated, and the leader should move into authoritarian mode, telling people what to do. The democratic approach works well most of the time because the leader is soliciting ideas and synthesizing feedback. In all teams, it is important for all members to articulate clearly which leadership type is most effective for them. In this way, whoever becomes the leader can adapt to the needs of the members. It is much more difficult for a leader to be effective if she doesn't know how you like to be treated. If you are the one who is selected to be the leader, you will need to finesse your skills. Try to move out of your normal comfort zone if you rely on only one of these styles. Be fair to everyone and use the appropriate leadership style at the right time. You need to help your group feel that you care about their success and well-being.

— **Professional Perspective** —

The single most important skill one needs to perfect in order to be successful in a team environment is learning how to listen. It's very easy in chaotic, high-stress situations and corporate meetings to stay focused on what you as an individual have on your mind. Inevitably, everyone in your group falls into that trap, and it becomes almost impossible to make any forward progress. In addition, most people get caught up in being vocal about their own ideas with no one actually listening to what is being said. Lots of time, energy, and good ideas get lost. The trick to listening successfully and effectively in a team environment can be summarized in three steps. First, absorb what is being said by the other group members. Second, incorporate the good ideas and thoughts you hear with your own. Finally, present your clear and concise ideas on how to accomplish your team's goals to the rest of the group. If you follow these steps, you will consistently be seen as a valuable leader within your team.

Apprendre à écouter aux autres est le talent le plus important à développer lorsque l'on considère le travaille en groupe. Dans un environnement chaotique, bruyant et tendu, et aussi dans les rendez-vous incorpores, il est facile de rester fermé sur soi plutôt que de se tourner vers les autres. Il est inévitable, alors, pour chaque membre de l'équipe de rester dans son propre monde et tomber dans ce cercle vicieux où il est impossible d'aller de l'avant. De plus, tout le monde a tendance à parler uniquement de ce qui le préoccupe individuellement sans avoir personne à l'écoute. À maintes reprises, les idées intéressantes se perdent dans l'aliénation du groupe, et l'énergie de chacun est gaspillée. Pour apprendre à écouter de façon efficace, on peut utiliser une astuce simple qui se déroule en trois étapes: d'abord, absorbez ce qui vient d'être dit par les autres membres de l'équipe. Ensuite, rassemblez les bonnes idées et les pensées intéressantes que vous venez d'entendre et les synthétiser avec les vôtres. Finalement, exprimez vos idées de façon claire et précise à votre équipe, et expliquez sereinement les étapes nécessaires pour atteindre les objectifs que le groupe s'est fixé. Si vous suivez ce procédé, votre équipe vous considérera invariablement comme l'une des têtes pensantes les plus compétentes au sein du groupe.

—Robert C. Weigand
Technical Manager, Studio and Field Operations
ABC

— **Professional Perspective** —

The power you possess as a potential leader is awesome. People generally follow a leader until given a reason not to. A potential leader must have the highest ethical standards, seek and accept responsibility, and have a real passion for his or her team. If you bring these traits to your role, you will translate potential into real leadership.

—Timothy I. Martindale
President, Kiemle-Hankins Co.
Captain, U.S. Army (Retired)

SELECTING A LEADER

Leaders can be appointed, or they can emerge. There are always situations where you end up becoming the leader whether you want to or not. Think about the problems that happen if the group or a supervisor selects a person with the wrong skills. Imagine if you, the shy person, are appointed as the leader. Will the group function in the same way if either DeShara or Tony is appointed? What will be the dynamic between George, who has the organizational skills and wanted to be the leader, and any other team member who is elected? If tasks are assigned to the wrong people, member hostilities arise.

Ethical Considerations

You are leading a group that has put together a proposal. Your efforts are highlighted in a newspaper article; however, the article discusses the proposal as something that you have done. There is no mention of a committee. What should you do?

_____

_____

_____

_____

It is important to choose a person with the right skills to be the leader. This person should desire the leadership role and provide evidence of leadership experience. Skills without desire don't yield effective leadership. Those who want to lead but have no evidence of appropriate skills are not effective either.

As you select a leader, review the group's skills list. Some groups try to shirk the responsibility of choosing a leader. However, having a leader is important. Think about the teams you've experienced. How often have individuals pulled their own weight? How often has there been no conflict? How often has everyone simply known what to do instead of needing someone to delegate tasks? How often has everyone been able to meet at a convenient time? The chances are your answers to these questions indicate the necessity for having a leader.

Critical Thinking

Pick a group member other than George. Write a description of what would happen if that person were selected to be the leader.

_____

_____

_____

_____

_____

_____

Your group decides to select George because he wants to be the leader, and he offers evidence of having led other groups effectively. As he talked about his previous experiences, his communication style provided evidence that he thinks in an inclusive manner, and he appears to be direct and warm. In addition, he is the only member of the team who made direct eye contact with every member while he was explaining his background. The first thing George does after being selected is to thank everyone for the opportunity to lead the group. He begins with a brief motivational statement about the project, working together, and the group's mutual goal.

— Professional Perspective —

The best leaders are passionate about their chosen field and are prepared to make the commitment needed to succeed. In addition to management skills, a leader must also impart:

- **Character:** Words, actions, and ethics define the character of a leader and the way people respond to them. Admired leaders give and receive the respect needed to succeed. You must be willing to do what is right.

- **Vision:** A vision is much more than a good idea. It creates a long-term perspective. Innovative leaders break with tradition and embrace change. You cannot be inhibited by a fear of failure.

- **Motivation:** It is imperative to learn how to listen and ask the right questions. This will enable you to understand and address individual needs and strengths when seeking support.

Not everyone can be, should be, or for that matter, wants to be a leader. The decision to be a leader is a matter of balancing your proficiency skills with professional and personal goals.

John W. Nichols
Executive Director
The Art Museum Partnership

TASK VERSUS SOCIAL ELEMENTS OF TEAMWORK

As you begin the task, it is important to remember that teamwork involves task and social elements. *Task elements* relate to the project on which you are working. *Social elements* include chatting with one another, asking if people are doing well, and joking around. Some people are very social all of the time and nothing gets accomplished. Other people are so task oriented they can't even say hello. They call the group to order immediately, get to the business of the day, and then get angry when someone cracks a joke. Neither of these approaches works well. In order to work effectively on a team, you need to have a good mix of task and social elements.

As the meeting progresses, George says, "First we need to exchange phone numbers and e-mail addresses. Then, we need to set up a schedule for meeting times. After that, we need to decide on our group roles. Finally, we can start working on the project." George asks you to record this information and to e-mail it to the rest of the team. You tell the other members they will receive their e-mails by 10 PM. As secretary, this will be your first test of credibility with the team. If you fail to e-mail the information by the deadline, they will know they cannot count on you. Your follow through is critical.

Critical Thinking

Where do you fall on the task-social continuum? How will this help your team?

Task Oriented   Socially Oriented

◄───►
1   2   3   4   5

KEEPING PROPER RECORDS

How do you keep *proper records*? Most groups start with a meeting agenda. The agenda can be formal or informal depending on the team. Most agendas include the following items:

- A start time
- Correction and acceptance of previous minutes
- Announcements
- Reports from team members
- Unfinished business from previous meetings
- New business that must be accomplished
- An ending time for the meeting

Surely, you have attended meetings where nothing was accomplished. The leader began with, "What are we doing today?" and no one remembered what had been decided previously. An effective leader creates an agenda; this shows respect for team members because the leader is organized, prepared, and unwilling to waste their time. This is a test of credibility for the leader. If the leader can create, distribute, and stick to an effective agenda, the leader will earn every member's respect. If you finish the meeting early, the leader can dismiss the group. In this way, members who wish to socialize may do so, but others may choose to leave. Sticking to an agenda shows respect for everyone's time.

You should always have a formal record of decisions the team makes. You will find, even in working on a class project, keeping notes of decisions will save you a lot of time and future conflict. In order to keep proper records, the secretary should have the date, a list of who attended the meeting, what time the meeting was called to order, a notation of every item discussed, who initiated the idea, and what decision was reached. The secretary may also keep a record of every vote. The secretary concludes minutes with the phrase "Respectfully Submitted" and signs his or her name. If the minutes are distributed by e-mail, keep a signed original copy for the records.

The secretary should make sure minutes are formally written, with no abbreviations. All names should be spelled and recorded correctly. In business, use only last names. The secretary should proofread the minutes carefully before submitting them to the team. Remember, minutes are a legal document of the proceedings. Everyone should take responsibility for reviewing and correcting the minutes before approving them.

Some miscellaneous tips for record keeping include keeping a file folder of all agendas, all copies of the minutes, copies of all e-mail correspondence, copies of all memos, and copies of any handouts from team members. You should also put a date on all information you receive so you know when you received it. The secretary's goal is to keep all information concerning the project in one file.

Reality ✔

There are times in the workforce where your notes and conversations from a group meeting are considered to be confidential. You will need to be careful to adhere to the policy or agreements related to confidentiality that your team or organization establishes. It is common for people who do not comply with a confidentiality agreement to be fired.

MOTIVATING TEAM MEMBERS

Before getting to the task, George says he wants to discuss **motivation**, the spark that causes a person to act. Team members have already shared their individual goals. George says he will do his best to keep everyone motivated and on task, but members are also responsible for motivating themselves to get their assigned work completed. If everyone works diligently, the group will be satisfied with the final product and have interpersonal harmony. Juan, being creative, says he is motivated by pizza. The team laughs. But rather than let it go, he says, "No really, in my computer programming task group, we ordered food, and everyone was much happier and less cranky after they snacked."

Motivation can come in many forms. Some people are internally motivated. Others are motivated by a break in routine, food, or the comments of team members. It is important for team members to discuss motivational ideas and decide what might work for everyone. Those who think they are already motivated and don't need this discussion are fooling themselves. Teams can lack motivation at some point during a project and for a variety of reasons. The initial discussion regarding motivation should be revisited whenever motivation dips.

Critical Thinking

What motivates you when you are working on a team?

_____

_____

_____

— **Professional Perspective** —

Two skills are critical when motivating people: self-awareness and the ability to flex your style to meet the needs of others. Few managers truly understand the impact of their behavior on employees. Managers typically utilize one managerial style (*command and control*) to manage a diverse workforce with unique needs and talents.

During his term as mayor of New York City, Rudy Giuliani elevated the command and control managerial style to an art form. He cleaned up New York City and, in the process, alienated many of his constituents. On September 11th, he demonstrated the ability to flex his style to meet the needs of the people. He listened, communicated goals clearly, reached out across party lines, and gave careful consideration to the opinions of others. As a result, Rudy Giuliani emerged as an international leader, and New York City emerged to rebuild after a devastating tragedy.

As future leaders, the most important thing you can give to your employees is attention, feedback, and development. We all know how to practice command and control management. Unfortunately, we've had great role models. When you find yourself relying too heavily on this approach (and realize that you are de-motivating your employees) think of Rudy Giuliani, and flex your style.

—Maryellen Lurie
Principal
Maryellen Lurie & Associates, Inc.

PLANNING FOR MEETINGS

Planning is part of effective teamwork. A team member must be responsible for coordinating the details for the meeting site. In selecting a space (whether a room in the library, a meeting room on campus, or some other space), make sure it contains the technology your team needs. For instance, some university classrooms have computers and projection equipment that allow the team to watch as another member is typing information. As the team discusses and develops ideas, all members can observe the process. Everyone should be comfortable in the meeting space. There should be space to set things—a large table that allows you to display information for the meeting. You need to make sure the lighting is sufficient for everyone. Are there enough electrical outlets to plug in any equipment you may need? Is there air-conditioning? Will it be too cold? Are you in a place where Juan can have his pizza? Don't forget record keeping as you make these plans. It may be important for you to have a university receipt stating you have reserved the space. This can save you a lot of time if others challenge your right to be there or if you need to have a door unlocked.

As an individual member, make sure you are 100 percent prepared for whatever is scheduled on the agenda. You should have read the minutes of the previous meeting, so you can identify corrections and can vote to approve them. You should have reviewed the agenda, so you know what is planned. Be sure you have prepared a concise, accurate report for your portion of the task. You also need to have completed all of your assignments. Team members get irate quickly when individuals make excuses for why their work is not done. This shows great disrespect to your team members and is rarely tolerated in the corporate world. There are often severe consequences for not being prepared in business.

— Professional Perspective —

The foundation of team building lies in good communication. I take a group of 20–30 people who may or may not know each other and ensure that over a limited period of time (1–3 days) they function as a team. In live television, details are critical. A lot of pieces must come together properly and in the correct order for a live remote to be successful. I provide my crews with a detailed written plan of the project.

You must preplan well, share all information with team members, and remain calm to be effective in building a team.

—Jim Benson
President
Vision Quest Productions

The team approach to working together requires diligence in interpersonal skills. Members must be honest in sharing their needs with others and responsible for competently completing their assignments related to the task. It is also important to develop a sense of group pride in the quality of work generated. Everyone must be self-motivated and held together by a firm, yet positive, leader. Team members become role models for each other when they display excellent verbal and nonverbal skills. Team moments happen, and when they do, they become memorable. Once interpersonal skills unite the team, it is ready for problem solving. However, if the team is not united the problem-solving process will be more difficult.

Reality ✔

Tony doesn't meet a deadline, so George and DeShara no longer trust him. They begin to do his work, because they are afraid it won't get done. Their decision subdivides the team. George and DeShara are more focused on the grade and the quality of the project than on the cooperation of team members. This begins a downward spiral for the team. When Tony comes to the next meeting with work in hand, he finds that George and DeShara have already done the work. Tony feels excluded from the group and begins to withdraw. Meanwhile, George and DeShara begin to complain they have to do all the work.

This is a perception problem. Often when we have heard students complain about doing all of the work in a group, we hear from other team members that those people wouldn't allow them to do any work. In order to be successful as a team, you must find ways to trust, to encourage, and to motivate each other.

THE REFLECTIVE-THINKING PROCESS

The **reflective-thinking process** is derived from John Dewey's (1910) classic work, *How We Think*, in which he described five basic steps in scientific reasoning. The reflective-thinking process has been adapted into a variety of problem-solving models. Gerald Phillips developed The Standard Agenda—"the most complete, the most flexible, and a time-tested method for problem-solving discussion" (Young, Wood, Phillips, & Pedersen, 2007, p. 11).

The Standard Agenda has six steps that take the group through the reflective-thinking process.

Let's take a common problem—parking on campus, for example. Most students would agree parking on campus is a problem. So what is the first thing you hear people say when you tell them we need to solve the parking problem? Build a garage! Make more spaces! Take out the flowerbeds! These are all solutions, but it is possible none of these suggestions will solve the problem.

The purpose of the reflective-thinking process is to influence the type of communication that takes place during problem solving. There are a few key steps in the use of reflective thinking that must be followed to allow a group to arrive at an optimal solution. The group members must understand the procedure. They must also be flexible enough to work back and forth between the steps. This process improves the natural process of decision emergence.

Step 1: Understanding the Charge

Group members must understand their assignment. We have seen numerous groups, both at the student and professional level, begin problem solving before the members realize what it is they are supposed to accomplish.

Understanding the charge means being able to answer the following questions: What is the goal of the group? Who formed the group and why? What resources are available to the group, including financial, material, technological, and human support? When must the group make its final report? What form must the report take? Who gets the report?

⇨ Try It! ⇦

The instructor says she'll give your group $30 to go out for dinner. You must use The Standard Agenda to solve the problem of where you will go. Write the charge and answer the questions in step one.

_____

_____

_____

_____

_____

_____

Step 2: Understanding and Phrasing the Question

Once the group members understand their mission, it is time to define the problem. Often group members assume everyone understands the problem—after all, who doesn't understand the parking problem on campus? Well, think again. What is the problem? Often the dialogue runs like this:

Yip: What is the parking problem?
LaKeesha: There are no spaces.
Yip: There are plenty of spaces on the far perimeter of campus.

> LaKeesha: Okay, there are no spaces close to my classroom.
> Yip: If you get here at 7 AM, you can park as close as you want.
> LaKeesha: Okay, there are no spaces close to my classroom at times convenient to me.

And so it goes. So what is the problem? If we simply said lack of spaces, then we might build a parking garage at an astronomical cost to students and faculty. Maybe if the problem had been better defined, we could solve it with less expense. Consider the example that there are too many classes scheduled between the hours of nine and twelve. If we redistributed those classes more evenly, perhaps there would be less people on campus at those times, thereby eliminating the parking problem.

So, in this phase the group must determine exactly what the issue is that requires a decision. To do this effectively, the members should establish a discussion question. Discussion questions are usually phrased in the following manner: Who should do what about what? So an effective discussion question could be:

What recommendation can we make to ensure convenient parking for all students and faculty?

An effective discussion question sets the foundation; it does not offer a solution. An *ineffective* discussion might be:

What recommendation can we make to increase parking spaces?

⇨   **Try It!**   ⇦

What discussion question will your group use for the dinner problem?

_____

_____

Step 3: Fact Finding

During fact finding, members should collect as much relevant information about the issue as possible and exchange the collected information with each other. To achieve these goals, interactions must focus on (1) critical examination of the facts by all members, (2) whether the facts should alter the phrasing of the original discussion question, and (3) whether enough information has been gathered to proceed.

To be effective problem solvers, you must collect all the necessary facts. It is often difficult to determine when you are actually finished with this stage. Let's follow our parking example. We would need to find out:

How many spaces are available?
How many people need them?
How many people park illegally?
How much money is available for a solution?
What are the causes of the problem?
Are there any limitations?

⇨   **Try It!**   ⇦

List all of the facts you need to examine in order to solve the $30 dinner problem effectively.

_____

_____

_____

_____

_____

_____

Step 4: Establishing Criteria

By now members are usually ready to jump to a solution, but everyone still needs to go through one more step. Criteria are the standards by which we judge things. Everyone uses criteria; you have standards by which you judge restaurants, movies, music, and so forth. Instructors have standards by which they judge speeches, assignments, papers, and exams. Instructors cannot just put a "B" on a paper because it "feels" like an above-average paper. Instead, they need to know what they are looking for and how they'll know it when they see it. Criteria tell us how we know a good solution when we see it.

The standard form for criteria is "Any solution must. . . ." You would substitute words for "solution" as necessary. Instructors say, "In order to receive an A, any paper must . . ." and they would finish with a list:

Have fewer than three punctuation errors
Cover all of the concepts assigned
Be written well

Note the difficulty with one of these criteria—how do instructors define "written well"? The first two criteria are objective; the third is subjective. Let's go back to our parking example. "Any solution must . . ."

Go into effect by January 2012
Be acceptable to faculty, staff, and students
Cost less than X (be sure to define X!)

Do not move on from the criteria step until you have defined and prioritized all criteria. Definition is important so we have objective, concrete statements. Prioritization is important in case you have more than one solution that meets the same number of criteria. If two solutions meet only two of the criteria above (Solution A is acceptable to all and costs less than X, but can't be in effect until 2015, while Solution B goes into effect by 2012, costs less than X, but is not acceptable to students), you need to be able to tell which is the better solution. So you need to have your criteria set up in terms of priority—in this case we may say that cost is first because without the money, we cannot do it. Acceptability is next because we are concerned about morale on campus. We are more concerned with acceptability and cost than with the start-up date, so it becomes criterion number three. Once we've determined the prioritization, we can see that Solution A is our better choice.

Different solutions will be rated higher depending on how you set up and prioritize your criteria.

⇨   **Try It!**   ⇦

List and prioritize the criteria for solving your dinner problem.

_____

_____

_____

_____

_____

_____

Step 5: Discovering and Selecting Solutions

In this step, you will brainstorm a list of solutions and select the best one. Notice that we do not even mention the idea of solutions until this step. You must gather your facts and set up your criteria before you consider the solutions. After those steps have been completed, brainstorm solutions. In our parking example, we might come up with: build a garage, provide a shuttle, provide a health campaign giving students a bonus for walking from a parking lot a mile away, pave lawns to create more space, and so on. Remember, no idea should be evaluated while brainstorming.

Next, we systematically evaluate each of our solutions against each of our criteria. It is often useful to make a chart.

Solutions ⟶	Garage	Shuttle	Campaign	Pave Lawns
Criteria Any solution must . . . Cost less than $40,000				
Be acceptable to all				
Be in effect by 2012				

At this point, the group needs to discuss whether or not, and to what degree, each solution matches each criterion. Take criterion 1; would a garage cost less than $40,000? No. Would a shuttle? Yes. Would a campaign? Yes. Would digging up and paving over lawns? No. The group would need to provide facts to account for these conclusions.

Once the group has applied all the solutions to the criteria, it should become evident which solution is best. Let's assume the group made the following assessment after careful deliberation.

Solutions ⟶	Garage	Shuttle	Campaign	Pave Lawns
Criteria Any solution must . . . Cost less than $40,000	N	Y	Y	N
Be acceptable to all	Y	N	N!	Y
Be in effect by 2012	N	Y	Y	Y

It becomes obvious the shuttle is the best solution. The garage only meets one criterion and does not meet our first-ranked criterion of cost. The next two are equal. However, when we look at the strength of the matches, we find people are significantly more opposed to walking a mile with the health campaign than they are with taking a shuttle.

Keep in mind there are numerous ways to evaluate criteria. For one project, a group of students used the reflective-thinking process to find the best gas station in town. After collecting the facts, they developed a list of criteria by which to evaluate the stations. Note their criteria are in order of priority, so the ones higher on the list get more points than the ones lower on the list.

Gas Station Criteria Evaluation System

Price of Regular Unleaded Gasoline—10 points
  10 points = $3.05–$3.10
  7 points = $3.11–$3.15
  4 points = $3.16–$3.20
  2 points = $3.21–$3.25
  0 points = higher than $3.25

Acceptance of Checks
  9 points = Yes
  0 points = No

Number of Pumps
  8 points = 8 or more pumps
  6 points = 6 or 7 pumps
  4 points = 4 or 5 pumps
  3 points = 2 or 3 pumps
  0 points = 1 pump

Atmosphere
  7 points = Outstanding (how would you define this?)
  4 points = Fair
  0 points = Bad

Roof Over the Pumps
  6 points = There is a roof
  3 points = There is a partial roof
  0 points = There is no roof

Clean Bathroom
  5 points = Would actually use the bathroom
  2 points = Would only wash your hands
  0 points = Would not use the bathroom or no bathroom available

Window Cleaner
  4 points = If available

2 points = If available, but the water is dirty
0 points = If not available

Car Wash
    3 points = Good condition, clean, and usable
    2 points = Fair condition, moderately clean, and usable
    0 points = Bad condition and not usable or not available

Air Pump
    2 points = If available and there is no charge
    1 point = If available and there is a charge
    0 points = If not available

ATM Machine
    1 point = If available
    0 points = If not available

Using points is just one method for evaluating solutions with the criteria established in step 4. There are many other ways in the reflective-thinking process to measure solutions by the criteria.

⇨ Try It! ⇦

List the dinner solutions and evaluate them against your criteria:

Solutions ⟶				
Criteria Any solution must . . .				

Step 6: Preparing and Presenting the Final Report

The last phase is reporting your findings. The report will be in the format requested by the person who formed the group. If you must submit a written report, please refer to the appendix. Group presentations will be discussed later in the chapter.

When Does Reflective Thinking Yield a Bad Solution?

Do not be lulled into a false sense of security. The Standard Agenda helps people to make the best decisions possible through systematic thinking. However, there are times when a group doesn't use The Standard Agenda effectively. Beware of these pitfalls:

Members do not accurately assess the problem
Members do not gather all the necessary facts

Members do not accurately analyze the facts
Members fail to construct a good set of criteria
Members do not systematically apply the solutions to criteria

MEETING DOS AND DON'TS

While there is no comprehensive list of what you should and should not do in group meetings, we offer these suggestions:

- Be on time.
- Stick to the topic.
- Leave personal issues behind.
- Be prepared.
- Have handouts ready, if appropriate.
- Give an update of where you are on the project.
- Be positive when you ask questions of other members.
- Remember, the goal is to stay on task.
- Remember the difference between being critical of an idea and criticizing an idea or person.
- Don't keep a critique to yourself to appear to be popular.
- Use the proper tone when being critical of an idea.
- Be honest about what you can/can't do.
- Follow through.
- If you are having difficulty, say so as early as possible, so other members can help you.

TYPES OF GROUP PRESENTATIONS

There are a number of group presentations, but we will mention four: symposium, roundtables, panels, and forums. The **symposium** refers to a presentation where the group is in front of an audience, and each person gives part of a prepared speech. There should be an introduction, a conclusion, and transitions between the speakers. The speeches should all be approximately the same time length and should flow so that they appear as part of a greater whole. Everything that was discussed in the chapters on informative and persuasive speaking apply in this type of presentation. You need to think of the entire presentation as a whole with each person presenting a main point or section. Therefore, in a group of five, for instance, one person might give the introduction, the next three people would each present the main points, and the fifth person would present the conclusion.

The **roundtable** discussion consists of a moderator and group members having an actual discussion. The moderator can be a group member but can also be someone from outside the group. In a symposium, members prepare their remarks on a portion of a topic; in a roundtable, participants must be prepared to discuss the entire topic. A roundtable discussion is similar to a polite discussion among knowledgeable peers; there is generally no audience. This is a popular television format for journalists discussing topics of national interest (in this case, there is an audience, of course, but not in the studio). A roundtable discussion may be used for focus-group research where there is a set of prepared questions and a moderator who leads the discussion. Focus-group research is designed to get information from a group of people concerning their opinions or knowledge on a particular topic. They are commonly used in market research for advertising.

A roundtable discussion made up of expert panelists that is held in front of an audience is generally referred to as a ***panel*** discussion. Participants must enter the discussion fully informed about the topic. A moderator is used to keep the discussion moving, usually with preplanned discussion points. The panelists hear the reaction of the audience as they speak. Some panel discussions allow questions from the audience near the conclusion of the presentation.

Forum discussions involve the audience. Any talk show that you see usually has a forum component because the host asks the audience for input or questions. You can add a forum to the above presentations as well. Therefore, you may find a presentation advertised as a symposium-forum, meaning there will be a prepared presentation given by multiple people, but when it concludes, they will take questions from the audience. Panel-forums do the same thing. Forums are also known as town meetings. You will find town meetings are used in political campaigns as well as in organizations and universities.

Tips for the Presentation

There are numerous tips that can make your presentation stand out. Every member should be in professional attire and dressed in similar colors. Dressing alike has definite psychological advantages because your group appears united. Be aware of your nonverbals during a group presentation. If everyone is in front of the audience, it is essential that every member's attention is riveted on the speaker. As soon as members doodle, talk to one another, or fidget, they compromise the credibility of the entire group.

Be sure to practice the presentation. Many groups have each member design a portion of a presentation. If you don't plan this as a team, members often look ridiculous when they repeat the same information. The verbal and physical transitions from one member to the next should look polished, reflecting good teamwork. It is extremely difficult to work individually and make a presentation look like a synthesized project. A post-analysis critique is essential during this phase. If everyone just presents and then says "great job," no one really listened critically for the flaws in the others' presentations. Remember, just because you deliver information does not mean the presentation has been successful.

Follow the guidelines in chapters 7–9 for public speaking; visit the actual space where the group will be presenting. Learn where the electrical outlets are and the best way to use the space so there will be no mistakes during the presentation. Sometimes team members find they have differing definitions of professional attire. You should have every member practice in their professional attire. Shoes may make noise, blouses may be too low cut, and ties may not be tied properly. Eliminating these nonverbal issues before the actual presentation will help everyone to remain calm and professional during the actual presentation.

Summary

Teamwork can often be problematic. It takes skill and patience to solve problems and integrate personalities into a cohesive team. There are occasions when it will seem difficult to accomplish a task by working in a group instead of working on your own. However, at many points in your career you will have to work in a group. Learn the necessary skills to have a good team experience. Once you make effective choices and are committed to a team and the task, you should have a solid, rewarding experience.

— Professional Perspective —

The personality traits best suited for teamwork involve a sense of the greater good of the project over your own personal comfort or gain. Retaining this focus is not always an easy thing to do, especially when ego is involved and much of the production process is subjective. But whether you're talking about the production process or building a house, I think the universal traits that everyone needs to succeed as members of a team who are striving for a common goal are focus, commitment, and the ability to see the forest for the trees. In other words, what's the endgame? You need to keep your eye on the prize and not let setbacks and distractions knock you off course.

You also need to have the ability to really listen to people. I mean really listen so you can read what's going on between the lines. It's hard to resist putting forth your own opinions and visions, but sometimes you have to put those aside, buy into the vision of the group, and go for it! A sense of humor also helps.

—Gene R. Sower
Vice President, Production
West Glen Communications, Inc.

Key Words

authoritarian leaders	preparing and presenting the final report
democratic leaders	proper records
discovering and selecting solutions	reflective-thinking process
establishing criteria	roundtable
fact finding	social element
forum	symposium
groups	task element
laissez-faire leaders	team contract
member's needs	teams
motivation	understanding and phrasing the question
panel	understanding the charge
planning	

Crossword 13: Working in Teams

Across

1. Once written, this guides the team through the problem-solving process. A team must be prepared to revise it as they move through the steps and gather new information.

2. One of the most complete procedural problem-solving models is called the ____.

12. A procedure originally described by John Dewey in 1910. Most problem-solving agendas are based on this description.

13. Special groups working together to achieve a goal by using a procedure.

15. A roundtable discussion held in front of an audience and with knowledgeable group members is called a ____.

16. As a team leader, Jill knows taking a minute to find out what each member's ____ are will help her to work more effectively with each person on the team, because she can adapt her leadership style to accommodate them.

17. To be successful, group members must perform functions such as problem solving, record keeping, and analyzing data. These are ____ functions.

20. A leadership style where the leader tells the members what to do and expects them to follow obediently.

21. It is important to inventory individuals' ____ so you know who is best at doing what.

Down

1. When Brett asks team members for their opinions and then synthesizes the ideas, he is using a ____ leadership style.

2. A group presentation where each member has an individual "mini-speech."

3. A written document where team members state rules, roles, strengths, and goals.

4. These are standards by which we judge solutions.

5. Your team must understand the ____ before it can begin to do any problem solving.

6. The ideal is for individual group members to share the same ____, but even if they don't, by simply discussing them, cohesiveness should improve.

7. An important, but difficult, task of the team leader is to provide team ____. This will be different for each person. Members have a responsibility to tell the leader what will work for them.

8. When the leader doesn't pay much attention to the group and lets them do their own thing, this is called ____ leadership.

9. A presentation involving the participation of an audience.

10. Group members need to have a little time to talk to one another, joke around, and just vent. These are all ____ functions of the group.

11. One of the biggest mistakes groups make is failing to keep ____. This results in members trying to remember what happened at a previous meeting.

14. A presentation where members get together without an audience and discuss a topic.

18. In this step of The Standard Agenda, you must gather all of the information necessary to solve the problem.

19. If you don't ____ your criteria, it could be difficult for your team to decide which solution is best.

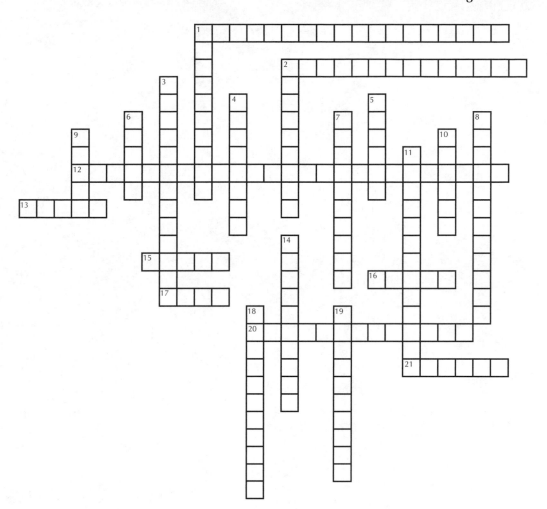

CHAPTER 14

Final Thoughts

You'll never really know what I mean and I'll never know exactly what you mean.

—Mike Nichols

Can you remember leaving for your first day at school and how you felt as you lost sight of your parents' faces? The butterflies in your stomach as you faced the unknown? You probably were an emotional mix of excitement and anxiety as you walked away from your home environment to face new people, a new situation, and new information. Whom would you meet? Would you like them? Would they like you? Would you be able to adapt to this new learning experience? All of these childhood concerns may seem light-years away now and possibly a little silly in hindsight when you compare that memory to what you have accomplished since then. And yet, that early experience was the foundation for every communication encounter in your life.

Each person you meet, each move you make, and each business that employs you will take you back to that first memory. Of course, the rules of communication are more complex as an adult, but the new situations you constantly encounter can be compared to your going-to-school experience. There are thousands of interpersonal moments to absorb and challenges to face throughout life, but a communicator who adapts to personalities and environments can effectively handle any situation.

Your self-confidence and fundamental nature are rooted in your home and your home community. This environment gives you a set of attitudes, beliefs, and values with which you can develop personal standards of conduct. As you advance in maturity and career, some adjustments in your fundamental nature may occur. These are decisions you must make as you meet a diverse culture you never imagined facing when you were a child. Success is rooted in personal accomplishment, and your self-confidence grows as you find yourself capable of reaching various goals.

Communication errors are made throughout life. You take calculated risks each time you speak publicly, write, or meet strangers. Other people interpret everything you do (just as you judge other people by your own standards).

Their interpretation of your communication abilities helps them decide if they want you as a friend, a colleague, or an employee. We can misjudge others through verbal and nonverbal channels just as they can misjudge us. It is for this reason that our fundamental nature may need some adjustment as we move forward in life.

As you read about and study a topic, you soon discover how much information you never knew. The key to better communication is making good decisions about new facts and information. If research convinces you a belief you hold is incorrect, then don't be afraid to change your mind. Rather than hold onto old beliefs because they are comfortable, embrace change. This is where learning helps you adjust your fundamental nature. A good communicator is truthful and adheres to the basic premise that he or she should be honest with every receiver or audience.

Nonverbal adjustments in adult behavior take appropriate thought, patience, and practice. For example, when we are young we don't give a great deal of thought to our appearance. Once we begin to focus on a possible career, however, we begin to make adjustments to our personal appearance, including our wardrobe and physical movement. Our role models become the heads of companies or departments we want to work in, and we find a way to adjust our appearance to be accepted. This adjustment is not always a complete makeover. It is important to communicate your own personality, but there may be some nonverbal elements that should definitely change so you can be perceived by decision makers as someone who has experience at their level. Your adjustment can be as simple as a new hairstyle or a different color scheme for your wardrobe. These are nonverbal commitments you make to become successful in your career.

Let's say you aren't as well organized as you could be with your personal effects. At work, other employees may think you are messy when they see a cluttered desk or office. They may think you are a poor image for the company and decide clients should not see your office space. This may not be a fair perception about you, but they make this value judgment anyway. Nothing is ever said about it, but their reaction colors their interactions with you. This could hurt your future with the company if one or more of the people holding this perception are in decision-making positions. You need to be self-critical. Engage in intrapersonal communication and make adjustments that will assist you in being seen as a professional. Each nonverbal move you make is seen and judged in some way by other people. Take risks—but also assume responsibility for the reactions you create with your behavior.

Perception checking is a critical skill. Whenever you wonder why someone did something or said something, ask a question. Do not attribute meaning to another person's actions, because your perception may be incorrect. Don't waste your time and energy worrying about hypothetical possibilities when a simple question can provide an answer. If the paralanguage of an answer still bothers you, ask another question. Why add stress to your life by imagining possible answers? Don't be afraid to ask questions and discover the truth. It's better to clarify your perception of an incident, so you can move forward to other issues.

Your pursuit of an education should excite you to explore the meaning of words in our culture and in global cultures. As an educated person, you are responsible for the effect your communication has on others. The more you read, the better you will be at using the proper words to explain your thoughts clearly in both spoken and written forms of language. However, words need to be examined as part of a complete thought. A complete thought tells a listener or reader what your message means. When you are the listener, don't isolate a word and react to it out of context. You must listen to a message and analyze its impact once it's complete. To do otherwise is unfair to a communicator or reveals an inability to listen and follow an argument.

Learn to express yourself effectively within your profession. Remember to eliminate any jargon if you speak to audiences who are not familiar with the language of your profession.

— Professional Perspective —

You never know the hand life will deal you, so you never know what words you'll need to know. In the age of the Internet, all the planet's population is a click away. No borders, no boundaries, no separation by country, race, sexual orientation, etc. If you don't understand what people are saying, you can never really know what they mean or understand the unsaid words lying beneath the surface of the sentence. Without the words you never know how to feel—or what you feel is inappropriate more times than not. Without the words you're obeying a master who uses them to his or her own purpose. Words allow you to distinguish between lies and truth, love and humiliation. Words allow you to understand yourself.

Words took me from New York City's South Bronx to Spain, Colombia, England, the Hawaiian Islands, Puerto Rico, France, Germany, Austria, Hollywood and Beverly Hills, China, Egypt, Greece, Italy, Mexico, Belgium, Switzerland, and San Marino. Who would have thought? Who would have known? Dream.

Nunca sabes lo que te espera en la vida, así que nunca sabes que palabras vas a necesitar. En la edad del Internet la población del mundo está a un clic de distancia. No hay fronteras, ni limites, no hay separación por país, raza, orientación sexual, etc. Si no entiendes lo que la gente dice, jamás podrás saber lo que verdaderamente quiere decir, ni podrás comprender el significado de lo que se deja entredicho. Sin las palabras, no puedes saber que es lo que sientes, o lo que sientes no es apropiado la mayoría de las veces. Sin las palabras, te sometes a la voluntad de un amo que las usa para su propio fin. Las palabras te permiten distinguir la verdad de la mentira, el amor de la humillación. Las palabras te permiten entenderte a ti mismo.

Las palabras me llevaron del Sur del Bronx de la ciudad de Nueva York a España, Colombia, Inglaterra, las Islas Hawaianas, Puerto Rico, Francia, Alemania, Austria, Hollywood y Beverly Hills, China, Egipto, Grecia, Italia, México, Bélgica, Suiza, y San Marino. ¿Quién lo hubiera pensado? ¿Quién lo hubiera sabido? Hay que soñar.

—Edward Gallardo
Playwright

There is another important decision to make about words as you mature professionally. They need to be pronounced properly. You need to analyze the speech patterns you absorbed in your childhood. The pronunciation and grammar you learned make you a part of that community. As you move beyond that community, you may need to adjust your articulation of some local sounds and develop more standard pronunciation to be understood. This is a decision only you can make, but it is an important one. The telephone is a common channel for employment and business communication— a receiver of your voice should not be able to identify you by region or ethnic background. You don't know what a stranger is thinking as she hears your voice. Don't give anyone the opportunity to form prejudicial impressions based on your speech. By simply mispronouncing a word in a conversation, a listener could think you are not well educated or are not experienced in your field. Of course this is unfair, but you allow this decision to be made against you by not modifying your speech pattern. Perceptual decisions are made in seconds. Don't give anyone the chance to consider you unqualified because of vocal habits you can adjust but fail to recognize. When teachers or colleagues make suggestions for vocal change, think about what they are saying. Word pronunciation is easy to check in a dictionary. The choice to change is yours. Choose wisely.

Spoken words are interpreted as others listen to you. Therefore, the quality of your voice, its energy and pace, plus your articulation and pronunciation, influence others' reactions to your message. People enjoy listening to others who speak well. The spoken form of communication is extremely important, but, you also must master using words well in written communication. It is important to have a solid writing style that makes you easy to follow as people look at your words and think about them. Clarity in your writing is absolutely critical. Just think about all of the technical channels you currently use to convey a written message: memos, IM, e-mail, reports, articles, evaluation forms, and employment forms. How is your spelling? How is your grammar? Do your word choices connect properly with the receiver?

Once your thoughts are written, receivers can reread the material as many times as they wish. This is why you must proofread every message for accuracy, clarity, and style. We take the time to proofread and analyze material in a report or an article knowing it will be in print. But occasionally we fail to recognize that electronic writing needs the same high degree of critical analysis before hitting the send button. Typos and incomplete thoughts can lead to improper understanding of a message. Even more damaging, they can cost you your career in many professional areas. There are individuals who refuse to read anything with a typo. Electronic messages are not private. They are stored in corporate electronic archives and can be retrieved by anyone. Unintended receivers can read your thoughts and messages. Therefore, keep your written thoughts professional and accurate.

Handwritten notes, application forms, memos, and thank-you notes do not have the automatic security of spell-check to alert you to errors. You must know how words are spelled. It is embarrassing to have colleagues discover you don't know how to spell when they read your handwritten notes and suggestions on reports. Even if you plan to use word-processing software and think all of your bases are covered with spell-check, a power failure could force you to write a report by hand to meet a deadline. In addition, spell-check corrects only misspellings, it won't tell you if you have used "here" instead of "hear." If there are spelling errors, you will have created an impression that will be remembered and difficult to change. This affects your credibility. Remember that you do not determine whether you are credible or not; other people make that decision about you. One mistake and your credibility is at risk.

The greatest challenge in using words effectively is to succeed in having other people understand your message as you intended it to be understood. Language should always be appropriate and organized to convey your message. You should also choose the best channel to send a message to another person or group of people. The intent of all communication is to help a receiver comprehend your analysis of a topic. Spoken speech is an extemporaneous exchange; you only have one opportunity to make the message clear. Your vocal pace, quality, and delivery of the message is critical. In written language, receivers can review your thought process as many times as necessary to understand your meaning. This gives written language an advantage over spoken language for audience comprehension. An inattentive reader can review your thoughts again, but a lazy listener misses your point entirely. Spoken and written communication should work together in helping you reach your audience; you need to build a strong foundation in both skills to be perceived as an excellent communicator and colleague.

> *It is a luxury to be understood.*
> —Ralph Waldo Emerson

We receive feedback about our behavior, thought process, use of language, and knowledge. The choices we make in selecting which pieces of information to accept or reject in adjusting who we are and what we want to become are very important. The external world seems to impose suggestions continuously about what we should do and what we should think. It is up to us, however, to make choices about our communication abilities and make the necessary adjustments to be successful. The consequences of our choices influence our future. This is not a frightening thought at all. It simply reminds us to take seriously how we communicate and how we listen to the external world.

Our lives appear to get more complicated as our careers advance and family responsibilities increase. The best solution is to learn to manage time more effectively and set priorities regarding life's important issues. One way to use time better is to know how to listen effectively to messages and then pick an appropriate way to react to those messages. Some messages can be ignored; other messages require action. Experience helps us to select the right words and behaviors to respond to a message, plus it helps us to select the appropriate channel for a response. We strongly support the use of face-to-face interpersonal communication for very important personal messages. When you take the time to see others and congratulate them on a job well done, console them, listen to them, or explain a difficult issue to them, you send a message of caring about them. What do you think about an employer who sends you a memo or e-mail saying your employment has been terminated versus an employer who takes the time to explain the issue to you directly? The consequence of the communication remains the same, but at least in the person-to-person meeting, you have a feeling there is some concern for you as a person. It is important to recognize the need for voice and physical presence in your communication style. Yes, it requires more of your time, but it also tells people you care about them. This is an important personal choice to make as an effective communicator.

Listening is a vital skill for personal growth. Don't superimpose a preconceived idea onto the thought a family member or colleague is sharing with you because you feel pressed for time. You owe it to other people to evaluate their ideas fairly before you respond to them. This is what interpersonal communication is all about. Do your best to analyze what they would like you to do or think and then find the proper words to respond to their needs. Family dialogue is stronger and business dialogue is stronger when we listen critically and evaluate a proper course of action prior to responding to another communicator's message. We are rarely alone in decision making. Compromises are usually necessary, but everyone must feel good about their compromises in interpersonal and team efforts for relationships to remain strong.

You have a greater chance for long-term personal success if your communication style can blend into a business culture that is globally diverse and a world that is becoming much smaller through cyberspace.

— Professional Perspective —

These are skills and insights I have developed and come to understand as necessary when dealing with clients in the music-promotion business as it pertains to achieving airplay at radio stations. I come across many, many different situations and people. I try to incorporate all of these insights into my conversations and presentations when dealing with clients.

1. Know what you believe.
Have total belief, conviction, and knowledge in what you are communicating. Don't simply articulate a brief summary or outline of your skills. Go into great depth and detail about what you have to offer. Give examples of your successes. Illustrate how your skills will benefit a person/business and how they benefit your current company, business, etc.

2. Be an optimist.
If you are upbeat and happy, your comments will come across to others as important and necessary. Thus, you become important and necessary to them. Smile and look people in the eye when you talk to them. It shows confidence. No one likes a sourpuss.

3. Research and prepare.
Know your client's likes and dislikes. What does the company/person stand for? Know and understand their needs inside and out. Realize corporate and personal situations can change on a daily basis and quite often do. What was once necessary can often be outdated within seconds—especially in a fast-paced business environment. Always be prepared for change, accept it, and move forward.

4. Have follow-through.
Do what you said you would do for people. If you do this on a consistent basis, they will trust you.

5. Display honesty, charm, and personality.
These qualities can go a long way to make people comfortable. Don't be obsequious, but be yourself and allow others to be the same way. You will find that people respond to others who know who they are rather than to those who put on airs and falsehoods. In today's corporate environment, shuck and jive no longer work.

—Lance Walden
Northwest Regional Radio Promotions
Universal Republic Records

We talked about the word *adjustment* earlier. Adjustment requires that you research various topics. There are times when you need to check out people and resources yourself without relying totally on the information given to you by others. This is an issue of personal responsibility and integrity. Reading and research can assist you in evaluating the information other people give you for truth, accuracy, and fairness. This is lifelong homework you need to do to stay on top of critical issues and decision-making choices. Whenever you are the decision maker, the consequences of communication choices sit on your shoulders alone. It is in your own best interest to recognize when you need to do personal research before you make a decision.

Communication is power. You use it with your family, friends, colleagues, and significant others in the workplace, job interviews, team environments, religious establishments, and clubs. You want to be liked by everyone, but that is not always possible. Communication is a personal challenge. Set your own standards for verbal and nonverbal message delivery. If you discover new techniques to improve your style, adopt them and use them effectively to build your own performance. Remain thorough and fair in every decision you make. It would be nice to think we can change other people or know what they really think, but we can't. We can only know ourselves.

When you learn to use language and behavior well, you are seen as an effective communicator. Mistakes in communication can happen. Analyze your error immediately and make sure not to repeat it. Everyone makes mistakes, but over the length of a career you will experience more successes than failures if you concentrate on the consequences of your messages.

You took a risk in communicating to the outside world when you went to school for the first time. You made it. Remember that. Every day gives you more insight into who you are and what you might become. It is important to accept the possibilities of success and move forward. Listen, observe, and analyze those around you. Absorb the good qualities they possess, if possible, and make them part of your communication strategy. You will be evaluated by the communication choices you make just as you evaluate the choices others make. Do not take words and behavior for granted. They are the keys to personal success. Success is within your reach, but you must constantly fine-tune your communication skills to meet ever-changing global needs and realities.

> *Communication is something so simple and difficult that we can never put it in simple words.*
>
> —T. S. Matthews

Writing the Final Report

(Adapted from *Group Discussion: A Practical Guide to Participation and Leadership 4/E* by Kathryn Sue Young, Julia T. Wood, Gerald M. Phillips, and Douglas J. Pedersen, 2007, pp. 154–158)

As you plan to write the final report, your strategy is important. Many groups try to divide the work and have everyone prepare a different part, but the same problems are inherent in group writing that are evident in group presentational speaking.

1. Group members have different writing skills. The differences result in some sections of the report being stronger and others weaker.

2. Group members have their own writing style. A reader knows immediately when the writing style shifts in the middle of a report.

3. Group members sometimes do not complete their work. If one person is in charge of an entire section and becomes MIA, the work will be incomplete.

If you choose to divide the work anyway, keep in mind you'll need time at the end for extensive editing to achieve a readable flow and to correct any errors. Since most groups are pressed for time as a deadline approaches, they often rush the written report—resulting in substandard results.

You can accomplish the writing in a number of ways. Many groups designate a writer or cowriters for their report. Usually this is someone who had a lighter load earlier in the project. If you use only one or two writers, it is imperative the other group members be available to offer ideas, suggestions, moral support, or snacks.

As one writer completes the rough draft, another person can begin the initial editing. Having two or three people involved in multiple revisions almost always guarantees a tighter, more professional report. When your group thinks the report is complete, have another person, who is not in the group, proofread the work for errors and clarity.

This may sound like a lot of work—it is. If you are used to turning in first drafts of your writing, break the habit. Too many groups put numerous hours of work into their projects but turn in a sloppy draft as their final report. Keep in mind that your credibility is enhanced or diminished by the written presentation of your work.

Here are some key guidelines for avoiding common writing errors.

- Make sure that you read all of your writing out loud. This will help you to find punctuation errors.
- Do not use contractions in formal writing. Don't should be "do not."
- Watch out for style shifts with group writing.
- Be sure to cite all articles properly.
- Know the difference between "definitely" and "defiantly." "Defiantly" is the first option that comes up in spell-check for Microsoft Word. "Defiantly" is definitely a different word than "definitely."
- "Nowadays" should never appear in your writing.
- A lot is two words (not alot).
- Be sure to number all pages.
- Be sure to use headings and subheadings in your writing.
- Be sure to use a preview and review if appropriate.
- Two complete sentences are joined by a conjunction, preceded by a comma.
  The dog ran, and the cat sat. The rat jumped, but he did not bite.
- Know which compound adjectives are hyphenated.
  My hard-hearted boss would not give me a raise.
- Create dashes by typing *two* hyphens with no space before or after the hyphens—see what I mean? (Software programs such as Microsoft Word can automatically convert two hyphens into the em dash [—].)
- Professional reports normally look better on heavier paper (25 percent cotton bond).
- Any time you use section dividers with plastic tabs, be sure they are typed. You can format them on a computer program.
- Above all, edit numerous times, proofread numerous times, and have someone else look over the writing.

— Professional Perspective —

As a supervisor in a human services agency, part of my responsibility was to review case notes documenting services provided to clientele. I was frequently amazed at the poor spelling, grammar errors, and unclear writing exhibited by caseworkers who were college grads, some with Master's degrees. The notes, used to develop client treatment plans, were often read by doctors, lawyers, judges, and juries and affected their decisions as well as their perceptions of our staff.

—Roberta J. Miller
Casework Supervisor, Retired

Bibliography

Alberti, R. E., & Emmons, M. L. (2001). *Your perfect right: Assertiveness and equality in your life and relationships* (8th ed.). Atascadero, CA: Impact Publishers.

Andersen, P. A. (1999). *Nonverbal communication: Forms and functions.* Mountain View, CA: Mayfield.

Barker, L., & Gaut, D. (2002). *Communication* (8th ed.). Boston: Allyn & Bacon.

Basic resume formats. (n.d.). Retrieved October 20, 2003, from www.bazarorissa.com/jobs/resume/Resume%20Formats.htm

Battle of Breed's Hill/Bunker Hill. (n.d.). Retrieved October 20, 2003, from Worcester Polytechnic Institute, Department of Military Science Web site: www.wpi.edu/Academics/Depts/MilSci/BTSI/Hill/

Bayless, O. L. (1967). An alternate pattern for problem solving discussion. *Journal of Communication, 17,* 188–197.

BBC News. (2003, October 17). Short workers lose a small fortune. Retrieved February 13, 2004, from http://news.bbc.co.uk/go/pr/fr/-/1/hi/health/3200296.stm

Beatty, M. J. (1988). Increasing students' choice-making consistency: The effect of decision-rule-use training. *Communication Education, 37,* 95–105.

Beebe, S. A., & Beebe, S. J. (2003). *Public speaking: An audience centered approach* (5th ed.). Boston: Allyn & Bacon.

Beebe, S. A, Beebe, S. J., & Ivy, D. K. (2004). *Communication: Principles for a lifetime* (2nd ed.). Boston: Allyn & Bacon.

Beebe, S. A., & Masterson, J. T. (2003). *Communicating in small groups: Principles and practices* (7th ed.). Boston: Allyn & Bacon.

Benjamin, J. (1997). *Principles, elements, and types of persuasion.* Belmont, CA: Wadsworth.

Berg, D. M. (1967). A thematic approach to the analysis of the task-oriented, small group. *Central States Speech Journal, 18,* 285–291.

Borchers, G. L. (1968). John Dewey and speech education. *Western Journal of Speech, 32,* 127–137.

Bormann, E. G. (1994). Response to "revitalizing the study of small group communication." *Communication Studies, 45,* 86–91.

Bormann, E. G., & Bormann, N. G. (1996). *Effective small group communication* (6th ed.). Edina, MN: Burgess International Group.

Boroditsky, L. (2001). Does language shape thought?: Mandarin and English speakers' conceptions of time. *Cognitive Psychology, 43,* 1–22.

Brickman, G. F., & Fuller, L. E. (1986). *Organizing for impact: A practical guide for the public speaker.* Dubuque: Kendall/Hunt.

Brilhart, J. K. (1966). An experimental comparison of three techniques for communicating a problem-solving pattern to members of a discussion group. *Speech Monographs, 33,* 168–177.

Brilhart, J. K., & Galanes, G. J. (1998). *Effective group discussion* (9th ed.). New York: McGraw-Hill.

Brilhart, J. K., & Jochem, L. M. (1964). Effects of different patterns on outcomes of problem-solving discussion. *Journal of Applied Psychology, 48*, 175–179.

Brinkman, R., & Kirschner, R. (2002). *Dealing with people you can't stand.* New York: McGraw-Hill.

Brotman, Barbara. (2007, June 14). Senn graduation truly a world party. *The Chicago Tribune*, pp. 1, 23.

Bush, G. W. Rose Garden Press Conference June 14, 2006. Retrieved June 13, 2007, from http://www.whitehouse.gov/news/releases/2006/06/20060614.html.

Cathcart, R. S., Samovar, L. A., & Henman, L. (1995). *Small group communication: A reader* (7th ed.). New York: McGraw-Hill.

Centers for Disease Control and Prevention. Intimate Partner Violence: Overview. Retrieved March 18, 2007, from http://www.cdc.gov/ncipc/factsheets/ipvfacts.htm

Clegg, B. (2001). *Instant interviewing.* Sterling, VA: Stylus.

Cline, R. J. W. (1990). Detecting groupthink: Methods for observing the illusion of unanimity. *Communication Quarterly, 38*, 112–126.

Coombes, Andrea. (2004, January 27). Bilingual job seekers rise above the crowd. *Chicago Tribune*, sec. 3, p. 4.

Crowell, L. (1953). Criteria are critical. *Western Journal of Speech, 17*, 245–248.

Daniels, Aubrey C. (2000). *Bringing out the best in people.* New York: McGraw-Hill.

DeNoon, Daniel (2004). "Child Antidepressant Use Skyrockets: Use Growing Fastest in Preschool Kids." Retrieved June 7, 2007, from http://www.webmd.com/content/article/85/98399.htm.

DeVito, J. A. (2002). *Essentials of human communication* (4th ed.). Boston: Allyn & Bacon.

DeVito, J. A. (2003). *Essential elements of public speaking.* Boston: Allyn & Bacon.

DeVito, J. A. (2003). *Human communication: The basic course* (9th ed.). Boston: Allyn & Bacon.

Dewey, J. (1910). *How we think.* New York: D. C. Heath.

Dewey, J. (1933). *How we think: A restatement of the relation of reflective thinking to the educative process* (2nd ed.). Boston: D. C. Heath.

Douglas, J. (1951). *An experimental study of training in problem-solving methods.* Unpublished doctoral dissertation, Northwestern University, Evanston, IL.

Douglas, J. (1953). Problems in measuring problem-solving in discussion. *Journal of Communication, 3*, 20–24.

Doyle, T. (2004). *Communication unbound.* Boston: Allyn & Bacon.

Duffy, D. (1999, January 15). Cultural evolution [Electronic version]. *CIO Enterprise Magazine.* Retrieved October 18, 2003, from http://www.cio.com/archive/enterprise/011599_rah_content.html

Dunn, D. M., & Goodnight, L. J. (2003). *Communication: Embracing difference.* Boston: Allyn & Bacon.

Edenborough, R. (2002). *Effective interviewing* (2nd ed.). London: Kogan Page.

Ehninger, D. (1943). A logic of discussion method. *Quarterly Journal of Speech, 29*, 163.

Elliot, H. S. (1927). *The why and how of group discussion.* New York: Association Press.

Ellis, D. G., & Fisher, B. A. (1993). *Small group decision making* (4th ed.). New York: McGraw-Hill.

Engleberg, I. N., & Wynn, D. R. (2000). *Working in groups: Communication principles and strategies* (2nd ed.). New York: Houghton Mifflin.

Fellingham, C. (2003, August). Extreme beauty. *O, The Oprah Magazine,* pp. 158–160, 182–183.

Fisher, B. A., & Beach, W. A. (1979, Summer). Content and relationship dimensions of communicative behavior: An exploratory study. *Western Journal of Speech Communication, 43*, 201–211.

Fisher, B. A., & Ellis, D. G. (1990). *Small group decision making: Communication and the group process* (3rd ed.). New York: McGraw-Hill.

Fletcher, L. (2004). *How to design and deliver speeches* (8th ed.). Boston: Allyn & Bacon.

Freedman, R. (2002). *Bodylove: Learning to like our looks and ourselves.* Carlsbad, CA: Gürze Books.

The freedom trail—Road to American independence. (n.d.). Retrieved October 20, 2003, from www.bostonuk.com/history/and_trail.htm#header

Frey, L. R. (1994). Introduction: Revitalizing the study of small group communication. *Communication Studies,* 45, 1–6.

Frey, L. R., & Barge, J. K. (Eds.) (1997). *Managing group life: Communication in decision-making groups.* New York: Houghton Mifflin.

Galanes, G. J., Adams, K., & Brilhart, J. K. (2004). *Effective group discussion: Theory and practice* (11th ed.). New York: McGraw-Hill.

Galanes, G. J., Brilhart, J. K., & Adams, K. L. (July, 1999). *Communicating in groups: Applications and skills* (5th ed.). New York: McGraw-Hill.

Gass, R. H., & Seiter, J. S. (1999). *Perspectives on persuasion, social influence, and compliance gaining.* Boston: Allyn & Bacon.

German, K. M., Gronbeck, B. E., Ehninger, D., Monroe, A. H. (2004). *Principles of public speaking* (15th ed.). Boston: Allyn & Bacon.

Gormley, John. (1987). The idea for visually looking at organizational patterns was developed by John Gormley and shared with KSY at The Pennsylvania State University.

Gouran, D. S. (1982). *Making decisions in groups: Choices and consequences.* Glenview, IL: Scott Foresman.

Gouran, D. S. (1990). Evaluating group outcomes. In G. M. Phillips (Ed.), *Teaching how to work in groups* (pp. 175–196). Norwood, NJ: Ablex.

Gouran, D. S. (1991). Rational approaches to decision-making and problem-solving discussion. *Quarterly Journal of Speech,* 77, 343–358.

Gouran, D. S., & Hirokawa, R. Y. (1986). Counteractive functions of communication in effective group decision-making. In R. Y. Hirokawa & M. S. Poole (Eds.), *Communication and group decision-making* (pp. 81–90). Beverly Hills, CA: Sage.

Grice, G. L., & Skinner, J. F. (2004). *Mastering public speaking* (5th ed.). Boston: Allyn & Bacon.

Griffin, C. L. (2004). *Invitation to public speaking.* Belmont, CA: Wadsworth.

Hagevik, S. (2000). Behavioral interviewing: Write a story, tell a story. *Journal of Environmental Health,* 62(7), 61.

Half, R. (1993, November). How do you prepare for nonstandard interviews? *Management Accounting,* 75(5), 12.

Hall, E. T. (1966). *The hidden dimension.* New York: Doubleday.

Hall, E. T. (1968). Proxemics. *Current Anthropology,* 9, 83–109.

Hamilton, C. (2003). *Essentials of public speaking* (2nd ed.). Belmont, CA: Wadsworth.

Harnack, R. V., & Fest, T. B. (1964). *Group discussion: Theory and technique.* New York: Meredith.

Harper, N. L., & Askling, L. (1980, June). Group communication and quality of task solution in a media production organization. *Communication Monographs,* 47, 77–100.

Hart, R. P. *Signposts on the road to effective communication.* Unpublished classroom handout available from Department of Speech Communication, Purdue University, West Lafayette, Indiana.

Hart, R. P., & Burks, D. (1972, June). Rhetorical sensitivity and social interaction. *Speech Monographs,* 24, 75–91.

Hirokawa, R. Y. (1980). A comparative analysis of communication patterns within effective and ineffective decision-making groups. *Communication Monographs,* 47, 312–321.

Hirokawa, R. Y. (1983). Group communication and problem-solving effectiveness: An investigation of group phases. *Human Communication Research,* 9, 291–305.

Hirokawa, R. Y. (1988). Group communication research: Considerations for the use of interaction analysis. In C. H. Tardy (Ed.), *A handbook for the study of human communication: Methods and instruments for observing, measuring, and assessing communication processes* (pp. 229–245). Norwood, NJ: Ablex.

Hirokawa, R. Y., & Pace, R. C. (1983). A descriptive investigation of the possible com-munication-based reasons for effective and ineffective group decision making. *Communication Monographs, 50,* 363–379.

Howell, W. S., & Smith, D. K. (1956). *Discussion.* New York: Macmillan.

Ingols, C., & Shapiro, M. (2003). *Your job interview.* New York: Silver Lining Books.

Ivy, D. K., & Backlund, P. (2004). *GenderSpeak: Personal effectiveness in gender com-munication* (3rd ed.). New York: McGraw-Hill.

Jaffe, C. (2004). *Public speaking—Concepts and skills for a diverse society* (4th ed.). Belmont, CA: Wadsworth.

Janis, I. L. (1972). *Victims of groupthink.* Boston: Houghton Mifflin.

Johnson, A. (1943). An experimental study in the analysis and measurement of reflec-tive thinking. *Speech Monographs, 10,* 83–96.

Johnson, A. E. (1942). *An experimental study in the analysis and measurement of reflective thinking.* Unpublished doctoral dissertation, Northwestern University, Evanston, IL.

Jurma, W. E. (1979, November). Effects of leader structuring style and task orientation characteristics on group members. *Communication Monographs, 46,* 282–295.

Kangas Dwyer, K. (1998). *Conquer your speech fright: Learn how to overcome the ner-vousness of public speaking.* Belmont, CA: Wadsworth.

Keen, C. (2003). Workplace rewards tall people with money, respect, UF study shows. Retrieved October 20, 2003, from http://www.mapa.ufl.edu/2003news/heightsalary.htm

Keltner, J. W. (1947). *An experimental study of the nature and training of skill in prob-lem recognition and formulation for group discussion.* Unpublished doctoral dis-sertation, Northwestern University, Evanston, IL.

Keyton, J. (1999). *Group communication: Process and analysis.* Mountain View, CA: Mayfield.

Kilmann, R. H., & Thomas, K. W. (1977). Developing a forced-choice measure of con-flict-handling behavior: The MODE instrument. *Educational and Psychological Measurements, 37,* 309–325.

Kleiner, B. M. (1993, September–October). Managing communication successfully in your management system [Electronic Version]. *Industrial Management, 35*(5), 18(3).

Knapp, M. L., & Hall, J. A. (2002). *Nonverbal communication in human interaction* (5th ed.). Belmont, CA: Wadsworth.

Knapp, M. L., & Vangelisti, A. (2000). *Interpersonal communication and human rela-tionships* (4th ed.). Boston: Allyn & Bacon.

Koerner, B. I. (2003). What does a "thumbs up" mean in Iraq? Retrieved June 6, 2007, from http://www.slate.msn.com/id/2080812

Kohrs Campbell, K., & Schultz Huxman, S. (2003). *The rhetorical act: Thinking, speak-ing, and writing critically* (3rd ed.). Belmont, CA: Wadsworth.

Krugman, P. (2003, January 21). A touch of class. *New York Times.* Retrieved June 6, 2007, from http://select.nytimes.com/gst/abstract.html?res=F30C10F839540C728 EDDA80894DB404482

Kursmark, L. "The benefits of behavioral interviewing: How to get behind candidates' facades." Retrieved May 2, 2007, from http://content.monster.com/articles/3485/ 16602/1/home.aspx

Language guide. (n.d.). Retrieved June 13, 2007, from http://www.specialolympics.org/ Special+Olympics+Public+Website/English/Press_Room/Language_guide/ default.htm

Larson, C. E. (1969). Forms of analysis and small group problem-solving. *Speech Mono-graphs, 36,* 452–455.

Larson, C. U. (2001). *Persuasion: Reception and responsibility* (9th ed.). Belmont, CA: Wadsworth.

LaRusso, D. A., & Tucker, R. K. (1957). Discussion outlines and skill in reflective think-ing. *The Speech Teacher, 6,* 139–142.

Luft, J. (1969). *Of human interaction.* Palo Alto, CA: National Press Books.

Lumsden, G., & Lumsden, D. (2003). Communicating with credibility and confidence: Diverse people, diverse settings (2nd ed.). Belmont, CA: Wadsworth.

Martyna, W. (1978). What does "he" mean—Use of the generic masculine. *Journal of Communication*, 28, 131–138.

McBurney, J. H., & Hance, K. G. (1939). *Principles and methods of discussion.* New York: Harper & Brothers.

McBurney, J. H., & Hance, K. G. (1950). *Discussion in human affairs.* New York: Harper & Brothers.

McCroskey, J. C. (2001). *Introduction to rhetorical communication* (8th ed.). Boston: Allyn & Bacon.

McGaan, L. (2003). *Communication: Functions, perception, self-concept.* Retrieved October 19, 2003, from http://department.monm.edu/cata/McGaan/Classes/cata101/Perception-SelfConcept.101.htm

McKerrow, R. E., Gronbeck, B. E., Ehninger, D., & Monroe, A. H. (2003). *Principles and types of public speaking* (15th ed.). Boston: Allyn & Bacon.

McLean, S. (2003). *The basics of speech communication.* Boston: Allyn & Bacon.

Metcalfe, S. (2004). *Building a speech* (5th ed.). Belmont, CA: Wadsworth.

Meyers, R. A., & Brashers, D. E. (1994). Expanding the boundaries of small group communication research: Exploring a feminist perspective. *Communication Studies,* 45, 68–85.

Moody, J., Stewart, B., & Bolt-Lee, C. (2002, March). Showcasing the skilled business graduate: Expanding the tool kit. *Business Communication Quarterly,* 65(1), 21.

Morreale, S. P., & Bovee, C. L. (1998). *Excellence in public speaking.* Belmont, CA: Wadsworth.

Morreale, S. P., Spitzberg, B. H., & Barge, J. K. (2001). *Human communication: Motivation, knowledge, and skills.* Belmont, CA: Wadsworth.

Natalle, E. J., & Bodenheimer, F. R. (2004). *The woman's public speaking handbook.* Belmont, CA: Wadsworth.

National Institute of Mental Health. (n.d.). *The numbers count: Mental disorders in America.* Retrieved June 6, 2007, from www.nimh.nih.gov/publicat/numbers.cfm

O'Hair, D., & Stewart, R. (1999). *Public speaking: Challenges and choices.* New York: Bedford/St. Martin's Press.

O'Hair, D., Stewart, R., & Rubenstein, H. (2004). *A speaker's guidebook* (2nd ed.). New York: Bedford/St. Martin's Press.

Oliver, R. T. (1997, Spring). "The way it was—all the way": A documentary accounting [Electronic version]. *Communication Quarterly,* 45(2), 1(130).

The Oxford American college dictionary. (2002). New York: G. P. Putnam's Sons.

The Oxford American dictionary and thesaurus, American edition. (2003). New York: Oxford University Press.

Parvis, L. F. (2001, May). The importance of communication and public-speaking skills. *Journal of Environmental Health,* 63(9), 44.

Pavitt, C. (1993). Does communication matter in social influence during small group discussion? Five positions. *Communication Studies,* 44, 216–227.

Peter, L. J. (1977). *Peter's quotations: Ideas for our time.* New York: William Morrow.

Phillips, G. M. (1965). PERT as a logical adjunct to the discussion process. *Journal of Communication,* 15, 89–99.

Phillips, G. M. (1966). *Communication and the small group.* Indianapolis: Bobbs-Merrill.

Poole, M. S. (1981, March). Decision development in small groups I: A comparison of two models. *Communication Monographs,* 48, 1–24.

Poole, M. S. (1990). Do we have any theories of group communication? *Communication Studies,* 41, 237–247.

Poole, M. S., Holmes, M., Watson, R., & DeSanctis, G. (1993). Group decision support systems and group communication: A comparison of decision making in computer-supported and nonsupported groups. *Communication Research,* 20, 176–213.

Poundstone, W. (2003). *How would you move Mt. Fuji? Microsoft's cult of the puzzle—How the world's smartest company selects the most creative thinkers.* New York: Little, Brown.

Propp, K. M., & Kreps, G. L. (1994). A rose by any other name: The vitality of group communication research. *Communication Studies,* 45, 7–19.

Putnam, L. L. (1994). Revitalizing small group communication: Lessons learned from a bona fide group perceptive. *Communication Studies,* 45, 97–102.

Pyron, H. C. (1964). An experimental study of the role of reflective thinking in business and professional conferences and discussions. *Speech Monographs,* 31, 157–161.

Pyron, H. C., & Sharp, H., Jr. (1963). A quantitative study of reflective thinking and performance in problem-solving discussion. *Journal of Communication,* 13, 46–53.

Rothwell, J. D. (1998). *In mixed company: Small group communication* (3rd ed.). New York: Harcourt Brace.

Sapir-Whorf-hypothesis redux. (2002, Winter). *ETC.: A Review of General Semantics,* 59(4), 456.

Scheidel, T. M., & Crowell, L. (1979). *Discussing and deciding: A desk book.* New York: Macmillan.

Schultz, B. G. (1996). *Communicating in the small group: Theory and practice* (2nd ed.). Boston: Allyn & Bacon.

Seibold, D. R. (1994). More reflection or more research? To (re)vitalize small group communication research, let's "just do it." *Communication Studies,* 45, 103–110.

Seiler, W. J., Beall, M. L. (2003). *Communication: Making connections* (5th ed.). Boston: Allyn & Bacon.

Sellnow, D. D. (2003). *Public speaking: A process approach.* Belmont, CA: Wadsworth.

Sharp, H., Jr., & Milliken, J. (1964). Reflective thinking ability and the product of problem-solving discussion. *Speech Monographs,* 31, 124–127.

Sheffield, A. D. (1926). *Creative discussion: A statement of method for leaders and members of discussion groups and conferences* (3rd ed.). New York: Association Press.

Shockley-Zalabak, P. S. (2006). *Fundamentals of organizational communication: Knowledge, sensitivity, skills, values* (6th ed.). New York: Pearson and Allyn & Bacon.

A short cut to better spoken English. (n.d.). Retrieved October 18, 2003, from http://www.msnbc.com/news/981625.asp

Silk, S. (1994, January). Making your speech memorable. *Association Management,* 46(1), 59.

Simpson, R. H. (1960). Attitudinal effects of small group discussions. *Quarterly Journal of Speech,* 46, 415–418.

Sprague, J., & Stuart, D. (2003). *The speaker's handbook* (6th ed.). Belmont, CA: Wadsworth.

Starbuck, J. J. (2000, January). Ginger and peppermint. *Better Nutrition,* 62(1), 44.

Stott, R., & Cordelia, B. (2000). *Speaking your mind: Oral presentation and seminar skills: Speak-Write series.* Boston: Allyn & Bacon.

"That's so gay" prompts student lawsuit. Retrieved June 6, 2007, from http://www.msnbc.msn.com/id/17388702/?GT1=9145

Timmons, W. M. (1941). Discussion, debating, and research. *Quarterly Journal of Speech,* 27, 415–421.

Too, L. (2002). *Lillian Too's flying star feng shui for the master practitioner.* London: HarperCollins.

Trenholm, S. (2002). *Thinking through communication: An introduction to the study of human communication* (3rd ed.). Boston: Allyn & Bacon.

Tubbs, S. L. (1997). *Systems approach to small group interaction* (6th ed.). New York: McGraw-Hill.

Ulloth, D., & Alderfer, R. (1998). *Public speaking: An experiential approach.* Belmont, CA: Wadsworth.

Vasile, A. J. (2004). *Speak with confidence: A practical guide* (9th ed.). Boston: Allyn & Bacon.

Verderber, R. F., & Verderber, K. S. (2002). *Communicate!* (10th ed.). Belmont, CA: Wadsworth.

Verderber, R. F., & Verderber, K. S. (2003). *The challenge of effective speaking* (12th ed.). Belmont, CA: Wadsworth.

Von Bertelanffy, L. (1968). *General systems theory.* New York: Braziller.

Voorhees, R. (2002). *Old age is always 15 years older than I am.* Kansas City, MO: Andrews McMeel.

Wagner, R. H., & Arnold, C. C. (1950). *Handbook of group discussion.* Boston: Houghton Mifflin.

Wall, V. D., Jr., & Galanes, G. J. (1986). The SYMLOG dimensions and small group conflict. *Central States Speech Journal, 37*, 61–78.

Weaver, M. (1999, April). Make your point with effective A/V. *Computers in Libraries, 19*(4), 62.

Weinberg, H. (1959). *Levels of knowing and existence.* New York: Harper Brothers.

Wilmot, W. W., & Hocker, J. L. (1998). *Interpersonal conflict* (5th ed.). New York: McGraw-Hill.

Wilson, G. L. (1998). *Groups in context* (5th ed.). New York: McGraw-Hill.

Wood, J. T. (1977). Constructive climate in discussion: Learning to manage disagreements effectively. In J. W. Pfeiffer & J. E. Jones (Eds.), *1977 Group Facilitators' Annual Handbook.* La Jolla, CA: University Associates.

Wood, J. T. (1977, June). Leading in purposive discussions: A study of adaptive behavior. *Communication Monographs, 44,* 152–165.

Wood, J. T. (1998). *But I thought you meant . . . : Misunderstandings in human communication.* Mountain View, CA: Mayfield Publishing.

Wood, J. T. (2001). *Gendered lives: Communication, gender, and culture* (4th ed.). Belmont, CA: Wadsworth.

Wood, J. T. (2003). *Communication in our lives* (3rd ed.). Belmont, CA: Wadsworth.

Wood, J. T. (2004). Communication mosaics—An introduction to the field of communication (3rd ed.). Belmont, CA: Wadsworth.

Wood, J. T. (2004). *Communication theories in action* (3rd ed.). Belmont, CA: Wadsworth.

Wood, J. T., Phillips, G. M., & Pedersen, D. J. (1986). *Group discussion: A practical guide to participation and leadership* (2nd ed.). New York: Harper & Row.

Young, K. S., Wood, J. T., Phillips, G. M., & Pedersen, D. J. (2007). *Group discussion: A practical guide to participation and leadership* (4th ed.). Long Grove, IL: Waveland Press.

Zarefsky, D. (2002). *Public speaking: Strategies for success* (3rd ed.). Boston: Allyn & Bacon.

Zeuschner, R. (2003). *Communicating today: The essentials.* Boston: Allyn & Bacon.

Ziegler, H., & Lawler, J. (2003). *Feng shui your workspace for dummies.* Hoboken, NJ: John Wiley & Sons.

Index

Accents and dialects, 152
Accommodating style of conflict resolution, 100
Action-requesting step, in MMS, 184
Active listening/feedback, 85–86
Actuation messages, in persuasive speaking, 170. *See also* Audience
Ad hominem fallacy, 187–188
Adaptability, 11, 84
Adaptors, 56–57
Adjustment, 246
Advertising
  appeal to authority in, 190
  bandwagon approach in, 189
  importance of clear expression in, 34
  Monroe's Motivated Sequence in, 194
  persuasive messages targeting culture, 164
Affect displays, 55
Aikens, M., 105
Allen, J., 203
Ambiguity, 33–35
Analogy, 134, 187
Andaloro, V., 8
Anderson, T. W., 27
Andrulonis, J. M., xi
Anger, emotional appeal of, 192
Answering machines, 90
Appeal to authority fallacy, 190
Arguments
  from analogy, 187

biased, ethical considerations about, 191
  causal, 188–189
  circular, 189–190
  inductive, 186
  reasoned, 186–190
Aristotle's building blocks of persuasive messages, 179–194
Aromatherapy, 60
Articulation, 151–152, 243–244
Artifacts
  job interviews and, 205
  organizational culture and, 69
  personal vs. physical, 67–68
Attention step, in MMS, 183
Attention, selective, 16, 83–84
Attention-getters, 139–141, 183
Attire, and first impressions, 205–207
Attribution theory, 19, 22–25, 52
Audience
  analysis, in persuasive speaking, 172–173
  credibility assessment of speaker by, 142–143
  demographic analysis of, 123–125
  egocentric nature of, 141–142
  keeping the attention of, 144
  Monroe's Motivated Sequence, 182–186

need, identifying and satisfying, 183
  physical setting of, 125–126
Audio aids, in speeches, 141
Auditory Verbal Therapy, 83
Authoritarian leaders, 221
Avoiding style of conflict resolution, 99

Baker, M. C., 38
Bandwagon fallacy, 189
Behavioral interviews, 208–209
Benson, J., 228
Bernum, B. A., 20
Bibliography, 146
Body movement, 52–53
Brainstorming, 117, 120, 158–159, 232
Brainteasers, 210
Buchanan, R., 143, 154
Bullying, 99
Burks, D., 41
Burrows, L. L., 59
Business cards, significance in Japanese culture, 208

Causal arguments, 187–189
Cell phones, 91
Channels, defined, 5
Character and leadership, 224
Christie, R. H., 62, 208
Chronemics, 57, 59–60
Circular argument, 189–190
Circumstances, as communication context, 6
Citations, 145, 180
Claims, 180–181, 186–187
Clarke, C. L., 86